OLD WHISKEY AND YOUNG WOMEN

R. MARC KANTROWITZ

FONTHILL

To

JOHN "JACK" MOSCARDELLI, ESQUIRE
8/14/45—2/19/13

*If every attorney were like him the legal profession
would be the most revered in the nation.*

&

JUDGE KENT B. SMITH
3/11/27—10/31/12

A judge's judge with an unmatched love of people and history.

Both are sorely missed

Fonthill Media LLC
www.fonthillmedia.com
office@fonthillmedia.com

First published 2015, reprinted 2016

ISBN 978-1-62545-108-8

Typeset in Minion Pro
1 SJOUFEBOECPVOEJOUIF 1 *X SPVQ96 , XX UFSS SPZEPCFT 3 XX: :

Contents

Introduction

A reader of my column, *Law 'n History*, sidled up to me one afternoon and commented that she really hated history in school but loved my articles. I thanked her for the compliment. Later I thought about what she had said. Why is it that she, along with so many others, doesn't like history? History is, after all, stories about people, and what could possibly be more compelling? Indeed, the best-selling magazines and most popular movies often focus exclusively on people and the myriad predicaments in which they find themselves.

One problem might be how dryly the subject is taught in our schools; all broad strokes with insufficient focus on the many often fascinating foibles of the individual. Simply put, the "human" taken out of humanity, the "his" (as well as her) out of history.

What follows is my perhaps feeble attempt to return history to the people. I confess that I am no historian; rather, I am a writer in search of a good story. And history is overflowing with them. Nearly all the tales I tell gripped the nation at the time they occurred. Imagine if you will the #1 movie star today being accused of murder. Unquestionably, the news coverage would be never-ending, 24/7. Yet, in a hundred years, not only would the incident be forgotten but so too would the #1 movie star. Such is the fate of Roscoe Fatty Arbuckle, America's most famous star at the start of the twentieth century. No one was bigger. Yet today few know who he is. Ask anyone under thirty about Jean Harlow and Lana Turner, two major Hollywood stars who were infamous in their time, and prepare to be met with blank stares.

In researching these various stories, I learned how little people know about even the most famous of past events and what they do know is often wrong. Myself included.

My fear is that I will perpetuate the myths and misconceptions. History is, after all, an after-the-fact retelling of a story that is often clouded, even at the time of its occurrence. My view is further colored by my belief that people are generally the same today as they were hundreds of years ago; the smart, wise, and generous vying against the petty, vengeful, and stupid. At times, intelligent people do dumb things and wise people act foolishly. A wife conspiring with her lover to murder her husband, for instance. Sadly, a tale as true today as it was in 1788 when the comely and intelligent Bathsheba Spooner did just that.

In a sense, the themes running throughout the book are common—nothing lasts forever (except for a chosen few, such as Marilyn Monroe, Al Capone, and Charlie Chaplin, who have somehow ingrained themselves in our national consciousness); crimes and trials of the century are forgotten by the next century; the more things change, the more they remain the same; and, as history repeats itself, one may predict the future by learning from the past.

With these observations in mind and with apologies to all historical figures unintentionally maligned, I now take you, in the pages that follow, to the biggest stories in America when they occurred: the most notorious murder cases, the greatest sex scandals, and the most dastardly schemes ever perpetrated. I hope to raise the dead; to bring life to what was once vibrant. Join me as we travel back to the sizzle, sparkle, and pop of history.

R. Marc Kantrowitz

I

TINSELTOWN AND SHOWBIZ

A S MUCH AS WE MIGHT wish it weren't so, the rich and famous, especially those in show business, are different than the rest of us. Too much sex, drugs, alcohol and violence. Indeed, too much of everything. Like the blockbusters in which they were filmed, the lives of the stars are often larger than life itself.

It wasn't always like this. Way back when it was far worse. More drugs, more sex, more violence. Cocaine was more abused in the 1920s than in the 2010s. Sex was so prevalent that a major studio in the early 1900s had to be shut down for a few weeks to allow its many employees to recover from the venereal disease spread by an ambitious young starlet.

And those inhabiting high society often acted the same, as evidenced by one of America's foremost architects, Stanford White, who designed some of our nation's most revered buildings and structures. He also liked naked young ladies gently gliding back and forth on red velvet swings.

1

Thaw Ices White

So scandalous was the trial of Harry Thaw that the House of Representatives passed a resolution calling for President Teddy Roosevelt to ban the postal service from delivering newspapers that carried accounts of its lurid testimony. After all, it wasn't every day that the loony son of a multimillionaire fatally shot a world-renowned socialite in front of a large, partying crowd. And all over a woman.

*   *   *

Born in 1853, the victim, Stanford White, Stanny to his friends, was the most prominent architect of his day. He was a man who brought beauty, class and stature to each project on which he worked. He designed some of New York City's most notable churches, towers and clubs, including the Washington Square Arch and the second version of Madison Square Garden—the very building in which he was killed. His New York Herald Building was modeled after the Doge's Palace in Venice. He was also responsible for Boston's Public Library, Trinity Church and the Hotel Buckminster in Kenmore Square, as well as numerous other highly regarded structures throughout America.

A noted connoisseur of the beautiful and stylish, he took leisurely trips to Europe, searching for antiques and art for both himself and for his many wealthy clients. His eye for beauty extended far beyond inanimate objects, however. He was kindly and courtly and selectively sexually avaricious. Though married and a father, he led the life of a carefree bachelor in Manhattan, bouncing between his many social arenas and his different residences. Upset that clubs closed at a certain late hour, he and his cronies founded The Brook, which never shut its doors. His lifestyle and those of his friends mirrored the times. In 1898, America was just entering a golden age of wealth and excess, a land led by the Carnegies, Rockefellers and Vanderbilts. And Stanford White comfortably immersed himself in those circles, cavorting with the wealthy as he designed their homes and businesses.

*   *   *

Famed architect and bon vivant Stanford White;
c. 1892.

Stanny both attended and hosted parties. At one such soiree, a scantily-clad, sixteen-year-old girl slithered out of a gigantic cake, much to the delight of the assembled guests. Many of the women White enjoyed were newly arrived in New York, searching for careers on Broadway. The well-connected White not only introduced them to producers and directors, but often paid for their lodgings and even their dental work. He even befriended the girls' mothers, who found him so charming and cultured that they never suspected any illicit behavior on his part. Little did he realize that one such dalliance would lead to his murder.

* * *

Evelyn Nesbit was born outside of Pittsburgh, Pennsylvania on Christmas Day in 1884, although her mother may later have shaved a few years off of her birth date to skirt around the child labor laws. A brother Howard joined the family of four, which was a happy one until Evelyn was ten or so, at which point her supportive and beloved father unexpectedly died. Poverty and hard times followed. To find work as a seamstress, Mrs. Nesbit moved to Philadelphia where the city discovered the beguiling beauty of her young daughter. Soon Evelyn was posing and establishing contacts. When the family relocated to New York City in 1900, Evelyn, with letters of recommendation and introduction in hand, quickly found herself again in demand.

As her photos circulated, her popularity soared and soon she graced the covers of the City's leading fashion magazines, as well as calendars, postcards and the canvases of artists. In short time, however, she grew bored with the idleness of posing and sought more action. The money she was earning was also surprisingly sparse. The lure and excitement of Broadway beckoned and, in short order, she climbed onto its stage, dancing in the chorus of a show.

The beguiling young lady at the center of it all, Evelyn Nesbit; (1906).

With her expanding horizons, she soon collided with Stanny. First at his parties and then in his bedroom. She was sixteen; he was forty-seven.

White, as was his practice, took what seemed to the outside world a paternalistic attitude toward Nesbit and her family and moved them into an upscale apartment. When Howard's educational needs grew, White paid for him to attend military school in Pennsylvania. The money woes of the Nesbit family had finally been suitably addressed.

With Nesbit inhabiting White's social universe, she met and dated other men. Her most serious affair involved one of the famous Barrymores, Jack, who, at twenty-one, was close in age to her. The handsome couple had an affair wherein she got pregnant and had an abortion. When Jack proposed marriage, she, at the behest of her mother and White, rejected him. At the time, he was not making much money and was not considered a good catch. As such, Evelyn's mother and White, for selfish and possessory reasons, pressured her to break-up with the love-struck actor-to-be. She did. She would not be alone for long.

* * *

The first time Harry Thaw gazed upon Evelyn on stage, he was mesmerized. So much so that he returned to the show, and then again and again—in all, seeing her perform over three dozen times. As his infatuation grew, he arranged to meet her. He was not disappointed. His ardor exploding, he showered the young actress with flowers and gifts. He could easily afford it. Mad Harry Thaw was the exceedingly wealthy, wild and unsettled son of Pittsburgh steel and railroad magnate, William Thaw, whose fortune, which continued to grow after he died in 1889,

The very wealthy and violent Mad Harry Thaw.

topped forty million dollars. With money came stature, even if undeserved. Evelyn, upon later meeting the family, found them unsophisticated, if not shallow. Like many of the nouveau riche, they craved respectability and public acceptance. One of William's daughters married into cash-strapped English nobility while another married the nephew of Andrew Carnegie. Harry, on the other hand, unbalanced and odd, brought disgrace. He drank, abused drugs, lavishly spent money and partied. He also savagely beat people who, for whatever minor and irrational reason, irritated him. His abuse of hotel workers and taxi cab drivers paled in comparison to his brutal violence toward young prostitutes, whom he enjoyed whipping. Money bought their silence.

His courtship of Evelyn took some years. As with others, he beat her. But he also showered her in money and the promise of an opulent lifestyle. When he proposed, she mulled over her options. She knew that her liaison with White would never lead to marriage. Indeed, if it ever became public, she felt—given the mores at the time—that she would be ruined both personally and professionally. Memories of poverty also darkened her view. Like Scarlett O'Hara screaming to the heavens, Evelyn swore she too would never return to its vile clutches. A fateful decision was made, which years later she explained: Thaw was the only really wealthy man to ask her to marry him. Boxed in, and armed with his promise to change, she, at twenty-one, agreed to his proposal and they wed in the spring of 1905. Shortly thereafter, they settled in the family mansion in Pittsburgh.

Despite winning the hand of a beautiful woman a dozen years his junior, Thaw's paranoia, fueled in part by his continuing consumption of cocaine and morphine, grew. And at the center of his warped antipathy stood Stanford White, the man who had deflowered his thought to be innocent wife. White had to be exposed, Thaw concluded, to save all young women. Mad

Harry even added a clause in his will to that effect, providing money to the victims of "White and other inhuman scoundrels." Detectives were hired to follow the unsuspecting architect, whose name was forbidden in the Thaw household. As Mad Harry gave in to the darkness, he irrationally concluded that White might retaliate and so, in self-defense, Thaw started carrying a gun. In fact, White, like so many others, barely paid him a thought.

∗ ∗ ∗

The evening of Monday, June 25, 1906, was a warm one, in the mid-70s. Despite it being early in the week, Thaw and Nesbit, temporarily passing through New York en route to Europe, were out hitting the night spots of the city. Soon, they found themselves in the rooftop theater at the top of Madison Square Garden—ironically a building White designed and in which he owned an apartment. A large crowd gathered to enjoy the debut of Mamzelle Champagne, a musical revue. Near the end of the performance, tenor Harry Short launched into "I Could Love a Thousand Girls," at which point Thaw nonchalantly wandered over to White's table, took out his gun and fired three shots.

Thaw held the weapon up high and slowly exited as the shocked crowd slowly realized that what they had witnessed was not part of the performance, but real and deadly. Screams rang out. Panicked theatergoers ran, knocking over chairs and tables in a mad scramble to escape. Those who kept their wits shouted for calm.

Thaw met his befuddled wife amid the frenzy. As he was quickly taken into custody, he offered no resistance, simply muttering, "He deserved it. I can prove it. He ruined my wife and then deserted the girl."

The show, as it turned out, was only beginning.

∗ ∗ ∗

The papers quickly glommed on to the sensationalistic story, covering every aspect of it. If facts proved to be unsupportive of a story, the story remained, and the facts were replaced by fiction. A great debate ensued. Was Thaw a cold-blooded murderer or one worthy of respect and admiration for upholding the honor of his wife? So titillating was the tale that soon the entire nation grew fixated.

As might be expected, privately the Thaw family was assembling the finest legal talent, which devised its strategy. As Thaw had undoubtedly committed the crime, his attorneys recommended claiming that he was insane.

The suggestion met with resistance from their reluctant client, and later his mother, who urged that the family be portrayed in only the most positive of lights. If Harry were found not guilty due to insanity, he'd be committed to a mental hospital. To avoid that embarrassment and outcome, Thaw and his family preferred that his attorneys pursue a defense of temporary insanity; that he was crazy when he pulled the trigger, but fully recovered at the time of trial. If successful, he would walk away a free man. At Harry's insistence, his doubting attorneys were fired and a new, more malleable team, assembled.

A New York killing on the front page of the *Washington Times*; (June 26, 1906).

*   *   *

Fed by the media, who often got misleading tips from the public relations mavens the Thaws had retained, as well as from the defense and prosecution teams, the masses clamored to attend the proceedings. Like ants materializing on spilled ice cream, they came. The trial started in January and quickly turned into a long-running spectacle, taking four months to conclude.

So infamous was the matter that the jury selection took over a week with over three hundred potential jurors being examined. The prosecution quickly presented its case, easily proving that Thaw shot White. And then the defense took over.

Thaw's position—that he was temporarily driven mad due to White "ruining my wife"—was supported by an army of experts and Nesbit herself, who demurely highlighted what had so blindly enraged her husband. On the day she started her testimony ten thousand people jammed the courthouse streets.

As the innocent, schoolgirl-like Evelyn took the stand, time stopped. One awestruck veteran newspaperman reported that she was "the most exquisitely lovely human being I ever looked at—the slim, quick grace of a fawn, a head that sat on her faultless throat as a lily on its stem, eyes that were the color of blue-brown pansies and the size of half dollars, a mouth made of rumpled rose petals."

In a soft voice, she told of the much older White plying her, a young girl, indeed a mere child, with drink and then, after she had passed out, deflowering her, in his opulent apartment; the room filled with mirrors and colorful lights, designed for seduction; of his velvet red swing in which Nesbit, as well as other barely clad young women, leisurely swung. She had entered his palace a virgin and left a wronged woman.

Politicians, ministers and genteel society howled at the lurid nature of the testimony. Legislatures around the nation demanded that such vile filth not be disseminated to the masses. The public, meanwhile, feasted on the entertainment.

In rebuttal, the prosecution countered, parading its own experts forward, asserting that Thaw was sane when he pulled the trigger and that Evelyn was not quite as innocent as she had let on. And on it went. When the testimony finally ended, closing arguments commenced, for three long days. It was now April. Winter had turned to spring.

The jury deliberated. After grueling and stressful hours, it reported that it was hopelessly deadlocked. Seven jurors believed the defendant guilty and deserving of the electric chair, while five held that Thaw was not guilty. A new trial was ordered.

*   *   *

The second trial started the following January. After reviewing his options, Thaw and his family agreed to a refined strategy, returning to the original advice given. His attorneys were now free to argue that Mad Harry was insane when he pulled the trigger and still insane at the time of trial. A verdict of not guilty by reason of insanity was surely preferable to being found guilty of first degree murder and executed as a result.

The second jury heard what the first had not—testimony about family insanity and from Thaw's mother, nurse, teacher and headmaster, of his longstanding irrational behavior. It worked.

Epilogue

Committed to an asylum and knowing he'd continue to reside there until experts attested to his mental recovery, Thaw schemed to get out, any way he could. If the legal road proved difficult, he'd take another.

On August 17, 1913, Thaw escaped, fleeing to Canada and once again finding himself on the front pages of newspapers throughout America. Quickly captured, he was turned over to the authorities in New Hampshire. When those in New York petitioned to have him returned, Thaw vigorously fought the extradition request, a battle which ultimately landed in the United States Supreme Court. In an opinion written by the august Oliver Wendell Holmes, Thaw was ordered back to New York.

In 1915, the year he and his wife officially divorced, Thaw's long fight for freedom was finally realized. Two years later he savagely beat and whipped a young man, for which he did another seven years in another asylum, this one in Pennsylvania.

In 1947, Mad Harry died. He was seventy-six and left a pittance from his large estate to Nesbit. Perhaps he was angry that she had divorced him. Or perhaps it was due to Nesbit becoming pregnant during his confinement.

As for Evelyn, she remained in show business, worked in vaudeville around the country and found some success. A second marriage to a fellow entertainer lasted but a few years. During the Roaring Twenties, she worked in speakeasies and dance halls around the nation. Along the way she wrote a book, developed a drug and alcohol problem and attempted suicide. In 1955, *The Girl on the Red Velvet Swing*, was released. Evelyn served as a consultant, having been paid fifty thousand dollars, for the highly fictionalized film. The truth would have made a better movie.

Near the end of her life, she summed up the trials as ones in which she testified to save a husband she didn't love for killing the man she did. She died on January 17, 1967, proclaiming until the end her undying love for America's grandest architect.

Tidbits

If, in fact, her date of birth had been doctored, then Nesbit started her affair with White when she was fourteen.

It was believed that White had a local photographer take naked pictures of his young paramours. At his death, to avoid further scandal, the pictures were destroyed.

Some thought that right after the shooting, Thaw uttered that White had ruined, not Thaw's wife, but Thaw's life.

During the trials, the experts were often asked lengthy hypothetical questions. One question took over ninety minutes to ask, filling thirty-nine pages of transcript.

President Teddy Roosevelt consulted with the Postmaster General concerning the request to restrict the press reporting the trial. No action was taken. Perhaps Teddy had more on his mind, being the father of his ever so vibrant and unconventional daughter, Alice.

Nesbit gave birth to a son in 1910. She insisted that Thaw was the father and conception took place during one of her visits with him. Given his wealth, Thaw's surroundings in the mental facility were notably superior to those similarly confined.

Thaw's sister's marriage to English nobility ended after five years. The marriage was annulled due to a lack of consummation. It appears that her effeminate husband may have been gay.

From his release in 1924 until his death over two decades later, Thaw slowly faded into obscurity.

In a testament to destiny, Thaw and his wife were merely passing through New York en route to Europe. White, who was supposed to be in Philadelphia for business, stayed in New York to have dinner with his college-aged son and a friend, both of whom were visiting from Harvard.

Our Next Tale

Scandal and objectionable behavior were not confined to New York. With the birth of Hollywood came the explosion of rumor, disgrace and dishonor. And at the head of the pack was one of America's earliest and greatest stars who soon found himself in the middle of a sensational killing. Hollywood would never be the same.

2

The Rape of Rapp

He was a superstar in Hollywood. A household name making a million bucks a year while the average American made less than a grand; as famous as Charlie Chaplin, Douglas Fairbanks and Mary Pickford. All of his fame and fortune, though, could not shield him from the unspeakable crime of which he was accused.

Word spread quickly. Roscoe Fatty Arbuckle had raped Virginia Rapp by inserting a champagne bottle into her vagina, rupturing vital organs resulting in her untimely death. Or maybe she was killed while engaged in unwelcomed intercourse with Fatty and his mammoth 275 pound girth. Or maybe it was all made up by an ambitious prosecutor with an eye on higher office.

Few people today know of Fatty Arbuckle, much like few people a hundred years from now will know of Tom Cruise, Eddie Murphy, Jon Stewart or Angelina Jolie. A century ago though, along with Chaplin, Roscoe Fatty Arbuckle was the nation's biggest comedian, literally and figuratively.

* * *

Huge even at birth, weighing in reportedly at sixteen pounds, in 1887 in Kansas, the blond-headed and fair-skinned Arbuckle developed into one surprisingly agile despite his great weight. He also came to possess a magnificent singing voice. Moving to California with his abusive and alcoholic father, ill mother and four siblings, he dropped out of school in the second grade and hid out at the local theaters, enraptured by what he saw. Soon, at eight, he was performing, and getting paid for it. In short time he became the lead act—singing, dancing, juggling and mugging for an audience awed by his talent. How could such a large boy move so gracefully and be so funny? And that voice!

He toured the Far East and the west coast. En route from Los Angeles to Long Beach to perform, he perchance met a petite, dark haired young woman boarding a streetcar. She too was an actor, named Minta Durfee and it became quickly apparent that, while only eighteen, she was strong-willed and sharp-tongued, telling the smitten Roscoe that, "I don't like fat men and I don't like blondes." Even when she discovered that they would be performing in the same show, her attitude didn't change. That is, until he jumped on stage, mesmerizing both

Roscoe Fatty Arbuckle (1887-1933) in costume.

the audience and her. Five months later, on August 6, 1908, she married her sweet, shy and impeccably dressed suitor. Only later did she realize that when he drank he changed. With a crowd, he often became outgoing; alone or with a select few, including Minta, he turned dark, moody and unpleasant.

✳ ✳ ✳

At the turn of the century, Hollywood was but a mere baby. Actors working there were looked down upon, the belief being that the truly gifted and worthy performed on stage. Those in the early industry often comported themselves in such a manner that even the local boarding houses warned against them: "No Actors or Dogs Allowed!"

It matured as it grew, though, and in 1913 business was booming. And Fatty was riding the wave, signing a contract with Mack Sennett, the creator of Keystone Studios and the Keystone Cops. Arbuckle's talent for comedy became readily apparent. He did his own stunts, moved nimbly about and became the funniest man in America, influencing Chaplin, befriending Buster Keaton and helping discover Bob Hope. If he did not create the legendary pie-in-the-face routine, he certainly popularized it, as he did dressing in drag.

Shy and sensitive about his weight, he hated his moniker and no one close to him ever called him Fatty. His manners, like his dress, were impeccable and he was almost chaste-like with women. Like his father, though, when he drank he turned into a different, far less likeable, person.

Hollywood was evolving, not all of it in a good way. Stories of wild parties, promiscuous behavior and excessive alcohol and drugs abounded. Even worse, that decadent lifestyle was being projected onto the screen. Soon temperance unions, women's groups and those in the clergy demanded an end to movies glorifying sex, drugs, adultery and divorce. The press gladly reported and exploited the stories of sin. And there were many: the drug-related death of the seemingly sweet and innocent starlet Olive Thomas, who was married to the hard-drinking and drug-abusing Jack Pickford; America's Sweetheart Mary Pickford, sister to Jack, who dumped her husband and quickly married fellow movie star Douglas Fairbanks; the morphine-addicted—and soon-dead—young, dashing, and handsome Wallace Reid; and the scandal of Chaplin's marriage to a pregnant sixteen-year-old.

Film executives, mindful of the bottom line and fearful of governmental intrusion, felt compelled to take strong action and turned to the former chairman of the Republican Party, Will Hays. Lured from his position as postmaster general of the United States, Hays soon became the feared "movie czar," promising to police the perceived runaway industry.

Against this backdrop, Arbuckle, who was now also directing and writing movies, remained impervious. He both held and attended parties, as did everyone in Hollywood. Rivers of alcohol flowed in the face of Prohibition and over the increasing roar of disapproval throughout Middle America. It was probably without much thought then that Roscoe hopped into his grossly oversized car, which came with a bar and toilet, and drove with director-actor Lowell Sherman and cameraman Fred Fischbach to San Francisco's fashionable meeting ground for the stars, the St. Francis Hotel. Now estranged from his wife Minta, Arbuckle set out to spend this 1921 Labor Day Weekend as a man about town.

Three rooms in the stylish hotel were rented—two rooms for the three men and the middle one for the party, which started and ran over the long weekend. Continually, people came and went, all the while drinking, dancing, and eating. Some even engaged in a quick tryst. On Labor Day Monday, Virginia Rapp popped in along with Maude Delmont, guests invited by Fischbach against the wishes of Arbuckle who knew of their horrid reputations.

Fatty's party was just beginning. It was one he would forever regret.

✴ ✴ ✴

When Roscoe excused himself from the loud bash to use the bathroom in his next door suite, he discovered a highly intoxicated Virginia Rapp, whom he knew to be an actress and part-time prostitute, vomiting in the toilet. In great distress, Rapp was placed onto the bed, from which she rolled off. Screaming in pain, she was returned back to the bed, where she vomited on herself. Hoping to provide some relief, Roscoe retrieved some ice to place on her burning body. Hearing the screams, Maude Delmont, who had just met Rapp that weekend, entered and saw Arbuckle putting ice on Rapp's stomach and thigh. They discussed Rapp's plight and agreed that she was merely drunk.

Suddenly Rapp let out a shriek that she was dying and hurt. Hearing the screams, Zey Prevon and Alice Blake rushed in. Delmont ordered that the bathtub be filled with cold water to help Rapp who was fading in and out of consciousness, rambling and feverish. Rapp then blurted out the hook the prosecution would later use to impale Arbuckle. Looking at Roscoe, she screamed, "Stay away from me! I don't want you near me. What did he do to me, Maudie? Roscoe did this to me."

The sexually charged Virginia Rapp (1891–1921) in a rather demure pose; (1920).

At the time, little sense could be made out of her incoherence. The cool bath calmed Rapp, who was moved to another room. Arbuckle meanwhile called the hotel manager and doctor, who upon examining the now calmer patient, diagnosed her as having had too much to drink. The party, with the loud Rapp now subdued, resumed in its earlier intensity. Arbuckle left to run an errand.

Over the next few days, nurses and two doctors, including the doctor to the well-to-do, Melville Rumwell, examined Rapp, surmising her problems to be related either to her bladder, vile bootleg liquor, venereal disease, a kidney problem or a severe infection. Rapp herself opined that it was due to excessive intercourse with a boyfriend. Her body bore no marks or bruises nor signs of violence or rape.

As time passed, Rapp grew sicker. One nurse, incensed over the lackadaisical manner in which Rapp was being monitored, quit when Delmont refused to contact Dr. Rumwell. When Rumwell was finally called, he examined the fading Rapp and hastily ordered her immediate hospitalization. Too late. She died on Friday. The cause—peritonitis, an acute infection caused by the rupture of the bladder. Despite not securing authority from the coroner's office, Rumwell conducted an autopsy and removed, and later destroyed, vital organs in the process.

With the death of Rapp, Maude Delmont lashed out, spurting out a tale of Arbuckle dragging Rapp into his room and raping her. With William Randolph Hearst leading the charge, every newspaper reported the incendiary allegations, which grew in intensity. Newspaper sales leaped, as did fabrications. Ice on the stomach became a champagne (or coke) bottle jammed inside the virtuous and defenseless victim. Some reported that it was Arbuckle's great weight that caused the fatal injuries. Soon the local district attorney, Matthew Brady, with eyes on the governorship, jumped in. In short order he had sworn affidavits from Delmont, Zey

Prevon and Alice Blake, all charging that Arbuckle had caused the death of Virginia Rapp.

And with that, America's most famous star was charged with murder and imprisoned, held without bail.

* * *

Many weaknesses in the case quickly bubbled to the surface, all in the form of scant evidence and shifty witnesses. Every time star accuser Delmont aka Montgomery aka Rothberg told her story, it changed dramatically. What didn't change was her lengthy rap sheet, consisting of fraud, extortion, bigamy and racketeering. Known as a blackmailer, her forte was setting up unsuspecting males and catching them engaged in compromising positions. Armed with the damaging evidence, she'd threaten to expose them unless her monetary demands were met. Sometimes she set up married men in the throes of a divorce to provide their wives with a golden opportunity to nab their wandering husbands in the nefarious act. Delmont even offered to testify in court, falsely if need be, if the price was right.

The very lovely victim also had a soiled background. Born out of wedlock in 1894, Virginia Rapp grew into a fetching and ambitious young lady who lived life to the left of the fast lane. Reportedly she had five abortions by the time she was sixteen. Engaged at seventeen to a forty-year-old, she gave birth to a baby girl. After her fiancée ditched her, she ditched the baby and eventually relocated to California where fame awaited her. In 1918, she was named Hollywood's "Best Dressed Girl in Pictures." In the town known for loose morals, Rapp was a poster child. One tale had her infecting so many movie studio employees with a venereal disease that production had to be shut down for a few weeks to give the infected time to heal and to shield the few who hadn't yet been exposed to her. When she drank she became lewd, loud and loose, often ripping off her clothes in a frenzy.

And with this ragtag army of evidence, the proceedings commenced.

* * *

District Attorney Matthew Brady, himself ruthless, ambitious and unlikeable, had his eyes set on the governor's office and the Arbuckle case was the fuel to propel him there. That his witnesses were unreliable and dishonest made his job difficult. When Zey Prevon and Alice Blake changed their stories he threatened them with perjury and imprisonment. Both quickly fell into line. Delmont, on the other hand, who frequently changed her renditions of the event was kept far from the grand jury, coroner's jury, and judge who heard the preliminary hearing. All three actions ended in the same result—reducing the charge from murder to manslaughter—much to the displeasure of Brady. Equally dismayed was Roscoe, who, knowing of his innocence, was crushed when he wasn't exonerated. At least though he was allowed to make bail.

Once freed, he quickly discovered that he was a pariah, not only in Hollywood where his friends were pressured by their studios and publicity agents to stay away from him, but by the public, which had turned violently against him. Depicted as a monster by the press, his

Fatty's mugshot; *c.* 1921.

movies were pulled from theaters throughout America. His bosses also shunned him, shutting him out of work.

Along with these crushing burdens, he also faced severe financial woes, including his hefty legal bills. Having spent so much money so lavishly, Fatty's creditors, fearful that the money well was about to run dry, came calling. Arbuckle neither had the funds to repay them nor the prospects of employment. He was in dire straits. And his agony would continue.

*   *   *

As the trial started, District Attorney Brady had Prevon, Blake and Delmont held in custody, shielding them from the defense and assuring that any forthcoming testimony would be to his liking. Notwithstanding his best efforts, the trial was going well for the defense even with Brady either filing or threatening to file perjury charges against any defense witness. When Arbuckle testified, he was subjected to a withering cross-examination, which he handled well. It appeared victory was at hand.

Until the jury got the case. One juror, Helen Hubbard, with undisclosed ties to the District Attorney's Office and who was convinced Arbuckle was guilty the day he was arrested, held out, refusing to even seriously deliberate or consider the testimony. She convinced another juror to join her. A deadlocked jury, 10-2 for acquittal. Arbuckle was devastated.

*   *   *

So convinced of a not guilty verdict at the re-trial, Arbuckle's team basically mailed it in, barely presenting a defense. Arbuckle didn't even take the stand. The result was predictable. Another hung jury, this one with the majority of the jurors voting to convict.

Knocked to their senses, in the third trial, the defense went all out. They demonstrated that evidence had been planted and witnesses pressured to lie. Roscoe testified. Maude Delmont did not. Indeed, at no point during any of the three trials did she testify. Delmont was, in the words of one of Arbuckle's attorneys, "the complaining witness who never witnessed."

The jury, which was out for less than ten minutes, not only rendered a verdict but surprisingly a statement:

> Acquittal is not enough for Roscoe Arbuckle. We feel that a great injustice has been done to him....
> [T]here was not the slightest proof adduced to connect him in any way with the commission of
> a crime.... We wish him success and hope that the American people will take the judgment of
> fourteen men and women that Roscoe Arbuckle is entirely innocent and free from all blame.

Epilogue

America and movie tyrant Will Hays were not so forgiving. Shortly after his acquittal, Arbuckle was banned from the movies and blacklisted. He was also charged federally with a liquor law violation. Even when the ban was officially lifted, he had difficulty finding work. At one point he resorted to using a pseudonym and worked behind the scenes. As for Rapp's cause of death, some opine it was due to a botched abortion set up by Delmont and performed prior to the party by Dr. Rumwell (which explains why he improperly performed the autopsy and destroyed the evidence).

A dozen years after Roscoe's court troubles, the sun of his career finally started to emerge from the blackened skies when Warner Brothers signed him, at the age of forty-six, to a movie contract. He reportedly exclaimed that it was the happiest day of his life. That night he died in his sleep.

Tidbits

Two lies from the affair prosper even to this day. The first, as per a statement by Delmont which she later recanted, had Fatty leering, chasing and yelling at Virginia that he was coming to get her. The other was the use of either a champagne or coke bottle to rape her, which was simply made up by the press.

Rather foolishly, Arbuckle underreported his income to the IRS, stating that he "only" made $250,000 a year, his salary from the movie studio. In fact, he made far more, as evidenced by his mansions, which he lavishly decorated, his six expensive cars and a specially built railway car which he used when traveling to promote his latest films.

Hays, the enforcer of morals, reportedly took bribes from whoever was seeking a favor. He also formed the Motion Pictures Producers and Distributors Association (MPPDA) which reviewed scripts and outtakes. A production code was established. Censorship was now in full bloom, presided over by the dictatorial Hays.

Rapp often used the last name Rappe, as it sounded more elegant.

Arbuckle married two more times. He never had any children.

The pseudonym Arbuckle used after he was blacklisted was William B. Goodrich. Ever the comic, the shortened name read, Will B. Good.

Matthew Brady never made it to the Governor's Office. He remained as the district attorney until he was turned out of office in 1943.

Arbuckle's partner in his early movies was Mabel Normand. Together they formed a comedic couple unparalleled at the time. Both found great fame at the time, and equal tragedy, which will be discussed in the next chapter.

Our Next Tale

While the second Arbuckle trial was under way, one of Hollywood's best known and highly respected directors, William Desmond Taylor, was murdered. The last person to see him alive was Mabel Normand, whom many thought had committed the horrific deed. In the end, she was only one of a bucket full of suspects.

3

A Murder with No Ending

In October 1908, William Tanner vanished, leaving behind his mystified and wealthy wife, Ethel, and their young child Daisy. A decade later Ethel finally saw the man who had deserted her, quite unexpectedly. Taking her daughter to a movie theater to watch the action-packed movie *Captain Alvarez,* Tanner, now with a last name of Taylor, heroically dashed onto the screen as the star of the movie. Ethel leaned over and whispered in her daughter's ear, "That's your father."

* * *

Tanner arrived in Hollywood penniless, after years on the road where he scratched out a living working a series of meaningless jobs. Once in Los Angeles, the handsome and soft-spoken gentleman with the British accent quickly established himself first as a leading man and then as an acclaimed movie director. Climbing to the top of his profession, he again veered wildly off course, enlisting in 1918 at the age of forty-six as a private in the British army to fight in World War I. Originally stationed in Canada prior to travelling to England, Taylor rose to officer rank in less than a year. The war ended before he saw any action. He did however incur the wrath of a noncommissioned officer, whom he caught purloining military property. A court-martial ensued with the NCO swearing vengeance against his accuser.

Upon Taylor's triumphant return to America in 1919, he received a hero's welcome and re-established himself as a major force in Hollywood, again making profitable and tasteful films. Three years later, on February 1, 1922, he was shot dead. The list of suspects grew quickly as did the mystery surrounding a man everyone thought they knew, but really didn't. And never would.

* * *

In 1872, William Cunningham Deane-Tanner joined two sisters, Nell and Daisy, when he was born in Ireland to a retired British military officer and his wife. Four years later, a brother Denis joined the Deane-Tanner clan, destined to follow in the footsteps of his enigmatic brother.

In 1890, at eighteen years old, young William set sail for America, where he knocked around the Midwest before landing in the theaters of New York City. He eventually met a fellow thespian, Ethel May Hamilton, who came from a wealthy family. The two married; the ceremony taking place on December 7, 1901.

While it might have been a difficult decision, Tanner left the stage, opting to work in an exclusive antiques shop on Fifth Avenue. In short order, he joined the blue-bloods of New York's high society. Along the way a daughter, Daisy, joined the seemingly happy and robust family. And then, on October 23, 1908, Tanner left to attend the prestigious Vanderbilt Cup Race on Long Island and vanished. Approaching, if not firmly ensconced in, middle age at thirty-six, Tanner was known to have "mental lapses," and many thought that he was in the midst of one and would turn up as quickly as he had disappeared.

Four years later his brother Denis, also an antiques dealer in New York, as well as a former member of the British military, travelled down the same dark road when he too eerily and suddenly disappeared, leaving behind his young family—a wife and two children. Soon financially strapped, Denis's wife Ada moved west, to California, to live with relatives.

✳ ✳ ✳

From the scratchy accounts that have been cobbled together, it appears that William shed his wealthy lifestyle and led a nomadic existence, working out west in a hotel and mine and even going as far as Alaska in search of gold. Some even had him returning to the stage in San Francisco.

After five years of wandering about in the shadowy vagaries of whatever world he chose to inhabit, Tanner surfaced in Los Angeles with a new name—William Desmond Taylor—and

The talented and famous movie director, William Desmond Taylor; (1872–1922).

purpose. Almost as mystifying as his disappearance was his career ascension, quickly appearing in the movies. Soon he was directing them, overseeing some of Hollywood's most famous stars. His meteoric rise perhaps is best summed up by the words of a detective who later investigated his murder, "William Desmond Taylor was at once the favorite and the mystery of the movie picture colony. A cultured, dignified gentleman with a charming personality and considerable magnetism, the men with whom he worked were devoted to him, and most of the women fell in love with him." So respected by his colleagues was he that he was named president of the Motion Picture Directors Association, which had recently come into existence.

With success came renewed fortune and Taylor soon found himself again comfortably associating with the highest levels of society, this time with those living three thousand miles away from his former haunts. He joined prestigious clubs, ate in the finest of restaurants with the best known of celebrities, and travelled in luxury.

As might be easily concluded, Taylor's celebrity was not confined to his locale. Starring in movies, his fame snaked throughout the nation, rudely shocking his now former wife Ethel while she innocently sat enthralled viewing an exciting movie in a darkened theater with her young daughter. Ethel had divorced the man who had abandoned her and now finally learned of his whereabouts when he bounded onto the wide screen.

When Taylor's former sister-in-law Ada, now living in California, learned of her former brother-in-law, she soon came knocking, demanding to know the fate of her Denis. Taylor feigned ignorance. He did, however, promise to help financially and started sending her a monthly allowance, up to the day he was killed.

∗　∗　∗

Upon his return from military service, Taylor moved into the upscale Alvarado Court Apartments on South Alvarado Street, Los Angeles. The U shaped complex consisted of eight tightly packed elegant houses, each with accompanying duplex apartments. Many involved in the blossoming movie business lived there, including the lovely Edna Purviance—a frequent co-star of Charlie Chaplin—and Douglas MacLean, a movie comedian. Within a few years, the stars realigned to the trendier galaxies of Hollywood and Beverly Hills.

Two years after moving to Alvarado Court, Taylor underwent stomach surgery and on the advice of his doctors, took a five week vacation, leaving for Europe on June 9, 1921. In his absence, he allowed Edward Knoblock, an accomplished writer, to stay in his house, along with Taylor's valet and cook, Edward Sands, a short and stocky twenty-seven-year-old who, by his jovial manner, masked a sinister soul.

Quickly, Knoblock came to dislike and distrust Sands. After a month, when Sands asked for a short vacation, ostensibly to marry and honeymoon, Knoblock readily agreed, knowing that Taylor was due back shortly. After the week ended, Taylor returned, Sands didn't.

Sands—who never did get married—took more than a non-existent honeymoon; he took Taylor's expensive car, clothing, money, jewelry and checks. Sands forged the checks and stole thousands from Taylor's bank account. Taylor hired a replacement, Henry Peavey, and filed charges that summer of '21 against Sands who was never apprehended.

* * *

On December 24, an envelope arrived at Taylor's residence. Inside, it contained tickets from a pawn shop in Fresno, California for some of Taylor's stolen property and a note: "Dear Mr. Taylor: So sorry to inconvenience you, even temporarily. Also observe the lesson of the forced sale of assets. A Merry X-Mas and a happy and prosperous New Year. Alias Jimmie V."

Alias Jimmie Valentine was a 1920 Metro picture based on an O'Henry story about a thief who reformed himself after meeting a woman. It also inspired a song that included the line "he's a pal of mine, an educated crook."

The pawn tickets were in the name of William C. Deane-Tanner. The note was in the handwriting of Edward Sands.

* * *

The last person, other than his murderer, who saw Taylor alive was Mabel Normand. Notwithstanding her diminutive stature—standing under five feet tall and weighing under one hundred pounds—she was a heavyweight, albeit an aging one, at twenty-nine in the film industry, having starred in several movies with Fatty Arbuckle and Charlie Chaplin. Despite her pioneer status—a female writing, directing and producing movies—her career

Within minutes of movie megastar Mabel Normand leaving Taylor, he was dead.

The angelic looking, love struck Mary Miles Minter. Did she kill the man she loved?

was in decline, due in part to health problems and an addiction to cocaine. Given her good looks and obvious intelligence, it was no surprise that she, like so many others, had a robust relationship with Taylor. She was different though. Taylor loved her, which did not sit well with the others who vied for Taylor's time and affection, including the young love-struck movie starlet, Mary Miles Minter.

Mary was born Juliet Reilly on April 25, 1902 in Louisiana and started acting at the age of five. At ten, she made her screen debut. To get around the child labor laws, Juliet's mother, Charlotte Shelby, stole the identity of a deceased relative, Mary Miles Minter, who had been eight years older than Juliet. From there, the career of the newly named, adorable, curly-haired blond child skyrocketed, becoming a true star at the very outset of the making of movies. She also greatly enjoyed the life, despite the strong protestations of her mother. At fifteen or so, Minter fell in love with a fellow actor twenty years her senior, James Kirkwood, who strongly returned her affections, expressing his amorous feelings in the many letters he wrote her. Mary soon found herself pregnant, which caused her mother to threaten Kirkwood with death. In short order Kirkwood was in England on another project and Mary was undergoing an abortion.

A few years later, in 1919, Minter starred in *Anne of Green Gables,* directed by Taylor, with whom the fatherless seventeen-year-old again fell madly in love. The event, as before, set off her domineering and unpleasant mother, who herself allegedly had designs on the handsome director.

* * *

On the unseasonably cool evening of February 1st, Normand, chauffeured in her luxurious car, came to visit Taylor at his home around 7:00 and stayed for approximately three quarters of an hour. Taylor had invited her over, wishing to give her two books he had earlier purchased. Both shared a love of literature, Normand's nurtured in large part by the older film director. During her brief stay, Henry Peavey, the cook who replaced the now-gone Sands, left. As an African-American and subject to Jim Crow laws, he had a curfew and had to be off of the streets.

Normand, at twenty-nine, had earlier met Taylor, in 1918, and the two developed a friendship that deepened after Taylor's military service and the end of his engagement, in 1919, to Neva Gerber, with whom he remained on good terms. Taylor kept a picture of Mabel on his mantel and a small silver locket with her picture on his person. When she confessed to a drug habit that uncontrollably gripped her and pleaded for Taylor's help, he arranged inpatient care for her in New York. So incensed with the rampant use of drugs in Hollywood, Taylor reportedly confronted drug dealers on the set of his movies and forcibly removed them. He also turned to the federal government for assistance, contacting the prosecutor in charge of drug prosecutions and asking him to crack down, starting with those supplying Normand, whose habit was costing her thousands a month.

Taylor left the door to his house slightly ajar as he walked Mabel out a fair distance to the curb. They chatted for a few last minutes as she climbed into her car. Taylor told her that he'd call her at nine. As her chauffer slowly drove her away, she playfully blew kisses at Taylor, who returned the sweet gesture. She ended by planting her lips on the cool window, laughing as she did so.

Taylor turned and walked back to his home, where a single bullet awaited him.

* * *

When Peavey reported for work on the 2nd, he opened the locked front door and moved inside, heading toward the nearby living room. Taylor's feet greeted him.

"Mr. Taylor?" No response. Peavey stepped in closer. Taylor lay on his back, still elegantly dressed from the night before. His arms lay at his sides. His legs stretched out straight; his left one six inches under a chair; his right one pushed up against and partially folding a portion of the rug. Some blood sat by his mouth. When Peavey's brain finally processed what his wide-open eyes saw, the horrified cook ran outside, hysterically screaming, "Mr. Taylor's dead! Help, help! Mr. Taylor's dead!"

The nearby neighbors came scrambling. Quickly, Charlie Eyton, Paramount's general manager, was alerted and he made arrangements for three trusted hands from the studio to immediately rush to Taylor's home and remove any potentially scandalous materials—letters and booze, which was illegal given Prohibition. As Detective Zeigler and a fellow officer were arriving from the Wilshire Police Department, the materials were leaving. A doctor, who coincidentally had been nearby tending another patient, noticed the commotion and joined it, offering his services. After a cursory look and unable to turn the body until the arrival of the coroner, he declared the death due to a stomach hemorrhage. As Taylor had been known to suffer severe stomach discomfort—Peavey just that morning was bringing over milk of

Did Charlotte Shelby, the domineering and ferocious stage mother of Mary Miles Minter, murder Taylor?

magnesia—Detective Zeigler wrote "Natural Causes" in his report. More ominously, he also noted what Taylor's next door neighbors—Douglas and Faith MacLean—told him about hearing what could have been a gunshot, or backfire from a car, the evening before.

Eyton came shortly thereafter and greeted Ziegler, who accorded the familiar studio executive great respect, even allowing him to travel upstairs. Eyton hustled up in search of any other potential embarrassments that were overlooked by the minions he had sent earlier. At this point, while it appeared that Taylor's death was tragically natural, Eyton, given the Fatty Arbuckle imbroglio, acted to protect the reputation of the studio.

Deputy coroner William Macdonald arrived shortly before nine and, with the help of Charlie Eyton, who oddly seemed to be everywhere, turned the body over. A pool of blood. A bullet wound on Taylor's back. Eyton blurted out, "Good God, he's been murdered! Someone shot him in the back!"

Upon later hearing the horrible news, Faith MacLean exclaimed, "So it was a gunshot!" She shuddered upon the on-rushing realization that not only had she heard the gunshot but she had seen the killer.

* * *

Around eight o'clock the previous evening, Faith sat in her living room knitting. Nearby her maid Christina Jewett tidied up. Without warning, a noise rang out, causing Christina to shout, "Oh, wasn't that a shot?" Faith, who had heard the sound, wasn't as sure, thinking it might have merely been a loud sound emanating from some nearby automobile. Regardless, Faith walked to her front door, opened it and looked out, focusing on the lit doorway, which sat cater-cornered to her close-by neighbor, Bill, as she, like others, referred to Taylor.

Faith gave various statements to the police, an early one being: "[He did not seem in a hurry. He] was the coolest thing I have ever seen. He was facing Alvarado Street [away from me], and as I opened my door, I saw him. He turned around and looked at me—and hesitated. Then it seemed to me that Mr. Taylor must have spoken to him from inside the house. Seemed like he [the stranger] pulled the door shut. He turned around and, looking at me all the time, went down the couple of steps that go to Taylor's house. I thought it was just nothing, none of my business. I closed the door as he started in between [our] two houses. He [turned left, walked in my direction and made a second left] toward the alley and Maryland Street [in the rear of Taylor's house]."

Later she told the district attorney that the person wore a mackinaw-type heavy coat, a cap and a scarf. MacLean stated that the person appeared to be a man, but a "funny looking" one. When pressed, she indicated that she had been on movie sets with her husband where she saw actors and actresses in make-up, who appeared funny looking. From this the police surmised that the murderer could have been a female.

In the alleyway by Taylor's house, cigarette butts were discovered. Jewett had even reported that she had heard footsteps in that area, as if a man was heavily pacing back and forth. With this the police concluded that the killer waited in the alley and entered Taylor's house when he walked Normand to her car. Shortly after Taylor entered, he was shot once. As reported, "[t]he bullet entered Taylor's left side, about where his elbow would be if he were standing naturally, the bullet angled steeply upward, ending up at the right side of the base of his neck." Powder burns on the back of Taylor's jacket indicated that the shot had been fired inches away. Had the killer come up right up behind him? Or, conversely, had Taylor been embracing someone shorter, who reached to the victim's side, gun in hand? The unaligned bullet holes in the left portion of Taylor's jacket and vest also led to disparate theories. One being that Taylor was shot as he sat, hunched over, at his nearby desk, his arms outstretched as he worked on his income taxes, the forms of which were spread out over the desk; another being that his arms were raised as if being robbed. Robbery, however, was quickly discarded given that apparently nothing was taken from either the apartment or Taylor, who at death wore an expensive two carat diamond ring and platinum watch. Seventy-eight dollars sat in the pocket of his expensive pants, which remained undisturbed.

*　*　*

Like vultures on a dying buffalo, the newspapers throughout America stumbled over each other, often highlighting titillation over truth. In Taylor's bedroom, steamy love letters were discovered—"Wouldn't it be glorious to sit in a big comfy couch by a cozy warm fire with the wind whistling outside, trying to harmonize with the faint strains of music coming from the Victrola…. I'd go to my room and put on something scant and flowing; then I would lie on the couch and wait for you. I might fall asleep, for a fire makes me drowsy. Then I would awake and find two strong arms around me and two dear lips pressed to mine in a long, sweet kiss." Alongside the letters, a flimsy pink silk negligee, emblazoned with the initials MMM.

Death took on a life of itself. A nationally known nubile heartthrob—Mary Miles Minter—a child really at nineteen, caught up in the lecherous web of conniving film director Taylor, nearly fifty. Papers flew off of the stands, exploiting and fantasizing about the relationship.

In fact Taylor, well aware of the youngster's hungry crush on him, sought to distance himself from her. The task proved a difficult one as, a few days prior to the murder, Minter appeared at his house at three in the morning, refusing to leave.

When she heard of the death, Minter rushed to capture one last private moment, traveling first to his home and, upon discovering that his body had already been removed, to the morgue. Put off for a few days, she was finally allowed to see the man she worshiped. Sobbing uncontrollably as she gingerly touched his ice cold body, she screamed out, "God, please take me! They've crucified Jesus! They've crucified my mate! Who could've done this to him?"

Little did she know that many would come to believe that the killer was her very own mother, Charlotte Shelby.

* * *

The police initially focused on Edward F. Sands, Taylor's thieving assistant. The more they dug, the dirtier Sands grew. His real name was Edward Fitzgerald Snyder and, at seventeen, he enlisted in the Navy, from which he was dishonorably discharged after serving a year in the brig for embezzlement. Over the course of the next five years, he enlisted in various branches of the military, often under an alias, and always deserted. Ultimately, he moved to Hollywood, changed his name to Sands and found employment at Paramount, which, finding him an agreeable chap, recommended him to Taylor.

* * *

A story spread that Sands and Denis, Taylor's missing brother, were one and the same. The tale festered despite it clearly being untrue, given the nearly two decade age difference between the two, as well as their vastly different body types—Sands short and stocky, Denis tall and lean.

Regardless, other suspects soon elbowed Sands to the side, although he remained the chief target. Reports flew in of a man stopping by a gas station and asking the attendants where Taylor lived; another of a man seemingly waiting for a streetcar on the corner of 6th and Alvarado, but not boarding one when it arrived, instead walking to the rear of Taylor's house, all the while transferring an object from his left hip pocket to his right jacket pocket.

The police considered all angles—love, jealously, revenge, blackmail and even sexuality, given that Peavey, definitely, and Sands, perhaps, were "queer persons." Indeed, the illiterate Peavey was due in court that week for some indecent incident that occurred in a nearby park shortly before. That mystery keys, discovered in the apartment, opened nothing that could be located led to press speculation that they were for some love nest where Taylor carried on nefariously.

The drug slant remained a sharp one, with reports flying in from throughout the nation that angry drug dealers killed Taylor to avenge his intrusion into their racket. Strangely, the press not only reported this, but, adding drama to the sexual element, falsely turned Taylor's anti-drug crusade into one in which he was a pusher, using drugs to enslave defenseless young women.

A farmer reported that on the day before the murder, he picked up two hitchhikers, who had sworn vengeance against an overzealous Canadian officer named Bill—a man they said had caused them to be imprisoned during the War—and were travelling to Los Angeles to carry out their murderous deed. One even showed a .38 caliber gun, which used bullets similar to the type used in the actual killing.

Some thought the cook Peavey was the killer. For his part, Peavey was certain that Normand killed Taylor; that the two had argued on that last night. Meanwhile, a dozen confessions floated in from an assortment of people who clearly had nothing to do with the murder.

When Taylor's estate was probated, his accountant, who was confident of Taylor's wealth, discovered he had far less money than anticipated. Counting every asset, his worth was under twenty thousand dollars, a substantial sum at the time but low for a man making $35,000 a year. The diminished estate led investigators to consider that the victim had been blackmailed and when he refused to continue paying, death resulted. Like all other leads, this one too withered and died.

Shortly into their investigation, District Attorney Thomas Lee Woolwine, a good friend of Charlotte Shelby and the recipient of large donations from the studios, strangely took the homicide investigators off of the case and ordered that the evidence be held in his office. Soon those materials were transferred to his home, where they disappeared. Among the lost items were three strands of blond hair, which had earlier been determined to have belonged to Mary Miles Minter, found on the death jacket of the fastidious Mr. Taylor.

* * *

Charlotte Shelby was the ultimate stage mother, perversely obsessed and highly protective of her meal ticket and daughter Mary Miles Minter, who really did not enjoy her role in the movies and the heavy demands made upon her. If Mary were to be exploited, Shelby was the one to do it, going so far as to even confine Mary to her room when the circumstances called for it.

Foul-mouthed and unpleasant, Shelby threatened anyone who she perceived as a menace, including Taylor, with whom her daughter had fallen deeply in love. Regardless of the vast age difference between the two, and Taylor's relationship with Mabel Normand, Shelby confronted the director in front of others, screaming, "If I ever catch you hanging around Mary again, I will blow your goddamned brains out!" Shelby owned a .38 caliber gun and knew how to use it. During the investigation, Shelby failed to cooperate and even left California. Witnesses had her knowing about the murder prior to it being publicly announced. When the police planted a story in the papers about a spiritualist visualizing the killer as the mother of a famous mother star, Shelby's attorney, paper in hand, appeared at the DA's Office demanding to know who the spiritualist was and whether she had she named anyone. Years later, when the case was re-opened, Shelby repeatedly lied about her feelings toward Taylor, characterizing him as others had—a marvelous human being.

In time, Mary and her sister Margaret, given their financial exploitation, sued their mother. During court proceedings in 1937, explosive testimony had Margaret, an alcoholic who Charlotte had committed to a mental hospital the year before, accusing Charlotte, who herself had strong feelings toward Taylor, with the murder. In response, Shelby demanded that the then District Attorney, Buron Fitts, re-open the case, which he did. Damaging evidence against Shelby resulted. Her ex-chauffer, Chauncey Eaton, testified that after the murder Shelby handed him a .38 and asked him to remove and dispose of the bullets, explaining that she was doing it for the safety of her distraught daughter. Eaton hid the bullets in the basement on a beam. Fifteen years later Eaton led the investigators to the beam which still held the bullets. As for the gun, Margaret indicated that Shelby gave it to her mother, who threw it into a bayou in Louisiana, where the family originally lived. Whether the police ever looked for the gun where it was allegedly thrown is not known. What is known is that in the end, Shelby was never charged. Perhaps it was due to witnesses describing Taylor's killer as being 5 feet 9 inches tall and 165 pounds. Shelby stood 5 feet 2 inches and weighed around one hundred pounds. She also had an "alibi," claiming that she had been with Carl Stockdale on the night of the homicide. Stockdale for his part matched the description of the killer.

✳ ✳ ✳

Near the very end of her life, it was said Mabel Normand exclaimed, "I hope before I die that they find the slayer of William Desmond Taylor." It wasn't to be.

Every story should have an ending, satisfying or not, but at least neatly wrapping up all loose ends. How William Desmond Taylor lived and how he died has none and never will.

Epilogue

Although not having anything to do with the murder, Mabel Normand remained scandalized. Her troubles continued when, in 1924, her chauffer Joe Kelly, using Mabel's pistol, wounded Courtland Dines, the millionaire boyfriend of actress and Taylor neighbor Edna Purviance. Six years later, in 1930, Normand died, at thirty-seven, of tuberculosis, although some believe that drugs contributed to her demise.

A year after the murder, Mary Miles Minter, never happy as an actress, left show business at the age of twenty-two. She had appeared in over fifty films, most of which are today lost. After suing her mother, the two eventually reconciled; Shelby dying in Minter's home in 1957. That same year, Minter married. Her husband died in 1965. Mary lived in relative security but sadly was the victim of numerous burglaries; in one, she was viciously beaten. When she died in 1984, her neighbors could scarcely believe that their elderly and feeble neighbor had once shined brilliantly on the big screen. Like Mabel, she too has a star on the Hollywood Walk of Fame.

Neither Sands nor Denis were ever seen again.

Tidbits

In 1919, Taylor directed *Anne of Green Gables*, which was filmed in part in Dedham, Massachusetts. The movie, about a charming orphan adopted by a generous family, is based upon the novel of the same name, written by Lucy Maud Montgomery and published in 1908. Montgomery based the heroine, Anne Shirley, on a picture of Evelyn Nesbit, the love interest of Stanford White and Henry Thaw featured in the first chapter.

Upon learning of her father, Daisy, living in New York, wrote him in California. Shedding whatever desire he had to remain anonymous to his former family, Taylor wrote back. The two eventually met during the early summer of 1921. The reunion was a happy one and the two continued to correspond, happily looking forward to another meeting, which never happened.

Mabel Normand was due to marry her mentor and director Mack Sennett in 1915. When she found him in bed with actress Mae Busch, a scuffle broke out, resulting in Mabel suffering head injuries. Bleeding, she fled to the nearby home of Fatty and Minta Arbuckle, who took her to the hospital where she remained for several weeks. Needless to say, the engagement was called off. Mabel later, in 1918, gave birth to a stillborn child, the father being Samuel Goldwyn, with whom Normand made sixteen films from 1918–1921.

When the highly regarded actress Gloria Swanson, a good friend of the murdered Taylor (and one time lover of patriarch Joseph P. Kennedy), starred in *Sunset Boulevard*, her character—Norma Desmond—was reportedly named after Taylor and Mabel. The 1950 movie was nominated for eleven Academy Awards, winning three.

Margaret married film director Emmett J. Flynn in March 1937. Unfortunately, Flynn was still married at the time, which led to the marriage being annulled a month later. In June Flynn was found dead in his apartment. As King Vidor wrote in his book, "The similarities between the two crimes were frightening: two Hollywood directors, roughly the same age, killed under mysterious circumstances after being involved with a daughter of Charlotte Shelby's."

In 1923, an anti-drug film, *Human Wreckage*, was released. It opened with, "Dope in America is the gravest menace which today confronts the United States."

In the 1960s, the Alvarado Court dwellings were demolished and replaced by a supermarket.

Our Next Tale

When the silent movies went vocal, she became America's first sexpot to appear in them. The Blonde Bombshell even set a national fashion standard. At twenty-one she married one of the top creative geniuses at MGM. That he was twice her age raised some eyebrows. That he died three months later raised a whole lot more.

4

Things Are Seldom What They Seem

Upon discovering the grisly scene, MGM honcho Louis B. Mayer blurted out, "Oh my God, we can't have a murder." When the police arrived hours later, their job was made easy. A cursory investigation was conducted and it was quickly concluded that Paul Bern, the forty-two-year-old wunderkind movie producer, had taken his own life. They even had a suicide note.

Whispers, followed by a press conference held by Mayer, provided the reason for Bern's suicide. He could not sexually satisfy his twenty-one-year-old wife, "the reigning sex queen of the 30s," known variously as The Blond Bombshell, The Platinum Blond or simply Baby. Jean Harlow was that and more. At a time of strong social mores, she wore provocative outfits which highlighted her striking physical attributes. That her newly wed husband was impotent undoubtedly crushed him, leading him to take his own life. Or, at least, that's what the studio executives wanted the public to believe.

* * *

Harlean Carpenter was born in Kansas City, Missouri in 1911, to a headstrong mother, Jean Harlow, who obeyed her pushy and successful father and married a dentist, Montclair Carpenter, whom she did not love. It thus came as little surprise, even after the birth of a child, when the couple divorced ten years later.

With daughter in hand, Mama Jean Carpenter set off to Hollywood to make it in the pictures. When they arrived, Harlean enrolled in a private school. While the child prospered, the mother did not. Sadly, although still a young woman in her early thirties, she was too old for the movies. Armed with disappointment, the two person family returned to Missouri.

The eyes of Cupid were upon them however and quickly their fortunes turned, both finding love. Mama Jean to Marino Bello, a suave, self-promoting gadfly always on the lookout to make a quick buck, and sixteen-year-old Harlean, who ran away from a boarding school to wed twenty-three-year-old Chuck McGrew, the wealthy son of a well-connected family. Given her prematurely developed voluptuous figure, the justice of the peace surely had no idea that she was a minor. Mama Jean did however and she was none too pleased.

The young couple moved to Hollywood, in part to escape Harlean's disapproving mother. Not needing to work, they lived a life of comfort and leisure. They were young though, too young,

The beautiful and sexy Jean Harlow; *c.* 1930–31.

and problems unsurprisingly settled in. With her marriage starting to crumble and with little to do one day, Harlean jumped at the request of an actress friend for a ride to a movie studio for an appointment. After dropping her off, Harlean waited for her to return. Perchance a studio executive happened by and noticed the comely young lady. Her fate was sealed.

* * *

Harlean's difficulties with her mother were nothing more than the average teenager's with a parent. And when problems arose, the troubled child turned to the loving mother. Harlean split with Chuck and moved in with her mother and Bello, who both also ventured west. Her private life now settled, she turned to her professional one.

Harlean's first concern was her name; she needed a new one. After mulling several over, she concluded that none were better than her mother's maiden name. And a new Jean Harlow was born.

* * *

Compared to Baby Jean's roller coaster ride, the cultured and reserved Paul Bern led a far more serene life. Born in Germany in 1889, he and his family immigrated to America nine years later, ultimately settling in New York City. While there, Paul attended acting school. Bright and droll, he soon met a fellow student, the attractive and alluring Dorothy Millette. Soon the two were a couple, enraptured with one another. While Paul was finding love in 1911, Baby Jean was being born.

Ten years passed with Paul and Dorothy still together and still in love. And then tragedy. The time bomb of mental illness slowly ticking in Dorothy's head finally exploded, sending

The happy wedding of movie mogul Paul Bern
(1889–1932), and Jean Harlow (1911–1937), on July 4,
1932. In two months, Bern was dead. (*Corbis*)

Dorothy into a sanitarium. Her loyal lover vowed that she would receive only the very best of medical care.

While Paul would forever financially support Dorothy, he could do no more. Her illness took not only her sanity but her love. And with that, Paul left New York. Having decided that his future lay in working behind the cameras, not in front of them, Bern departed for Hollywood, where writing, directing and producing movies awaited him.

His talents were many and shortly after his move, he found himself at MGM and at the top of the heap. Working with his boss, the Boy Wonder Irving Thalberg, their studio MGM started releasing some of its greatest hits.

With Paul making movies and with Jean appearing in them, it was just a matter of time until the two rising stars collided. And then they did.

∗ ∗ ∗

A casting director brought Harlow by Bern's office for a meet and greet. Bern was immediately smitten; so too apparently Jean, who invited him to the premiere of her coming-out movie, *Hell's Angels*, a film directed by the iconic, and soon to be rather crazy, Howard Hughes. In typical Hughes fashion, the publicity department went into warp overload, which successfully resulted in thousands of movie patrons crowding the streets and packing the theater for its debut. Despite many critics panning her performance, few could deny that she possessed that undefinable "it" quality. And soon, throughout the nation, women, blinded by Jean's brilliant platinum hair, started emulating it.

Bern thought Harlow perfect for MGM's latest romantic comedy, *Red-Headed Woman,* and battled with a reluctant Thalberg about casting her. Thalberg, like others, thought Harlow a short-on-talent blond sexpot, who enhanced her talents by neither wearing a bra nor underwear and rubbing her nipples with ice to gain a desired appearance; worse in his view, she was being asked to change the color of her famous hair for the movie that was essentially a comedy. Bern, on the other hand, saw something and someone radically different; an actress who could not only act but act humorously if called upon. As he was wont to say, "Things are seldom what they seem." In Harlow's case, Paul was right. Thalberg gave in and Harlow was cast. The movie's release in June 1932 catapulted Harlow, becoming the first major sex symbol of the new-fangled talking movies.

One month later, on July 2, 1932, Harlow and Bern, to everyone's surprise, if not shock, were married. Not only was he, at forty-two, twice as old as his young wife, but they were seemingly so different; he a thoughtful, generous, laid back gentleman of culture and ordinary looks who shunned the spotlight; she an over-the-top sex kitten. To all, however, they seemed to be very much in love.

On September 5th he was dead.

* * *

An inquest was held in which relatively few significant witnesses appeared. Harlow, citing emotional strain, was not there. Testimony revealed Harlow leaving their marital home and going to her mother's for dinner while Bern stayed behind. The police told of the physical evidence—Bern, holding a gun in his right hand, found dead of a single gunshot wound to his head. While the location of a diary was discussed, surprisingly the suicide note itself was not. Regardless, the conclusion reached was a foregone one—"suicide ... motive undetermined."

MGM supplied the motive—impotency—and the press revealed the contents of the note discovered on his dresser bureau:

> Dearest Dear,
> Unfortuately [sic] this is the only way
> to make good the frightful wrong I have
> done you and to wipe out my abject humiliation.
> I Love You.
> Paul
> You understand that last night was only a comedy.

Bern, unable to sexually satisfy his beautiful young wife had committed suicide. The judgment then, and still the official version to this very day.

But untrue.

* * *

At all costs, the image of MGM and its stars had to be preserved and protected. Scandal was unacceptable. Taking care of the distasteful Bern matter went to the head of MGM security,

Whitey Hendry, and its publicity director, Howard "The Fixer" Strickling. Both were on the scene hours before the police. Both remained involved with the matter until it went away.

The inquest never heard from a neighbor, Slavko Vorkapich, who saw a limousine deposit a "woman in black" to Bern's house. Later Slavko heard loud voices, intermittently arguing and laughing. Nor did it hear any evidence concerning Dorothy Millette, the woman deep in Bern's background. Having lived together years earlier as husband and wife, Bern's earlier will left everything to "my wife Dorothy." If in fact they had been married and never divorced, the Bern-Harlow marriage was a bigamous sham, disastrous to the public image of MGM and its star.

After Millette left her sanatorium, she lived in New York City's famed Algonquin Hotel. Bern, as always, paid for her expenses. Still exhibiting signs of mental instability, Millette frequently irrationally threatened to join Paul in Hollywood to rekindle both their relationship and her acting career. She finally made good when she checked out of the Algonquin and traveled first to San Francisco and then Los Angeles. She was the woman in black. They argued and she shot him, using one of his guns casually displayed in his bedroom. She fled, leaving behind a single shoe never given to the police, into a waiting MGM limo, that Bern had earlier called. The voucher for the trip indicated that the chauffer drove his charge to San Francisco. As for the undated, ambiguous "suicide note," it was either forged or, more likely, it referred to a prior tiff between the parties. Most damaging, long after Hendry left the studio, he confided to a friend that he had arranged the murder scene to make it look like a suicide.

Epilogue

A few days after the murder, Dorothy Millette killed herself. She had boarded the Delta King, a boat sailing on the waters of the Sacramento River, and jumped overboard. Her body washed up on the shores of San Francisco. Penniless and about to be sent to a pauper's grave, someone quietly paid for her to be buried in an upscale cemetery. Her tombstone was simple, reading: "Dorothy Millette Bern 1886–1932." The donor? Jean Harlow.

Tidbits

So intent on protecting Harlow and portraying her sympathetically, false stories emerged in the press savagely attacking Bern, depicting him as an impotent and violent woman-beater.

Prior to her marriage, Harlow was democratic in her choices of escorts. She dated all types of men, including "The Al Capone of New Jersey," mobster Abner "Longie" Zwillman. Despite engaging in an affair, he privately spoke disparagingly of her. Stories abounded of his carrying strands of Jean's pubic hair in his wallet and giving other strands, encased in gold lockets, to gangster friends.

Shortly after Bern's death, Harlow engaged in a fairly open affair with heavyweight boxer Max Baer, who in a highly ballyhooed match in June 1933, defeated German heavyweight and Hitler-favorite Max Schmeling. To avoid the adverse publicity of a romance with the married Baer, the studio pressured Jean to marry a compliant Harold Rosson, a movie cinematographer. They were quietly divorced seven months later, in 1934.

Jean died in 1937, just five years after Paul. She was only twenty-six. Notwithstanding the more scandalous rumors of the cause of her death, it appears that she died of kidney failure.

The Boy Wonder Irving Thalberg, always sickly, also died at a young age, thirty-seven, in 1936. In his honor, the Irving G. Thalberg Memorial Award was created, which goes to "creative producers, whose bodies of work reflect a consistently high quality of motion picture production."

When young Jean Harlow went to school in Hollywood, one of her classmates, Irene, was the daughter of Louie B. Mayer. Irene later married David O. Selznick and both served in the Harlow-Bern wedding party. Selznick produced a number of classic movies, including *Gone with the Wind*.

F. Scott Fitzgerald wrote the original screenplay for *Red-Headed Woman*. When MGM ordered a rewrite, the assignment going to Anita Loos, Fitzgerald responded with a lengthy bender.

The November 1960 issue of *Playboy Magazine* published a Hollywood Babylon-type article by noted writer Ben Hecht. In it, Hecht casually wrote that everyone in Hollywood knew that Bern had not committed suicide, but rather was "the murder victim by another woman." The article rekindled the investigation but given that most of those connected with the incident were dead, it too quickly died out.

In the 1960s, hairstylist Jay Sebring rented what had been the Bern-Harlow house. One night when Jay was out of town, he allowed his good friend, Sharon Tate, to stay there. While in bed, she felt the eerie presence of not being alone. Suddenly she saw a ghost, who looked like Bern. Fleeing down the stairs, she saw another vapor-like figure—either of her or Jay—with a cut throat and tied to the stairway. Three years later, in her house less than a mile away, Tate, Sebring and three others were slaughtered by the Charles Manson Family.

Our Next Tale

The dashing, swash-buckling movie star Errol Flynn played Robin Hood, General George Armstrong Custer, Don Juan, kings, princes and pirates and various other devil-may-care action heroes. Millions loved both his movies and the star in them. In turn, the ruggedly handsome, hard drinking actor loved them back. Especially the ladies. Especially the young ones.

5

Old Whiskey and Young Women

He was the original Tasmanian devil: a charming rogue as dashing and devilish off the screen as he was on it. At a fit and muscular 6 feet 2 inches, 180 pounds, the seemingly permanently bronzed hulk, complete with a cleft chin and dimples, looked every bit the movie star that he was. Perhaps unknowingly being far more insightful than he intended, he described his life as, "I like my whiskey old and my women young." Little did he know he was describing his downfall.

* * *

Errol Flynn was born on June 20, 1909 in Australia. Tasmania to be exact. His father was a biology professor. For whatever reason, Flynn hated his mother, explaining perhaps a lifelong distrust of women. It didn't stop him however from loving them, often. His attentions and interests were invariably returned.

After a somewhat turbulent school career which found him in trouble for fighting and having sex with the daughter of a school employee, Flynn left for a succession of seemingly romantic jobs—prospecting for gold, working in a copper mine and on a tobacco plantation, before deciding to try his hand at acting. He landed his first role, a minor one filmed in New Guinea, in 1933. Two years later he married the French actress Lili Damita, who bore him one son. The lure of Hollywood beckoned and soon he was in America where good fortune awaited.

* * *

In the wake of MGM's popular *Mutiny on the Bounty*, Warner Brothers searched for a similar movie to make and settled on *Captain Blood*. When the studio's first choice dropped out due to a medical ailment, in flew the unknown Flynn, whose wife Lili fortuitously was good friends with the wife of the head of the studio. Little did the studio realize that its fictional character—that of a "devil may care philanderer"—fit Flynn, who was playing that role in real life, to a tee.

The public loved both the movie and its star and soon Flynn was cast in a movie that would forever define him. In *The Adventures of Robin Hood*, he again played the debonair swashbuckler. And now everyone in America knew him.

As busy as he was working—he often made three movies a year—and despite being married, his nightlife was hectic, active and never-ending. He partied and he drank, not necessarily in that order. Many of his female cohorts, whom he often met in the fast lane of show business, were attractive and young. It thus came as little surprise, to the Hollywood crowd at least, that in 1942, the year of his divorce, he was charged with statutory rape; of having sexual relations, at different times, with seventeen-year-old Betty Hansen, an aspiring actress, and sixteen-year-old Peggy Satterlee, a dancer at the renowned night-club The Florentine Gardens, which featured food, music, entertainment and scantily clad showgirls.

* * *

The trial, which ran for nearly a month in early 1943, resembled a Flynn movie, complete with a multitude of adoring fans mobbing the area in and around the courthouse. Starring in the role of his primary defender stood Jerry Geisler, the high-powered attorney to the stars, the rich and the famous. The jury was packed with women who, Geisler hoped, would be drawn to the charismatic defendant, who sat quietly as the two young girls recounted the lurid details from the witness stand. They both appeared, at the behest of the prosecutors, without makeup and modestly dressed, to highlight their youthful innocence.

The pretty Betty Hansen took the stand first and detailed the dinner she had with Errol at the home of one of his friends; of how she drank some foul-tasting drink which sickened her, whereupon Errol took her upstairs where they had sex.

Left: The dashing Errol Flynn with his equally vivacious wife Lili Damita; 1941.

Right: Deputy District Attorney Thomas Cochran questioning the comely under-aged sex "victim," Peggy Satterlee on January 20, 1943. (*Corbis*)

Satterlee, similarly, told the enraptured jurors that Flynn took advantage of her on his yacht. Indicative of their close friendship and sexual relationship, Flynn had earlier alternatively nicknamed her both "J.B."—for jail bait—and "S.Q.Q."—short for San Quentin Quail. On successive evenings, they engaged in unwelcomed relations on the gentle ocean, surrounded by the moon and the stars and various guests, none of whom she approached about any untoward advances.

On cross-examination, Geisler had a field day with both girls, which at some points had spectators either laughing or shaking their heads in disbelief. The witnesses confused their stories and readily admitted to sordid pasts and lying about their ages. They also told of an abortion and being the subject of an on-going criminal investigation.

Although he probably didn't need to, Flynn took the stand and casually testified that he never had sexual relations with the two. After the defense rested and the judge gave his final instructions, the case was left in the hands of the jury. After deliberating for thirteen hours, the jurors slowly entered a packed and now-tense courtroom. The verdict was rendered.

In a scene worthy of a Hollywood drama, bedlam broke out. The crowd cheered lustily as the defendant spontaneously leapt to his feet, a broad smile stretching his handsome face. Flashbulbs popped. Female admirers rushed to touch the star. His lawyers, also on their feet, congratulated both him and each other for a job well done. The judge rendered the final review when he told the jury, which had just presided over a lengthy trial involving the alleged ravaging of two young females, "I have enjoyed the case, and I think you have."

While similar scandals had wrecked careers in the past, this one had the opposite effect. Errol's popularity soared. Indeed, indicative of his devil-may-care persona and, like a cat always landing on his feet, a term was coined which found popularity throughout the world: "In like Flynn."

As always, Flynn remained in character. During the breaks of his trial, the bad boy spent much of his time wooing eighteen-year-old Nora Eddington, who worked in a nearby food stand. When she became pregnant, they wed. They had two children before divorcing in 1949.

Epilogue

A year later, in 1950, Flynn wed for the third time, this time to Patrice Wymore. Later, despite being married, he, as always, took up with another woman, this one an aspiring actress, Beverly Aadland. He even helped her secure a role in what would be his fifty-eighth and final feature length movie, *Cuban Rebel Girls*. Early in the affair, calling her by the nickname he had given her, he sighed, "Here I go again Woodsey." She was fifteen.

This romance however would not end like the others. A lifetime of drinking and carousing exacted its ultimate and expected revenge. His observation—"I've got a zest for living but twice an urge to die"—was astute. His good looks, like his career and health, faded as he bloated up and prematurely aged. He died in 1959, having just turned fifty.

Tidbits

Despite his swashbuckling image, Flynn was rejected from military service due to a myriad of health problems. At one point or another, he suffered from heart troubles, malaria, back pain (which he self-medicated with morphine and later, heroin), tuberculosis, and numerous venereal diseases. He came under criticism for not serving America, of which he became a citizen in 1942.

In all, Flynn had four children. His only son, Sean, became a noted war correspondent and went missing in 1970 in Cambodia. His body has never been recovered and he was thought to be killed by the Khmer Rouge.

Flynn enjoyed sailing and owned two yachts, the Sirocco and Zaca. Flynn first spotted the Sirocco while working in Sydney, Australia. In 1930, he and three friends sailed to New Guinea. Eight years later, he sailed it to Miami and later Jamaica.

The Zaca operated as a patrol and rescue ship in the San Francisco area during World War II. Flynn purchased it in 1945 and sailed it to Acapulco and the Mediterranean. In 1950, Flynn and third wife Patrice lived on board. After Flynn's death, the Zaca was abandoned in France and became known as a ghost ship. Locals claimed there were emanations of Flynn coming from the vessel and the sound of wild parties at night. These stories ended after a dual Anglican-Catholic exorcism in 1979.

His last appearance was on the Red Skelton television show on September 29, 1959. He died a few weeks later, on October 14.

Some controversial books have accused him of being a Nazi sympathizer and spy as well as being bisexual. The claims are probably false. Indeed, Flynn was a friend of Fidel Castro. His last film, as already noted, was *Cuban Rebel Girls*.

Our Next Tale

Movie star Lana Turner had it all—talent, husbands and ambition. She also had a gangster boyfriend, Johnny Stompanato, who thought nothing of smacking her around. One evening Lana's sixteen-year-old daughter Cheryl took umbrage at how Johnny treated her mother. To get her point across she jabbed him with a sharp knife.

6

The Movie Star and the Mobster

Married eight times to seven different men, Lana Turner epitomized the fast lane of show business. When she wasn't married, she was having affairs with many of Hollywood's leading men. The high life included partying, drugs, alcohol, abortions and an attempted suicide. It also included murder.

* * *

Lana Turner defined the meaning of "star." The platinum-crowned, sophisticated debutante sported garments perfectly tailored, fingernails impeccably manicured, and make-up flawlessly applied. Her soft, angelic, and graceful features pleasantly complemented her voluptuous figure and sensuous voice. Her many sparkling jewels bedazzled.

Behind the scenes at MGM, where she worked, things—like in the times of Jean Harlow—were not always quite as immaculate and luxurious. Lana was notoriously promiscuous and scandalous, having had several romances with celebrities such as Clark Gable, Frank Sinatra, Mickey Rooney, Tyrone Power and a host of others, which caused the publicity-conscious studio heartache and cover-up.

* * *

Lana Turner was born Julia Jean Turner on February 8, 1921 in a small mining town in Wallace, Idaho. Her porcelain complexion and blue eyes were tokens of her Scottish, Irish, Dutch and English heritage. Her father, John Virgil, a lighthearted man, earned a living occasionally in the mines and more often at the poker tables. His wantonness and gambling often left the family destitute. The family soon fell apart and Lana was forced to board with family friends. After a few additional years of hardship, Lana, her mother Mildred Frances Cowan, and Virgil relocated, landing in San Francisco in 1927. Three years later, Virgil won big shooting craps. When his body was discovered shortly thereafter the money was missing.

With her health starting to fail, Mildred was advised to seek warmer weather, which she did, moving in 1935, with fifteen-year-old Lana, to Los Angeles. They fit right in. It was the Depression and seemingly everyone was poor.

Dreaming of becoming a dress designer, Turner attended Hollywood High School. A month into her school year there, she innocently, if not mischievously, decided to skip classes. While enjoying a soda at the Top Hat Café, she was noticed by Billy Wilkerson—the founder of the highly influential Hollywood Reporter—who was mesmerized by her looks. Beauty, innocence, youth, provocation. A chance encounter in a soda bar. A career launched.

On February 20, 1938, Lana signed with MGM, the number one movie studio in America. Given her sexy looks and penchant for donning tightly worn sweaters, she was quickly dubbed The Sweater Girl. Since the company strove to exemplify a pure, all-American appearance, it went to great lengths to conceal Lana's excessive drinking, cigarette-smoking and nightclub-carousing.

Lana met her first husband, bandleader Artie Shaw, on the set of a movie in which she played a professional dancer. The talented and egotistical Shaw possessed an overbearing personality and hungry appetite for women. His philosophy for bedding a woman was either to marry her, which he did eight times, or merely propose it. Upon hearing of his marriage to Lana, Judy Garland, who thought she was in a serious relationship with Shaw, was crestfallen; so too Betty Grable, who then aborted their baby. His marriage to Lana lasted four months.

Lana's second husband, the tall and suave actor Steve Crane claimed to be a tobacco heir from Indiana and a member of Phi Beta Kappa. In fact, he came from a middle-class family whose father owned a pool hall and cigar stand. Crane lived off of his gambling profits, and mingled with the elite of Hollywood. An affluent philanderer, he wasn't divorced from his first wife when he married Lana. When that came to light, the marriage was annulled. Shortly thereafter they remarried. In that short marriage, Turner gave birth to her only child, Cheryl Crane, on July 25, 1943. Crane, hoping for a boy, was disappointed and left Lana at the hospital, a portent of things to come. Shortly thereafter they were divorced.

To counter Lana's partying, drinking and smoking ways, MGM used Cheryl as a prop, photographing mother and daughter, and portraying their star as an attentive and loving mother. In reality, Lana was far too occupied with filming and dating to devote time to her daughter. The star's temperament, like her mothering skills, was fickle, shifting from chipper cheerfulness to profound depression. To combat her down periods, she popped amphetamines.

It was during this time period that Turner, in 1946, rendered her greatest movie performance, that of Cora Smith in *The Postman Always Rings Twice*. The sexy young Cora, married to the middle-aged and unattractive Nick, is unhappily idling her life away as a waitress at a dusty, out-of-the-way dinner joint, when drifter Frank Chambers stumbles in. Soon an enthusiastic Cora has seduced a somewhat suspicious Chambers and together they successfully plot the murder of Nick to collect his insurance. The movie won Turner accolades. Of her co-star John Garfield, who played her lover, she complained that he wasn't good-looking enough.

In 1948 Turner married Henry Topping Jr., the millionaire brother of Dan Topping, who owned The New York Yankees. The nuptials came three days after Henry divorced his third wife, who had earlier been married to his brother Dan. The marriage, from 1948–1952, lasted longer than usual.

A year later, in 1953, Tarzan flew into Lana's life. Lex Barker, who played the jungle god, was sexy, charming and handsome. He was also a child molester who openly exposed himself

The Academy Award nominee Lana Turner who probably had far more lovers to her credit than the over fifty movies she made.

and masturbated and even raped ten-year-old Cheryl. Like all pedophiles, he threatened the young child, telling her that no one would believe her if she told and that she would be hauled off to reform school. She finally did and Lana threw her protesting husband out.

Turner's personal life, in its continual state of turmoil and mischief, soon collided with what had been her smooth-sailing professional one. Choppy waters lay ahead. A series of poorly received movies coupled with a movie industry under siege. Studios, which had created a monopoly, were ordered by the courts to sell the movie theaters they owned. Additionally, and more ominously, the growing popularity of television was threatening the entire film business. MGM reacted to the financial calamity by letting Turner go. Despite being one of its major stars, she was also one of its most expensive. The studio—her home really for nearly two decades—that had lavished and sheltered her, was now kicking her to the sidewalk. Lana grew resentful and bitter, complaining of her treatment and the obligation to repay hefty loans, leaving her financially vulnerable. She shared her growing woes with the bottle and grew more and more inebriated. Soon she was blaming Cheryl for some of her troubles, once going so far as to strike her. Cheryl left and moved in with her grandmother.

Still a talented and great beauty, Lana rebounded in 1957, a year which proved to be a watershed for her. She received an Academy Award nomination for best actress for her role in 20th Century's *Peyton Place*, a movie about small town America and its many hypocrisies.

Lana also began receiving incessant phone calls from a mysterious secret admirer, John Steele. She tried ignoring him, but Steele was insistent, sending her bouquets several times a week and turning to her friends, whom he had cultivated, for support. When Lana finally gave in and invited him over for lunch, he arrived, carrying a plate from her favorite restaurant and an engraved, diamond bracelet.

Lana Turner with her killer of a young daughter, Cheryl Crane, 1959. (*Library of Congress*)

The attractive and sexy but mysterious man's true name was Johnny Stompanato, who possessed many monikers—Handsome Harry, Johnny Stomp and Oscar (for the Academy Award size of his notable male organ). He worked for Los Angeles mobster Mickey Cohen. A dapper, lizard shoe-wearing nightclub regular, Stompanato squired older, wealthy women about town. He took their money and dumped them when they no longer served his purposes. A former Marine, he saw action during WWII in the Pacific. He had been married three or possibly four times, the first to a Muslim woman for whom he converted. In 1949, he married actress Helen Gilbert, who played a teacher in *Andy Hardy Gets Spring Fever*. As usual, Johnny was with an older woman, one with the experience of marriage. He was her fourth of seven husbands. The marriage lasted for less than six months. In 1953, he married Helene Stanley, the model for such Disney classic characters as *Cinderella*, *Sleeping Beauty* and the young wife in *101 Dalmatians*. That marriage lasted two years.

As enticing as he could be, Stompanato also possessed a mean streak of jealousy, which was easily aroused, and an equally strong temper. When gossip began swirling about Lana's relationship with her leading man, Sean Connery, on the movie set of one of her next projects, *Another Time, Another Place*, Stompanato confronted Connery, who, perhaps apocryphally, in true James Bond fashion, subdued the gangster, who quickly fled the scene. Stompanato took out his rage on Lana, with whom he now frequently argued. Forbidden to attend the 1957 Academy Awards, which were held on March 26, 1958, he barged into Lana's bedroom and slapped her, sending her crashing to the floor. Fearful of notifying the authorities, Lana didn't, afraid that Stompanato would carry out his threats to have her mother and daughter killed.

The tempestuous relationship incinerated a week later, on April 4, Good Friday, with yet another violent argument in Lana's bedroom and threats to cut her up. Concerned,

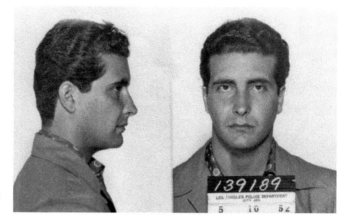

The 1952 mugshot of former Marine and mobster Johnny Stompanato, who got it from teenaged Cheryl Crane.

fourteen-year-old Cheryl knocked on the door, took her mother by the hand and led her from the bedroom. She begged Turner to get rid of her abuser. Lana told Cheryl of her great fear of Stompanato and went back into the bedroom. The arguing continued. Lana asked him to leave, a request that he refused. More threats. Lana crying. Cheryl went downstairs and retrieved a knife from the kitchen and traveled back to her mother's bedroom door. The argument grew even louder, the threats even more violent. Cheryl begged her mother to open the door. Finally she did. Cheryl saw Johnny with his hand up as if to hit Lana. Cheryl stepped into the room. Stompanato stepped into the knife. His eyes met Cheryl's as he slowly fell to the floor.

Lana phoned her mother, yelling for her to call a doctor. Cheryl called her father, screaming that something bad had happened and to get over to the house. The doctor came. Crane came. Stompanato was dead. A lawyer—the lawyer to the stars—was called: Jerry Geisler, who quickly arrived.

Cheryl's story to the police, when they responded, was that she was trying to protect her mother, whose own version of the incident had some discrepancies. Lana claimed that Stompanato was leaving, holding a jacket and shirt retrieved from a hanger. She insisted that Stompanato's hand was not raised as if trying to hit her.

Bail was denied, sending Cheryl off to juvenile hall. Her mother meanwhile grew distraught and gaunt and turned to sedatives to calm herself. Mickey Cohen argued that his associate's murder was suspicious and swore vengeance. And he quickly got it. Shortly after the stabbing, Stompanato's apartment was burglarized. Letters were stolen and leaked to the press, which delighted in printing missives from Lana to "My Beloved Love," "My Dearest Darling Love" and detailing "our love, our hopes, our dreams, our sex." Some even came from Cheryl, ending with, "Love ya and miss ya." Thanks to the handiwork of Cohen, the nation, from coast to coast, had now entered the world of Lana, titillation and all. And soon the questions arose.

Was Cheryl taking the rap for her mother? What was the real relationship between Cheryl and the man she killed? Why were there no fingerprints on the knife? Why was there so little blood, either in the bedroom, which showed no signs of disarray, or on Lana, who allegedly tended to her dying paramour? What really happened?

Famed attorney to the stars Jerry Geisler, with Marilyn Monroe at her 1954 divorce hearing with Joe DiMaggio. Did he help Lana clean up the Stompanato murder scene?

A week after the killing, a non-binding inquest was convened. Answers would be provided. The hearing room was packed. Of the 160 available seats in the courtroom, the press took 120. The networks and radio covered the event live. The public lined up at dawn to claim the remaining forty seats.

First called to testify, Mickey Cohen. When asked for the identity of the deceased, Cohen reverted to gangster form and took the Fifth. Medical evidence came next, revealing a single fatal stab wound caused by the eight inch blade of a kitchen knife. Death came quickly.

And then Lana, the star herself, in the role of her life. She fashionably dressed for the part—a gray silk suit, white gloves and a hat. Impeccable as always, not a strand of her radiant platinum hair out of place. Make-up artists, arriving at her home early that morning, saw to that. For an hour she slowly recounted the terror of the evening. Breaking down twice, she captivated her audience, of the tale of a beloved daughter accidentally stabbing an abusive thug of a man.

The jurors were moved. After a brief deliberation of less than half an hour, they returned their verdict—justifiable homicide.

Epilogue

Mickey Cohen, disgusted with the criminal justice system, exclaimed, "It's the first time in my life I've ever seen a dead man convicted of his own murder." Stompanato's family sued; the case was settled out of court. Cheryl, now estranged from a mother who failed to mother her, left to live with her grandmother. Two of Lana's movies at the time—*Peyton Place* and *Imitation of Life*—jumped in popularity at the box office, courtesy of the publicity surrounding the killing. Ironically, in *Peyton Place*, Turner wore some of the expensive jewelry Stompanato had lavished on her.

Lana laid low for a short time and, when the excitement dissipated, bounced back to her omnipotent self, marrying three more times: to Frederick May of the May Department Stores empire; to actor and producer Robert Eaton, whose primary asset, being ten years younger than Lana, was his ability to satisfy her in bed; and hypnotist and magician Ronald Dante, whose real last name was Peller, who skipped out of their marriage with a $35,000 check she had given him.

The Sweater Girl eventually reclaimed a bond with her daughter, and retired in 1983 after a glorious career in the limelight. She died in 1995 of cancer. Cheryl meanwhile engaged in a successful business career, wrote a book about the incident and fell in love with another woman, with whom she has spent decades.

Tidbits

Legend has it that Turner was discovered at Schwab's Pharmacy. In fact, it was at the Top Hat Café.

William Wilkerson, the man who discovered Turner, not only started *The Hollywood Reporter*, but he helped found Las Vegas. An inveterate gambler, he figured it was best to keep his losses in house. Married six times, the hard-working, hard-drinking, hard-gambling partier died in 1962 at seventy-one.

Wilkerson referred Turner to a talent agency owned by Zeppo Marx, brother of Groucho, Harpo and Chico. Zeppo and his wife Barbara divorced in 1973. Three years later Barbara married Frank Sinatra, one of Lana's many bedmates.

MGM intended Turner to be their next Jean Harlow, who had recently died. Like Harlow, Turner also has a Walk of Fame star, located at 6241 Hollywood Blvd.

Turner lost her Academy Award to Joanne Woodward who starred in *The Three Faces of Eve*. *The Bridge on the River Kwai* won Best Picture, Director (David Lean) and Actor (Alec Guinness).

Lana shaved off her eyebrows for her role in the movie *Marco Polo*. Allegedly, they never grew back.

Turner was a popular pin-up for the GIs fighting in World War II.
A Turner saying, "A gentleman is simply a patient wolf."

Earlier, Jerry Geisler defended Errol Flynn and Charlie Chaplin in their statutory rape trials. He also represented Marilyn Monroe in her divorce from New York Yankee great Joe DiMaggio.

Turner had just moved into her new residence a few days before, on a Tuesday. Stompanato helped her with the move.

In a book by one of her many male friends, Eric Root claims that Turner told him that she killed Stompanato after catching him in bed with Cheryl. Turner then enlisted the aid of attorney Geisler and another to clean up the very bloody murder scene. Geisler might also have destroyed some compromising pictures of Turner and Stompanato.

When Cheryl was two, the FBI discovered a plot to kidnap her. Undercover police personnel, posing as gardeners, repairmen and deliverymen, led to the capture of the potential kidnapper, who turned out to be a former cellmate of one of Lana's mother's half-brothers.

Our Next Tale

Everyone loved television star Bob Crane, star of the hit show, *Hogan's Heroes*. That he was a sex fiend threatened to ruin his career. In the end, it did far more. It ended his life.

7

Colonel Hogan

When the popular actor and former star of *Hogan's Heroes* left The Windmill Dinner Theater after his performance in the light comedy *Beginner's Luck,* he was dismayed to find that his car had a flat tire. His luck was running bad. With his fiftieth birthday around the corner and in the midst of a bitter divorce from his second wife Patti, Bob Crane, along with his companion and good friend John Carpenter, jumped into his car and drove it, flat tire and all, to a nearby gas station. The tire was replaced along with the attendant promising to repair the original one within a day. After Crane left, the employee started fixing the flat when he made an interesting discovery. The tire had been tampered with, its valve loosened.

* * *

Bob Crane was, in essence, like many in show business; handsome, fit and six feet tall. With his dark brown hair just starting to gray, Crane exuded a smooth-talking, glib and confident persona. He hid his insecurities—a lack of education, the need to be loved, and the expectation, like many successful and powerful people, of getting his way. His skin was thin however and when criticism bit, it left a deep scar. On the surface though, to his many fans, he was the epitome of an accommodating star—friendly, likeable and outgoing, only too happy to sign an autograph or have his picture snapped.

Crane also lived on the edges as a sex addict, if not fiend—into pornography and swinging and having sex as frequently as possible with the litany of women, married and unmarried, who wanted to be with a star, even one whose career was fading. Astoundingly open about his sexual proclivities, he gladly displayed his large white photo album, which he toted around from city to city, containing hundreds of Polaroid pictures of naked women. Most of those depicted were shown fellating him. While an egalitarian in the selection of his sexual conquests, he preferred his women blond, blue-eyed, young and large-breasted. Taking advantage of the blossoming video camera and equipment industry, Crane shot scores of his sexual encounters, many involving unsuspecting female partners. His videos and photos also frequently featured his friend John Carpenter, a video whiz, who had introduced Crane to the new technological age and often set up their many sexual romps and parties. While Crane was heterosexual, it was thought his crony swung both ways. The two shared a close

The sex crazed Emmy nominated television star Robert Crane; (1928–1978).

relationship; Carpenter arranging his work schedule in the electronics field to join Crane. While friends often thought the two stayed together, in his latest visit at least, Carpenter stayed at the nearby motel, a half a block away.

✴ ✴ ✴

Crane starred for six seasons on the highly successful television comedy *Hogan's Heroes*. He received two Emmy nominations before the well-received show was cancelled in 1971. Thereafter, Crane made guest appearances on various television programs, starred in two Disney movies and performed in dinner theater productions, most notably *Beginners Luck,* a play in which he starred and directed. It toured throughout the country for years, allowing Crane to find hundreds of willing sex partners, before ultimately landing in Scottsdale, Arizona at the Windmill Theater.

✴ ✴ ✴

After having his flat tire repaired, Bob and John travelled to Crane's nicely furnished two-bedroom apartment, where Crane placed a telephone call to his estranged wife Patti. Within minutes, the two were engaged in a battle, Crane yelling so loudly that his neighbors could hear him. After twenty minutes, Crane slammed the phone down. Soon he was back in his car, travelling with Carpenter to a local watering hole, Bogarts. Despite it being nearly midnight, the evening was just starting for Crane, who often stayed out late and arose early. He required little sleep. When he did, he slept extremely lightly. A door opening or a nearby sound would ordinarily jolt him awake. As was his habit, regardless of whether he was in or out, he always locked his apartment door, often employing both the ordinary door lock as well as the deadbolt.

At Bogarts Crane met a fan, Carol, who was soon accompanying him and John back to Crane's apartment complex. There, Carol got in Carpenter's car, which followed Cranes' to another bar, the Safari, where Crane had earlier made plans to meet another female friend,

Carolyn. Unusually, both Carpenter and Crane struck out with their companions, both of whom spurned sexual advances. It was a rarity for Crane not to score. Indeed he had just had sex the day before with yet another woman. If Carolyn had only been like the so many others, either accompanying Crane to his place or inviting him to hers, fate would have been kinder. It was now 2:30 a.m., the wee hours of Thursday, June 29, 1978, and Crane was in his apartment, all alone. His killer would soon join him.

* * *

When Crane did not appear for a noon interview, his co-star, Victoria Berry, who was also being interviewed, was concerned. It was unusual for Crane to miss such an event. She thus travelled to his apartment to ascertain that all was well.

Arriving at two o'clock, the attractive and sexy actress, wearing dark blue hot pants and a tight tee-shirt, knocked on his door, #132A. No one answered. She tried again. Still no answer. With some trepidation, she turned the handle. It opened, surprising her given Crane's well-known practice of always locking the door. Calling out his name, she heard nothing. She wandered the apartment, seeing nothing. Figuring he might be by the pool, she slightly drew back the window blinds and peered out. Still nothing. She travelled to his darkened bedroom and again called out his name.

Seeing a figure lying on the bed, she slowly approached. Like a car striking a mighty tree, the realization of what she saw suddenly and rigidly stopped her. An unrecognizable face, matted blood, a slow trickle from the nose. A dead body. Its head so mutilated, she didn't know of whom, or even its sex.

In a state of horror and shock, she fled, seeking help. A neighbor called the police. For a department without a homicide unit—given the town's paucity of killings—it was unprepared for what awaited.

* * *

It appeared that the victim had been brutally struck two times with a weighty metal object, initially thought to be perhaps a tire iron or golf club, but later opined to have been one of the tripods in Crane's apartment. That was the cause of death. A black cord, from a camera or electrical equipment, which had come from another room, had been wrapped and tied in a neat and tight bow around Crane's neck. One end of the cord had been cleanly severed as if cut by a sharp knife. There were no signs of a forced entry, a struggle or any defensive wounds indicative of Crane fighting off his killer. He had clearly been asleep when attacked. A semen-like substance rested on his leg, a single long black hair on his shoulder. On his bed, a large black bag lay open. Whatever had been in it, perhaps as the police later surmised, graphic pornographic pictures, had been taken. Blood from the weapon had been wiped off on the bottom of the bed sheet, forming the outline of a sword-like object.

Resting nearby, Crane's date book indicated that he was supposed to take Carpenter to the airport that morning at ten. In the closet a sealed envelope containing two pictures of naked women was discovered. In the master bathroom, the police found a photo developing lab. A strip of negative film in the enlarger depicted a naked couple engaged in intercourse. Black and white prints were later found to be missing. By the television sat stacks of cassette tapes. Crane's wallet was nearby. Robbery was ruled out.

Policemen walked haphazardly throughout the apartment, giving little thought of preserving the crime scene. One discarded the remains of a cigarette he had been smoking. Victoria Berry chain-smoked as she told her story.

And with the police in the apartment, the phone rang. It was John Carpenter. He did not inquire why the police were in his friend's room.

✳ ✳ ✳

Suspicion quickly fell upon Carpenter, who at 5 feet 8 inches and 165 pounds was slightly smaller than the victim with whom he habitually hung. Black-haired and dark, people often mistook the Native American as Mexican or Italian.

Carpenter's recent behavior, as the police soon discovered, had been odd. Prior to calling Crane's apartment, Carpenter uncharacteristically called Crane's son, just to check in. Carpenter had never done that before. Further, there was no reason for the call. Carpenter's actions that morning were also puzzling. He had rushed from his motel, the Sunburst, to the airport to catch his plane back to California. The motel staff noticed that he checked out early, seemed to be in a rush and was agitated and nervous. Wasn't Crane, as per his date book, supposed to drive him? The day before the murder, Carpenter, while in the swimming pool in Crane's complex, started karate punching the water, explaining to a nearby swimmer, "I have to take karate because of this temper of mine that just goes berserk."

And then there was the blood—a drop of it, similar to Cranes' type B—found on the passenger door of Carpenter's car; a maid telling of a bloody pillowcase and hand towel in Carpenter's room. How notable could it have been, however, given the maid's bland reaction of merely tossing the stained linens into the wash along with all of the other dirty laundry? A search for blood in Carpenter's room turned up negative.

A host of suspects lingered in the background, some more identifiable than others. There were all of the husbands and boyfriends, many undoubtedly enraged at Crane's sexual activities

Crane and second wife Patti Olson, who went by the far more glorious moniker Sigrid Valdis when she starred with Crane in *Hogan's Heroes*.

with their wives and girlfriends. That pictures and even videos were taken caused further anger.

One boyfriend, upon learning of his girlfriend's earlier romp with Crane, tacked a mutilated picture of the actor on her door. A husband, from Phoenix, had Crane followed, spooking him so much that Crane swore off the city. Or how about the bikers and assorted lowlifes who participated in the Crane orgies? Might one of them, for whatever perverted reason, have carried a murderous grudge?

Or perhaps it was a woman who did the deed, outraged upon somehow learning of being surreptitiously filmed, her gender serving as the key to Crane's apartment. What of a red-headed woman who stalked Crane after a sexual interlude? Did his highly estranged and emotional wife Patti, with whom he bitterly fought, have any role? Economically, she gained greatly from his death. Although she was vacationing in the state of Washington at the time, could she have nonetheless arranged his murder?

And what of Crane's lawyer and business agent who, as the investigation deepened, was discovered to be embezzling the actor's money?

Was the flattened tire of any significance?

While the questions and suspects were many, the police always came back to one—John Carpenter. As Crane's friend, he easily could have gained entrance to the apartment of the security-conscious actor. As for motive, a waitress had overheard the two arguing shortly before, supporting other evidence of Crane's desire to distance himself from his second banana. Indeed in his date book, Crane had crossed out future meetings after the 29th with Carpenter. Crane's use for Carpenter was further diminished now that Crane was as adroit with the video equipment as his mentor. While the police were poised to arrest Carpenter, the prosecutors resisted, given the lack of solid evidence; knowing something was radically different than proving it.

Thus the case sat, for years, slowly covering itself with the dust of a nation's and prosecutor's fading interest. And then, a major break. Another look at pictures of Carpenter's car door revealed matter that was thought to be brain tissue. The smoking gun. Carpenter was arrested and charged with the murder of Bob Crane. The arrest was easier than the trial, held in 1994, sixteen years after the homicide.

* * *

Like much of the evidence, the photo of the tissue was disputed. The original substance was not preserved so it could not be tested. Defense experts countered experts for the prosecution. In the end, nothing could be definitively proved. Sloppy field work added to the state's distress. Tests were not conducted—not of the semen found on Crane nor the crusty substance in his groin area; not on the actual brain matter found on Crane's pillow, nor the black hair found, and later lost, at the scene. A mover who was in the complex assisting a tenant had noticed a white male exit Crane's apartment and drive off. While not sure of the time, having arrived at 5:30 a.m. for six hours of work, he was sure that the man he saw was not the defendant. The defense pointed to other suspects, even the woman who found Crane—Victoria Berry, who was alleged to have committed the crime with her now ex-husband, Alan Wells.

The trial started after Labor Day and ended on Halloween. The verdict, not surprisingly—not guilty.

Epilogue

If the murder had occurred twenty or thirty years later, advances in crime scene preservation and testing, most notably DNA, would have fairly easily either convicted or exonerated John Carpenter. Sadly, the homicide occurred in 1978 and will likely never be solved. At seventy, John Carpenter died on September 11, 1998, to the end insisting upon his innocence. Crane's wife Patti, who had the motive and anger to kill also had an airtight alibi. She died in 2007 at seventy-two, never having remarried, and is buried next to Crane in a common gravesite in Westwood, California.

Tidbits

Patti Olson met her future husband on *Hogan's Heroes*, on which she played Colonel Klink's sexy blond secretary Hilda. Her professional name was the more exotic sounding Sigrid Valdis. She was a widow when she met Crane.

Despite all of his philandering, Crane was married throughout his adult life, first to Anne Terzian, from 1949–1970, and then to Patti, from 1970 until his death in 1978.

Hogan's Heroes, popular throughout its run and one of television's most successful syndicated shows, was the brainchild of Bernard Fein, who earlier played Private Gomez on the classic show *Sergeant Bilko*. Fein wanted his good friend Robert Hogan to get the lead role. Hogan didn't, but his name did. Also considered for the role were Walter Matthau and Van Johnson. Initially Richard Dawson was to play Hogan and Crane an enlisted man; John Banner, who ultimately played Sgt. Schultz, was first cast as Colonel Klink. Crane modeled the lead character after Hendley "The Scrounger," played by James Garner in *The Great Escape*. Three of the cast members of the comedy about a Nazi POW camp were Jewish—John Banner, Werner Klemperer (Colonel Klink) and Robert Clary (Louis LeBeau), and suffered greatly from Nazi rule. The late actor Richard Crenna was instrumental in Klemperer getting his role.

Co-star Richard Dawson introduced Carpenter to Crane on the set of *Hogan's Heroes*.

The medical examiner initially believed the murder to be a violent homosexual one.

A movie, *Auto Focus*, starring Greg Kinnear as Crane and Willem Dafoe as Carpenter, was released in 2002. It was based on the book, *The Murder of Bob Crane*, by Robert Graysmith, who also wrote well-received books about the Zodiac Killer.

II

KILLERS, CON ARTISTS AND GANGSTERS GALORE

CRIMINALS IN THE DAYS OF yore came, like today, in all varieties. Some flew solo while others worked in groups. Abe "Kid Twist" Reles belonged to organized crime, which the head of the FBI didn't even acknowledge until something spectacular happened in 1957.

Some criminals were really smart. Ponzi conned a nation. Others though, like Leopold and Loeb, weren't quite as bright as they thought.

Dr. John Webster, who lived far beyond his means, taught at Harvard Medical School. And when he couldn't pay his debts, he tried to kill his way out of his problem. Brahmins just didn't do that in 1849. When one did, the whole world took notice.

8

CSI 1849

The medical evidence was gruesome. "The head had been separated from the trunk just below the Adam's apple by sawing through the upper vertebra. All the bowels and stomach were gone." While various parts of the cut-up body were discovered in different locations, the head never was. Attached to the pelvis, recovered from a privy located underneath the building, were male genitalia and six inches of intestines from the rectal area. A leg here, a knee there, parts jammed into gutted larger pieces of body, and dislodged teeth and pieces of bone.

The identities of the victim and defendant fueled the shocking and grisly medical aspects of the case. The deceased, Dr. George Parkman, a non-practicing physician, spent his time overseeing the family's extensive business holdings. Indeed he was one of the wealthiest men in Massachusetts, if not America. The accused, Dr. John Webster, taught chemistry at Harvard Medical School. That Brahmins—a term coined by Dr. Oliver Wendell Holmes Sr., a friend of both men and Dean of the Medical School at the time—would behave in such a ghastly manner was unimaginable; or as one member of the upper class opined, "It was the most disgraceful event in our domestic history."

To the locals the shock went even further. For years they had heard dark tales of grave robbers stealing dead bodies and illegally selling them to the medical school for all sorts of imagined frightening experiments. And now the genteel, dignified and respected Dr. Webster was charged with the brutal slaughtering and dismembering of Dr. Parkman. All highly unnerving and sensational. And as the word spread, the world reacted. In short order, reporters from as far away as London, Paris and Berlin flocked to witness the murder trial of the century. Twenty years later, upon Charles Dickens' second visit to Boston, when asked what he wanted to see, his first request was the room in which Webster killed Parkman.

Little did anyone know at the time, but what would transpire over the course of a nearly two-week trial would have vast legal ramifications to this day, notwithstanding that the factual details, like parts of Dr. Parkman's body at the time, are largely lost.

* * *

Dr. George Parkman was odd. Unpleasant, brisk and impervious in manner, Parkman's personality matched his strange gait. He took purposeful steps, held his body up high, and at

The very odd and wealthy Boston Brahmin, Dr. George Parkman;
(1790–1849).

all times extended his jaw to the stars. A large stovepipe hat adorned his peacock-like head. Behind his back, people snickered, referring to him as Mr. Chin.

If Parkman weren't so "quite peculiar in manner and person," it is conceivable that today he would be considered one of the great innovators for the humane treatment of the mentally ill. His oddity was perhaps the unspoken reason he was not named to the post he coveted and desired, if not deserved, that of headmaster of Boston's first insane asylum. Rebuffed, he turned to managing the family fortune, part of which involved lending money.

* * *

John Webster stood in stark contrast with Parkman, although they were close in age; Webster, at fifty-six, being three years younger than his future foe. The good professor, who ironically gained his position in 1824 due in no small part to Parkman's support, was pudgy and gregarious, well-liked by his students, faculty and all those with whom he came in contact. His book, *Webster's Chemistry,* became a mainstay in the field. Married to a vice-counsel's daughter whom he met in the Azores in 1823, the family grew with the addition of four daughters, over whom their father doted. Wanting the best, and wishing to keep up with his friends and neighbors, he threw expensive parties and comported himself as men of wealth did. At one point, he could afford the lifestyle with monies gained via an inheritance. It was squandered away though, mostly on a mansion, quickly dubbed Webster's Folly, a far-too-expensive house that was eventually given up.

* * *

John Webster (1793–1850), the very
highly regarded Harvard Medical School
professor who murdered and dismembered
Dr. Parkman.

With funds insufficient to fuel his substantial needs, Webster turned to Parkman, who was quite content to lend his friend money, confident that he would be repaid. And at first he was.

Then one day, while casually strolling the wealthy streets of Boston's Beacon Hill, Parkman innocently learned from his brother-in-law, Robert Gould Shaw, that Webster's valuable mineral collection was up for sale. As if stepping on a sharp nail, Parkman viscerally reacted to the news. Parkman already owned the rights to the collection, which Webster had mortgaged as collateral for a loan. The news enraged the pious Parkman. What Webster was doing was dishonest and offensive and against the very laws of nature itself. How could Webster sell that which he did not own?

Parkman quickly confronted Webster, demanding his money.

Webster didn't have it.

The chase commenced.

Parkman traveled to Webster's home, his lab and even waited outside his classes. Give me my money. I want my money. I don't have it. I don't care. I'll sue you. You'll be ruined.

Chased and publicly embarrassed, Webster begged for forgiveness and pleaded not to be taken to court, which would be catastrophic. He needed to get his affairs in order. Time though, like his money, was running short.

* * *

On Friday morning, November 23, 1849, Webster trudged over to Parkman's home and suggested that they meet early that afternoon to discuss the situation. The conversation was brief and Parkman was agreeable. After running some errands, Parkman walked over to the medical school. Somewhere in the building Ephraim Littlefield, the school's janitor, was cleaning up.

* * *

When the very punctual Parkman did not return home that evening, his wife quickly grew concerned. She called her brother, Robert Gould Shaw, who tried to calm her. They waited a day and, when Parkman still had not returned, sprang into action, alerting the city marshal and carpeting the city with flyers.

Given Parkman's high profile and the hefty reward offered, Boston found itself turned upside down as thousands searched for him. Rumors abounded. He was robbed and killed; he was kidnaped and hauled off to a ship; he was killed by a debtor; Irish immigrants were to blame. Hungry eyes scoured every cove, crevice, cellar and dwelling.

All, that is, except the medical college, where Parkman was last seen entering but not leaving. Webster told of meeting briefly with Parkman, paying off his debt and sending him off. No one ever suspected that the well-respected doctor had anything more to do with the sad affair. Except the school's janitor.

* * *

Ephraim Littlefield wondered why the furnace in the professor's lab was running so high for so long; why Webster was uncharacteristically spending so many hours there; why the typically open lab was now locked; and why the water was running so constantly?

He took his concerns to the school officials, who encouraged him to find out what he could. Traveling outside and under the medical building, which was supported by stilts, Littlefield crawled through the structure's cold, dank and dark underbelly and slowly chipped and burrowed his way through thick brick. Breaking through, he was surely greeted by the foulest of smells inhabiting Webster's privy. Peering into the darkness, Littlefield noticed water slowly raining down from Webster's lab. Settling on the floor. Washing over a severed hip. And parts of two legs.

The discovery jerked him up and away, scrambling to his superiors, who urgently notified first Robert Gould Shaw and then Marshall Tukey. Soon the police swarmed Webster's lab, searched it and found various cut-up body parts. In the now cooled furnace, bones; in a small tea chest, a hollowed out torso stuffed tight, like a turkey at Thanksgiving, with part of a thigh.

Upon Webster's arrest, he blurted out, "What about Littlefield?"

* * *

Little is known of the janitor Ephraim Littlefield, who lived in the medical school with his small family, and performed dark deeds for the school far beyond those required of an ordinary custodian. He served as the purveyor of corpses, the man who brought dead bodies from grave robbers for the medical school's consumption. And more importantly, to make a few

School janitor and procurer of dead bodies, Ephraim Littlefield who broke the case. Or, did he have something to do with the killing?

extra bucks, he possessed the talent at chopping them up. Twenty-five dollars for a whole body, five for the head only, price negotiable for a leg or arm.

*   *   *

A medical tribunal was convened to determine the cause of death and identity of the individual. The panel did far more. After determining the assembled pieces were indeed those of Dr. Parkman and that he had undoubtedly been murdered, it unusually went one step further, naming Dr. Webster as his killer. The words shot out like a cannonball, striking the masses and convincing them that indeed Dr. Webster had committed this most foul deed.

So heinous the case, so reprehensible the defendant, that responsible attorneys refused any representation. When approached, Daniel Webster, Rufus Choate and Charles Sumner, the three criminal legal giants at the time, all declined the invitation to participate in the most infamous murder case in America. While putting forth plausible excuses, the bottom line was that everyone thought Webster guilty and no attorney wished to dirty his hands on so filthy a case. Still though, as Webster sat in jail, he was well fed and attended to and received a steady stream of friends and supporters.

With the assistance of the highest court in Massachusetts, the Supreme Judicial Court, before whom the actual trial would be heard, two attorneys were eventually corralled—Edward Sohier and Pliny Merrick, both highly respected civil practitioners. While Merrick had been a district attorney in the past, it was apparent that his trial skills were deficient. As a hand specialist would not perform heart surgery, neither a civil attorney nor an incompetent criminal one, should try a murder case. They did, with disastrous results.

*   *   *

The scene of the homicide—Harvard Medical School.

It is clear, in 1849, as today, what the defense should have been: Littlefield did it. He had no great love for Webster, had easy access to Webster's laboratory and was skilled at hacking up bodies. He would also benefit greatly by collecting a reward many times his annual salary.

Counsel ignored nearly two hundred pages of notes Webster had prepared, many countering Littlefield's anticipated testimony. When Littlefield testified about Webster's movements in the week following Parkman's disappearance, Webster had given his attorneys the names of those who would contradict the janitor's testimony. When Littlefield told the jury he was not interested in the reward, Webster identified a professor to whom Littlefield told an opposite story. Counsel used none of Webster's notes. Most egregious, the day after a handwriting expert testified, tying Webster to an anonymously penned, bogus letter falsely telling of Parkman's whereabouts, a second letter, obviously written by the same person, arrived. Clearly, Webster who was in jail at the time could not have written it. If he could not have written the second letter, the expert was wrong in saying he wrote the damning first one. His attorneys did nothing.

In contrast to the ineptitude of the defense, the prosecution was brilliantly represented by Attorney General John Clifford and, primarily, special prosecutor George Bemis, who was paid, as was permissible at the time, by Parkman's family. Faced with a murder without a body, the team employed and developed legal strategies and tactics that are routinely used throughout our nation today. As the Civil War was the first modern war, the Webster trial was conceivably the first modern trial. In just under two weeks, forensic dental evidence, handwriting experts, proof of character and reputation, consciousness of guilt, alibi, taking a view of the crime scene, juror bias and circumstantial evidence were all highlighted in one manner or another.

So compelling the case that sixty thousand persons—half the population of Boston—rotated in and out of court in ten minute intervals to witness the spectacle. Journalists flocked from near and far to report the grimy details to a thirsty worldwide public.

* * *

The conclusion was a foregone one. Or as one juror later opined, "Was there nothing more that could be said in Dr. Webster's defense?"

In closing, the defense, as always, stumbled and fumbled, arguing at length to find the defendant guilty not of murder but manslaughter. By admitting their client's involvement, but besieging the jury to return a lesser verdict, the attorneys sealed Webster's fate.

On the flip side, John Clifford effectively, over the course of an entire day, laid out in minute detail his strong, albeit circumstantial, case. When he finished at five o'clock, many thought that after so long a day the jury would be sent out to rest and retire, returning to hear the judge's instructions with a fresh and clear mind. It was not to be.

For three more hours, Chief Justice Lemuel Shaw, one of the most highly acclaimed justices in the nation, told the jurors what they must consider. As inept the defense, as brilliant the prosecution, nothing did Webster more harm than what Shaw told them. Like a prosecutor, he went over various points made by the defense and told the jurors to disregard them, including that the jury should not credit seven defense witnesses who testified that they had seen Parkman later that Friday afternoon, long after the time Webster allegedly killed him. Shaw even suggested that perhaps Parkman had been drugged, notwithstanding that there had not been any evidence of such an occurrence.

Notwithstanding that over 120 witnesses testified over eleven days, the jury took but a few hours to render the inevitable verdict.

✳   ✳   ✳

Supreme Judicial Court Chief Justice Lemuel Shaw, who many accused of a judicial lynching for the manner in which he presided over Webster's murder trial.

After Webster was sentenced to death, an earthquake of criticism rocked the judiciary, with its Chief Justice receiving the brunt. From one Philadelphia newspaper, "Judicial Murder in Boston." Perhaps in response, the judge sat down with the four attorneys and re-wrote history, changing in part the testimony of the witnesses and most importantly, the charge given the jury; from the actual to what it should have been. Prosecutor Bemis then published the altered account as the official one and from that version Chief Justice Shaw wrote the appellate opinion upholding the jury verdict. Little need be said about the wisdom of having those who reviewed the trial being the very same judges who presided over it; so too, on an altered record.

From fundamental fairness reduced to ashes came *Commonwealth v. Webster*, one of the most noteworthy judicial opinions in legal history. The shining definitions and points of law outlined in that opinion are still used to this very day. Unfortunately the jury hearing the case in 1850 never heard them.

Epilogue

On August 30, 1850, John Webster was hanged. Prior to his demise he confessed to the murder. Asking that he be buried in Mt. Auburn Cemetery, his lawyer Ned Sohier and others, fearing grave robbers, acted against Webster's wishes and secretly buried him in an unmarked grave in Copp's Hill Burying Ground in Boston. In 1853, Governor John Clifford, previously one of the prosecutors on the case, appointed Pliny Merrick, one of the defense attorneys, to the Supreme Judicial Court.

Tidbits

To this day, some working at Copp's Hill Burying Ground do not acknowledge, or even know, that Webster is buried there.

Some believe that Webster was in fact innocent and admitted to the crime for some unknown reason, whether it be spiritual or in the hope of somehow benefitting his family. Littlefield is pointed to as the true culprit. For his part, Littlefield testified that he was not interested in any reward and would never take it. One month later he did.

Robert Gould Shaw's grandson, also so named, led Massachusetts' all Black 54th Regiment to, as the movie name signifies, *Glory*, during the Civil War. The son of Oliver Wendell Holmes Sr., the head of the medical school, was Oliver Wendell Holmes Jr., who survived his many Civil War wounds, and went on to serve on the Supreme Courts of Massachusetts and the United States

Parkman years earlier sold Harvard the land on which the medical school was built, right next to Massachusetts General Hospital. MGH is still there, the medical school is not. Parkman also sold the surrounding land to the city, which constructed the Charles Street Jail. The facility was closed in 1990 and transformed into an upscale hotel.

One month after the Webster trial, the Sara Roberts school desegregation case was heard. In it, the now odious separate-but-equal doctrine was created. In 1851, runaway slave Shadrich Minkins was rescued from that same courthouse by sympathetic abolitionists.

In his appellate decision, Shaw gave birth to, and promulgated, such legal points that one may be found guilty of murder on circumstantial evidence alone and that a body is not always needed; the classic definition of reasonable doubt; the compelling value of consciousness of guilt; the sequestration of witnesses to ensure that they do not base their testimony on that of other, earlier called, witnesses; allowing the jury to view a crime scene; the use of demonstrative evidence—models and drawings—to assist the jury; and the use of expert testimony.

Private attorney and prosecutor George Bemis never married and moved to Europe where he wrote law books. He also endowed the Bemis Professorship of International Law at Harvard.

The friends of Webster raised money for his financially strapped family. Reputedly, Mrs. Parkman made a sizable donation.

Some years later, the Supreme Judicial Court abandoned its practice of serving as both the trial court in murder cases and the appellate court in reviewing its earlier-made trial decisions.

Our Next Tale

From a wealthy family in Connecticut, he was a brilliant student who attended Yale Medical School. When the Civil War broke out, he did what all good men did—he volunteered. As a doctor, he tended to the medical needs of the many wounded. In the end, it drove him mad. And the world of literature would never be the same.

9

What Does M-U-R-D-E-R Spell?

Lambeth Marsh in London was a crime-infested cesspool of humanity. Crowded tenements housed far too many people, living in, or at the edge of, poverty in a dank area smelling of rotten eggs. Notwithstanding the ongoing and overt violence of the area, gunfire was a rarity. The modes of mayhem included fists, knives, bricks, rocks and shanks. Thus, when shots rang out shortly after 2 a.m. on February 17, 1872, all took notice.

* * *

The hapless victim was thirty-four-year-old George Merrett, the father of six with number seven on the way. An underpaid, working nonentity, he rose early to heave coal into the roaring fires at the local brewery. On his final day of life, he bid his wife Eliza farewell and trudged off into the clear and cold night. Smoke from his pipe mixed with his cold breath.

Suddenly, loud cries shook the quiet of the early hour. George turned and focused on the source of the commotion and quickly realized that a thunderbolt of violence masked as a raging, screaming madman was headed his way. And gaining ground quickly. George turned and started to flee, glancing back in terror as he did. The unknown man suddenly stopped and pulled out a gun. Taking aim, he fired three shots. George fell dead.

* * *

The gunman did not attempt to flee and was quickly caught. William Chester Minor readily admitted to the deed, although he explained he had shot the wrong man. His intended target was someone who had broken into his room.

The authorities learned that the easy capture of the killer stood in stark contrast to the nature of the man, for Minor was no ordinary criminal. Tall and regal, the thirty-seven-year-old Minor was a doctor. He had attended Yale and served the Union as a surgeon during the war. Questions abounded as to how this well-educated and respected American wound up living in sordid decadence far from home. A hungry and highly-excited press pounced on the possibilities. So too quickly, the criminal court, which found itself facing a vexing puzzle.

* * *

An elderly Dr. William Chester Minor; (1834–1920).

That Minor lived in a district of easy women mirrored his behavior when he served in the military, where he first started frequenting the sleaziest parts of the cities in which he was stationed. Meeting ladies of the evening fed a voracious sexual appetite and gave birth to a number of venereal diseases.

Unfortunately for Dr. Minor, those illnesses paled in comparison to the horrors he earlier found on the front. In time, what he witnessed and went through pushed him closer to, and soon over, the line that separated madness from mere mental discomfort. His behavior grew more and more bizarre. In the evening, when he tried to sleep, his torments crested, washing over him as he vainly sought the comfort of night.

People were coming at him. Through the walls, the floors and even the ceiling. The injustices were as varied as the entries. They were there to steal, poison, molest and victimize him. To protect himself against these terrifying and unwanted intrusions, he took to carrying a gun for protection, placing it under his pillow for easy access.

In 1871, the military discharged him, provided a well-earned pension, and sent him on his way. In the hope of escaping his demons, he traveled abroad, planning to rest, read and paint his watercolors in Europe's finest cities. Instead, he lived in a seedy part of London, where prostitutes were plentiful and frightening people continued to come through the walls.

After days, weeks of torture, he reached the end of sanity. As day bled into night, another imaginary uninvited foe entered. Minor, fed up, grabbed his nearby gun and shouted at his tormentor, who fled. Minor gave chase, yelling and screaming at him, "You'll bother me no more!" Minor stopped, aimed and fired. His aim, unlike his sanity, was steady. The man fell dead. When Minor approached his fallen prey, he realized that he had shot the wrong man.

* * *

Broadmoor Asylum—Minor's home for decades.

As difficult the question of why, the solution turned out to be easy. The defendant was clearly insane. And to address his needs, Minor was shipped off to Broadmoor, the country's newest, and first of its kind, institution, specifically built for treating the criminally insane; the hope being that Minor would regain a modicum of mental stability. It was not to be. The weeks turned into months which grew to years and then decades. Nearly four of them. Thirty-eight years to be exact, becoming the facility's longest committed patient.

As the cultured Minor did not pose a threat, he was given two cells, one in which to sleep and the other in which to write and paint. Having the luxury of money, he collected books. Soon his cell looked like a library, complete with bookshelves and even a fireplace.

Feeling great remorse for his murder of an innocent young man, Minor, with the approval of the institution, soon started sending money to the victim's wife, Eliza Merrett. In time, she started visiting him, apparently somewhat taken with this seemingly harmless yet refined individual. When in passing he mentioned having some difficulty obtaining certain books in which he was interested, she volunteered to purchase them for him and did so on a monthly basis.

His love of reading would have a profound effect on the literary world.

* * *

In 1878, six years after the murder, a group of some of the smartest men in the world met in Oxford. They gathered with a lofty goal; indeed perhaps the greatest undertaking in the history of English literature—to identify and define every word in the English language. While the project originally started two decades earlier, it was not until now that the Oxford University Press stepped to the plate to publish it. Selected to head the august project was a man with an equally impressive name—James Augustus Henry Murray.

* * *

For the next and last forty or so years of his life, Murray worked on the daunting task. With a small staff and thousands of volunteers, the English language was slowly and meticulously cataloged.

One volunteer, who simply identified himself as being from Broadmoor, Crowthorne, Berkshire, grew to be one of the book's greatest and most dependable contributors, working tirelessly for twenty years and providing tens of thousands of entries. His name: Dr. William Chester Minor. And how did he likely learn of the project in the first place? From a flyer in a book purchased by Eliza Merrett.

Epilogue

One of the greatest accomplishments in literature is the 1st edition of the Oxford English Dictionary in which every English word is defined. It took nearly seventy years to accomplish this mammoth feat. In twelve volumes, over 400,000 words were defined using 1.8 million illustrative quotations. The first volume came out in 1884.

Sadly, Dr. Minor's nightly visitors continued to torture him and would do so for the remainder of his long life. He died at eighty-five at an asylum in America to which he had been transferred.

Tidbits

William was the son of highly intelligent and pious parents, who travelled as missionaries to the Far East. William, as a young teenager, was aroused by the scantily-clad, attractive local female population. Given his upbringing, it was highly sinful to relieve his sexual tension.

Joining the Union Army in 1863, the exposure to the brutalities of war and disease devastated him. What may have imprinted the scar of insanity in the doctor's psyche came when he was forced to brand a young and scared deserter with a boiling hot iron. As the boy screamed in terror and pain, the sensitive doctor permanently imprinted the letter D on the boy's face.

After the war he remained in the army. From 1866 onward, he slowly descended downward. He started to frequent houses of ill repute, carried a gun and started to think that people were out to get him. At thirty-four, he agreed to be sent to an asylum, where he stayed for eighteen months. Determining that he would never fully recover, the army discharged him, with a pension, concluding that his problems stemmed from his military service. In 1871, he spent a seemingly relaxing summer with members of his family in Connecticut before leaving for London and murder.

For years, Murray sought to visit his top contributor, who always put him off. Finally, refusing to take no for an answer, Murray travelled to Minor's location. Needless to say, Murray was a tad taken aback when he learned of Minor's background.

One of Minor's half-brothers, Thomas Minor, also a doctor, moved west and, after living in various locales, settled in Seattle, which elected him mayor. In 1889, he and a friend ventured out on a canoe trip and mysteriously and permanently vanished. A street and school bear his name.

In time, the widow Eliza Merrett took to drink and stopped visiting Minor.

Other notable patients at Broadmoor included Daniel M'Naghten, also referred to as McNaughton and McNaughtan, whose name was given to the test for insanity (The M'Naghten Rule); James Kelly, who some believe to have been Jack the Ripper; and Charles Bronson, one of the most violent criminals in Britain.

Our Next Tale

When the economy hit the skids in 2008, many blamed the banks and the greedy managers of the stock market. Keeping with our theme that the more things change, the more they remain the same, venture back to 1869 when the nation was plunged into an equally egregious economic downturn caused by the materialistic rich. And, as further evidence of our other theme that people do not change, at the middle of the brouhaha was a man in love with the wrong woman.

10

A Graveyard for Our Friends

Jim loved Josie who loved Edward who killed Jim. If only it were that easy.

Of the teeming masses who attended Diamond Jim Fisk's New York City funeral, it was difficult to decipher whether they were there out of sympathy or hatred or curiosity. After all, he had helped plunge the nation into economic turmoil with his Wall Street shenanigans on Black Friday, September 24, 1869. Odd that it wasn't one of those he financially ruined who killed him but a rival who bested him in the game of romance and revenge.

* * *

Perhaps it was fitting the multi-monikered Diamond Jim, Big Jim or Jubilee Jim was born on April Fool's Day in the year 1835 to a peddler father. Young Jim took up the same profession, quickly moving from the small pond of Vermont to the large lake of Boston and finally the mighty ocean of New York, all in the search of greater paydays and profits. He hit his stride during the Civil War, during which he successfully avoided military duty in favor of smuggling Southern cotton to the North. Undoubtedly he did it more for profit than patriotism.

Fisk loved the action, loved associating with those playing the game. And most of all, he wanted all to know that they were dealing with someone special. Fisk was a dandy. He perfumed his hair and waxed his mustache. His loud velvet coats and white silk shirts shared space with ostentatious shiny diamonds and gaudy rings worn on his stubby fat fingers. He punched the air with the stout cigars he smoked to make a point. Lest one didn't get the point, a not-too-subtle jab into the chest drove it home.

His friends were of equal wealth, drive and ambition. Wall Streeters. Dan "the Double-Crosser" Drew, who screwed people during the week and sanctimoniously attended church every Sunday, and the mysterious Jay Gould, who wished only to continually and quietly acquire fortunes, regardless of how they were gained.

Together the three teamed up to fight Cornelius Vanderbilt for control of the Erie Railroad. Although Vanderbilt was seventy-three and the richest man in America, he wanted more. If he gained control of the Erie, he'd have a monopoly of railroads and could charge whatever he wanted. Drew, who had a controlling interest in the railroad, had no intention of giving it up. As the wealthy Vanderbilt bought more and more of its stock, Drew merely illegally

Jim Fisk (1835–1872), the millionaire Wall Street manipulator who could neither walk away from a fight nor the woman he once lusted over, Josie Mansfield.

printed more and more shares. The watering of the stock left Erie shareholders blind to what was occurring. When the legal heat started to simmer, thanks to Vanderbilt having a few more corrupt judges in his pocket than his rivals, Drew, Gould and Fisk skipped town for New Jersey, taking the Erie corporate books and seven million dollars in cash with them. Lonely with all that money, Fisk summoned his girlfriend, Josie Mansfield, to join him.

* * *

Helen Josephine Mansfield, Josie, was born in Boston to a mother who dragged her to San Francisco in search of the riches of the Gold Rush. Her father disappeared, as did her subsequent step-father. Married at fifteen in the hope of escaping California, she and her actor husband split once that was accomplished. She returned to Boston, left for Philadelphia and moved to New York in search of the opportunities post-Civil War America promised. More charming and attentive than attractive, men were drawn to the flowing brown hair, oceany blue eyes and voluptuous figure of the vivacious twenty-two-year-old. Calling herself an actress provided her with the spectrum of job callings, from her unlikely performing on the stage to her more talented stints in the bedroom. When she spotted Diamond Jim in November 1867, she asked Madam Annie to introduce them. Despite having a wife in Boston, Jim immediately took advantage of the situation, which he always did if it involved women who interested him. This one was different though.

* * *

Josie Mansfield, a lady who shared her charms with many, including the murdered Jim Fisk and his killer, Edward Stokes.

The outcome of the Erie imbroglio was predictable. Drew tried to double-cross his partners, Fisk and Gould, who turned the tables on him, effectively gaining control of the Erie at Drew's expense. They set up shop in, of all places, an opera house on 23rd and Eighth in New York City, which had the added benefit of a nearby Josie, ensconced in an apartment paid for by Fisk.

Josie had arrived. Arm in arm with her lover and benefactor Fisk, they swirled around the intertwined worlds of business, politics and show business. And at the center of the universe sat Diamond Jim—rich, powerful and corpulent—features that young Josie could not help but notice.

* * *

William "Boss" Tweed ran New York City politics with an iron fist. Through Tammany Hall, the highly corrupt machine of the Democratic Party, he controlled all the graft and payoffs he could handle, which were considerable. With judges and the law on his side, it was only natural that Tweed would seek to align his interests with those of his rich insider friends, Fisk and Gould, and their railroad. It was a match mutually beneficial for all, a financial windfall for men already drowning in money. More was needed, though, as money was their oxygen.

Thus, in 1869, when Gould saw an opportunity to corner the gold market, he jumped at it, with his friends supporting his efforts. That his scheme might be catastrophic for the economy was not their concern. Simply, they sought to buy all of the gold, driving the prices precipitously up before it all came crashing down. Quickly, on what came to be known as Black Friday, economic scandal and ruin came to many with Gould and Fisk at ground zero.

An avalanche of lawsuits followed as they scrambled with their attorneys, searching for a way out of their self-made predicament.

With all of this blowing about, Fisk inexplicably introduced Edward Stokes, someone with whom he did business, to Josie. Stokes was young, fit and very handsome. That he was married with a child was an impediment of minimal concern. Soon Josie and Edward were taking full advantage of their newfound friendship. Fisk meanwhile, perhaps blinded by his business troubles, was oblivious to the match he himself had set up.

* * *

Josie was in a quandary. She wanted Stokes' body and Fisk's money. To that end, she wrote her soon-to-be former lover a letter, a common form of communication back then, asking for monies that Fisk told her he had invested on her behalf. Soon the letters, increasingly angry, were flying back and forth. Josie, for her part, observed that she had been faithful, in her own unique way, taking money from no one other than Fisk.

Diamond Jim, knowing he was being tossed aside, and aware of the rumors linking Josie with Stokes, refused her offer to settle the affair for $25,000, setting the stage for tragedy. Stokes, having learned some lessons from the snake himself, suggested blackmail. Having read some of the past letters Fisk had written to his lover, Stokes sensed a windfall of opportunity. Unless Fisk settled with Josie, she'd release his salacious letters to the press. Scandal would surely follow.

Fisk, never one to back down from a threat, and perhaps of the belief that he was already being crucified in the press, reacted in his characteristic bombastic manner. He sued Stokes for some past business transgression. The gauntlet thrown down, Josie returned the favor and sued Fisk for money she claimed he owed her: $50,000. She also notified the press, claiming that she was being falsely accused by Fisk of attempting to extort money from him and that he should know better, given his past criminal transgressions, which she'd gladly expose, including the Erie Railroad and Black Friday shenanigans. The press salivated at their good fortune of a sex and business scandal involving a major player dropping onto their front pages. An over-anxious public eagerly devoured the on-going back and forth stories and allegations.

Soon even more lawsuits were launched, Fisk suing Josie and Stokes for extortion and, in return, being countersued for libel. Each side searched for the most biased judge before whom to file their suits. The threat of jail in such circumstances, an option in the 1870s unlike now, added to the tension of the parties and the entertainment to the public. Fisk, used to being arrested, kept a bail bondsman on staff, close-by.

As Josie's suit started in November 1871, a large audience jumped at the opportunity to be regaled in person, much like attending the theater. They were not disappointed. Fisk appeared in full military regalia, thanks to his buying an appointment as a colonel in the National Guard some years before. Josie took the stand and was questioned at length about being a kept woman, both past and present, including whether her step-father was also her pimp. Needless to say, all questions were met with denials, to the disbelief of many court observers. She did admit giving the Fisk letters to Stokes, but not to the newspapers, as well as meeting with Boss Tweed in the hope of settling the potentially explosive matter.

The spectacle of the trial from Thanksgiving to Christmas provided holiday fodder and frivolity—front page news, discussed by the rich and poor alike throughout all corners of the city and state. The people were getting their money's worth. Josie's lengthy and emotional testimony ended with her leaving the witness stand in tears, her reputation tattered but her story stubbornly intact.

Her paramour Edward Stokes testified next. It was now January 6, 1872, a Saturday, and court would adjourn early, at 2:00.

The handsome thirty-year-old, appearing both bemused and confident at the same time, told of a platonic relationship with Josie. An affair was impossible, he explained, as he was, after all, a married man with a family.

After the court broke for the day, Stokes to his great chagrin learned that a grand jury, doing Fisk's bidding, had unexpectedly indicted him for blackmail. The news shocked and soured him. Fisk had made good on his mantra. He got even with those who crossed him, including people he even once held in high esteem. As he was known to utter, "We have graveyards for our friends."

Stokes travelled to the elegant and new Grand Central Hotel, the largest hotel in New York, catering to the well-to-do. Witnesses later suggested that he had tailed Fisk there. As Fisk started walking up one of the grand stairways, he spotted Stokes, standing calmly at its head, as if casually awaiting a friend. Before Fisk could react, Stokes pulled out a gun, shot his nemesis twice and quickly walked off, tossing the pistol as he did.

Stokes was swiftly apprehended. As Fisk slowly trudged down the trail of death, he identified Stokes as his assassin. Less than twenty hours after having been shot, with his wife, who had travelled quickly from Boston, and his many friends at his bedside, his journey ended. He was thirty-six.

The killer Edward Stokes (1840–1901), who also fell under the spell of Josie.

It was as if a head of state had passed. Thousands, many of whom had lined up hours before, watched the processional as it slowly travelled through the streets of a hushed and stunned city to a railway car that would carry Fisk to his final resting place in Vermont. His funeral epitomized his life: large and over the top.

* * *

Six months passed, an eternity for the tense Stokes as he wasted in jail, before his murder trial commenced in the summer of 1872. Picking a jury took days as all potential jurors knew of the killing.

When the prosecutor ended his case, he felt confident. A strong case had been presented. The defense was multifaceted, but one filled with potholes—self-defense with a dose of temporary insanity. Stokes had been in fear for his life. As the first defense witness called, Stokes told the jury precisely that and more. He had crossed Fisk and men who did that often did not live. At every opportunity, Fisk intimidated him, grinding him. When he inadvertently saw Fisk at the hotel, Fisk reached for something. A gun. And Stokes shot him in self-defense. That no gun was discovered by or near Fisk was yet another problem for the defense, a fact which would partially be addressed by their next witness: Josie.

All eyes watched as the main feature, the femme fatale, slowly made her way to the stand. Dressed the part of a vamp, her heavy jewelry accented her immodest attire. As she lifted the veil of her large black hat adorned by a blue feather which matched her earrings but clashed with her violet-colored gloves, she spoke softly.

"Yes, I was involved in a libel suit against Mr. Fisk. One night, December 15th to be exact, during the middle of the trial, Fisk appears at 10:15 in the evening at my apartment. He tells me to drop the suit and that he'll pay me. He also says that unless I return to him, he will kill Mr. Stokes. He even takes out an expensive looking pistol with which to do the foul deed. The offer is refused as he will not publicly acknowledge that I was telling the truth all along. I relayed the threat to Mr. Stokes, who was rightly scared given how dangerous and deadly Fisk could be."

The defense ended with expert testimony suggesting that Fisk died not from his gunshot wounds but from shoddy medical treatment, specifically the administering of opium to treat the patient's pain.

The theatrical closings provided the ending the public craved, with each side dramatically yelling out their points, the defense even going so far as to question why Boss Tweed and Jay Gould were not in court to support their deceased friend. The prosecution responded in kind, beseeching the jury to keep its eye on the ball and not be waylaid by the mud flung at the corpse of the murdered.

After receiving their instructions, the sequestered jurors commenced their deliberations. When a verdict was not reached on that Saturday evening, they were brought back into court on the Lord's Day, a day the court cannot sit, but did due to a special law passed by the legislature just for this case. Sunday passed with the jurors indicating that they were having great trouble agreeing upon a verdict. On Monday, they announced that while they had endeavored greatly, a verdict could not be unanimously reached. A mistrial was declared.

Mistrials are like ties in sporting events or kissing one's sister, satisfying to no one. In this case, a do-over. The retrial commenced six months later, in December 1872. A different jury, a different result. Quickly. Guilty of first degree murder. Nearly a year after the murder, Stokes was sentenced to death. He and his supporters were stunned.

Until the appeals court reversed his conviction, ruling that the jury had been improperly instructed. Round three.

In the interim, though, continuing financial concerns blossomed into the Panic of 1873, which pushed the proceedings aside. Stockholders, upset with the direction of the Erie Railroad, forced Gould out. With the Erie stock plunging, others stocks joined in the avalanche. Meanwhile, the graft of Tweed caught up with him, landing him in jail. At rock bottom, our nation, and other parts of the world, were in a depression.

Against this backdrop, no one much cared anymore about the on-going saga of the Stokes trial. Indeed, many who were now financially ruined blamed Fisk, among others, for their economic plight. At trial, a witness mysteriously appeared for the defense placing a gun in Fisk's hand. The prosecution questioned why it took so long for this key piece of evidence to surface. Regardless, Stokes was found guilty of manslaughter and sentenced to four years in jail. After serving three, his health suffered and he was released a year early. As for Josie, she was nowhere to be seen.

Epilogue

Josie fled to Europe. She also outlasted all who were involved in the drama. Tweed died in jail in 1878, smack in the middle of the kingdom he once ruled. Gould bounced back from his financial setbacks and went west, developing a railroad in that growing part of the nation. When he died in 1892, he was remembered as being one of America's most sinister figures. Stokes lasted almost a decade longer, dying in 1901, living in obscurity and fading into paranoia, sure that Fisk was tailing him.

Meanwhile Josie bounced back and forth between America and Europe, enjoying life. In London, in 1891, she married an American lawyer, whom she later divorced given his lack of sobriety. Over a half century after the Fisk shooting, she died in 1931, no one quite knowing how she was able to live the lifestyle she did without the benefit of either work or money. Buried in Paris, two local women attended her funeral. So too an older gentleman, distinguished looking, whom no one knew.

Tidbits

While working in Boston as a young man, Fisk worked at Jordan Marsh's department store, which was a famous Boston landmark before it was purchased by, and renamed, Macys in 1996. Fisk was fictionalized in the movie, *The Toast of New York,* made in 1937. Edward Arnold played the leading role; Cary Grant also appeared.

At fifteen, Fisk ran away from home and joined the circus.

On Black Friday, the federal government interceded, releasing some its gold reserves to halt the panic. Four years later, in 1873, not much could be done as depression hit and remained for nearly a decade. The Franco-Prussian War in Europe (1870–1871) and fires in Chicago (1871) and Boston (1872) contributed to the economic calamity.

Our Next Tale

When the term "serial killer" is uttered, invariably one thinks of a male. It is not always the case. Not today, not ever. Meet an early mass killer. A woman.

11

The Belle of Death

Lonely men came to the doorstep of Belle Sorenson Gunness one by one as if spellbound. They arrived with their life savings in hand in response to an alluring newspaper ad: "Comely widow who owns a large farm in one of the finest districts in La Porte County, Indiana, desires to make the acquaintance of a gentleman equally well provided, with view of joining fortunes. No replies by letter considered unless sender is willing to follow answer with personal visit. Triflers need not apply."

When Midwestern papers in the early 1900s carried this listing in their matrimony section, readers assumed that Belle was looking for a husband. The stout Norwegian-born mother and widow, twice-married, possessed all the appearances of a busy housewife in need of a helping spouse. Numerous eager men arrived. Many were never seen again.

* * *

The events that occurred on the quiet farm of Belle Gunness during a seven-year span starting in 1901 quickly became local folklore. While at times difficult to separate fact from fiction, a rough sketch of her life and crimes emerges. She was born Brynhild Paulsdatter Størset on November 11, 1859 in Selbu, Norway, and raised on a small farm by a poor farmer. At eighteen, it is believed she became pregnant, but miscarried after being attacked; traumatic events which greatly altered her personality.

In 1883, she left home for the greener and richer pastures of Chicago, where she joined her sister Nellie Larson. Adopting the American-sounding name Belle, she dreamed of luxury and comfort. She married fellow Norwegian Mads Sorenson and shortly thereafter they opened a confectionery store. Business was slow however, and within a year their shop mysteriously burned down. Insurance allowed Belle and Mads to buy a home, which also later burned. Another payout, another home.

The couple had four children—Caroline, Axel, Myrtle and Lucy. Caroline died in 1896, with Axel sadly following her two years later. While both had symptoms of colitis, an inflammation of the colon, they also bore signs of having been poisoned. They both also had life insurance policies as did Mads, who passed on July 30, 1900, the only day on which his two policies overlapped. Medical personnel who examined him initially suspected strychnine poisoning,

Left: A young Belle Gunness, born in 1859, aging into her prime killing years.
Right: An older Belle with her murdered children—Lucy, Myrtle and Philip, 1908.

but were overruled when Mads' doctor blamed his demise on heart failure. As such, an autopsy was deemed unnecessary. Belle used the $8,500 insurance award to buy a farm on the outskirts of La Porte, Indiana in November 1901 and moved there with her two surviving children, Myrtle and Lucy, along with an adopted child named Jennie.

Belle, slowly realizing her dreams of wealth and security, was quick to find a new husband. She married Peter Gunness, a Norwegian-born widower, in La Porte in April 1902. The marriage lasted eight months. Belle, now pregnant, blamed the untimely death of her new husband on his being struck on the head when part of a sausage-grinding machine fell from a shelf. Despite the implausibility of the story, the local coroner, after examining the body and considering the evidence, concluded that the death was indeed an accident. Belle received another insurance payout.

Belle, now a widow again, gave birth to her next child, Philip. Three years later, in 1906, when her adopted child Jennie dropped out of sight, Belle casually explained that Jennie had left for school in California. In fact, Jennie was much closer to home.

* * *

After Peter's death, Belle managed the farm by hiring workers. She also began taking out matrimonial ads. Neighbors recalled seeing middle-aged men coming to visit, but strangely never leaving. Other odd behavior had Belle digging in or around her large pig pen at night as well as periodically making large bank deposits.

In 1906, she hired a scruffy farmhand with a wide mustache named Ray Lamphere. Shortly, he fell in love with Belle and was openly jealous of the men who came courting. Such intrusiveness stifled Belle, who quickly fired him. Despite this, he continued to lurk about. Belle also felt pressure from another quarter. People were starting to ask questions. One, Asle Helgelien, was threatening to come to La Porte to search for his missing brother Andrew, whom Belle had lured into her home. Belle professed not to know where he was. While Lamphere had become troublesome, a visit from Asle Helgelien could prove disastrous.

* * *

Belle made an appointment with an attorney, ostensibly to draw up a will. During their conversation, she related to him that Lamphere was causing her problems, even going so far as to threaten to burn her house down. Belle also visited the local bank. After completing these rather mundane acts, Belle was never seen again.

* * *

On the evening of April 28, 1908, Joe Maxson, a handyman hired to replace Lamphere, jerked awake from a sound sleep to the strong odor of smoke in his room in Belle's house. He rushed to the door and flung it open. Flames consumed the hallway. Maxson yelled out but received no response. With fire lapping at his feet, he escaped, unscathed. The house wasn't so fortunate.

Farmhand Ray Lamphere, who like so many others, strangely loved Belle.

As the authorities combed the ruins, four bodies were discovered in the smoldering rubble. Three were Belle's children—Myrtle, Lucy and Philip. The fourth body was that of an older woman who could not immediately be identified for a sensible and, highly disturbing, reason. The body was headless.

* * *

Officials were split on whether the corpse was Belle's. Some opined that the body was too small. Local tailors, familiar with Belle's measurements, noted the dissimilarities. Conversely, teeth discovered in the ashes and examined by her dentist, were thought to belong to her.

The investigation lasted for weeks. Crowds gathered to watch as the authorities pored through the wreckage, soon pulling out corpses from the garbage-laden hog-pits within eyeshot of the house. At least ten men, two women and numerous bone fragments were found. The bodies had by-and-large been drugged, bludgeoned, dismembered with a meat cleaver and covered with lye to dissolve the remains. Some of the remains had been fed to the hogs. Among the dead was Belle's adopted child Jennie. So too Andrew Helgelien, identified by his grief-stricken brother Asle.

The coroner concluded that the headless woman was that of Belle, who, some later opined, had, while living, processed some of the human remnants through her sausage grinder and fed the meat to her unsuspecting neighbors.

The magnitude and brutality of the crimes propelled the story nationwide. A steady stream of visitors, including journalists both local and foreign, traveled to La Porte, which had now become carnival-like, complete with ice cream and souvenir stands, picnic areas and guided tours. Children skipped school to snoop around and watch. Business was booming. Hotels thrived. Restaurants served "Gunness Stew." Postcards with photos of the "murder farm" and household items purportedly from the Gunness home were sold at inflated prices. La Porte, French for the door, was derisively being referred to as Gunnessville. Ballads and skits were written and performed.

* * *

Town officials, wishing to return their town to the sleepy haven it once was, moved to quash the repulsive uprising by solving the mystery. A headless corpse remained; so too the bodies of three children. In short order, former handyman Ray Lamphere was arrested and charged with four counts of murder and arson.

With thunderous anticipation, the trial started on November 9, 1908 to a packed courthouse. Tickets were sold for admittance. Overflowing crowds spilled over into the hallways and onto the lawn.

The identity of the headless corpse was a central issue at trial. The prosecutor, R. N. Smith, launched a ferocious assault upon the defendant, attacking him with reports of his troubles with Belle. Defense attorney Wirt Worden countered, reducing the case to a simple one; Lamphere could not have killed Belle for the simple reason that she was still alive. Dramatically,

Worden issued a summons for her to appear. Asle Helgelien's threats, Worden argued, had scared Belle into faking her own death and fleeing. Her plan all along was to escape and frame Lamphere for the killings. Lamphere even had an alibi, claiming that he was at the home of Elizabeth Smith, a black woman known as the town recluse, at the time of the fire. Smith was not allowed to testify, presumably because of her gender and color. Lastly, Worden addressed the teeth found in the ruins. A local jeweler testified that while the fierce heat of the fire had melted the gold plating on several watches and other items of jewelry, the gold in the dental bridgework had emerged from the fire almost undamaged.

The defense was a solid one, Lamphere being aided by the conflicting evidence and mixed public opinion surrounding Belle's purported death. When the verdict came down after two-and-a-half weeks of testimony, it reflected a compromise. Lamphere was found guilty of arson, but not murder. The tenuous evidence of Belle's demise wasn't enough to convince the jury that she was indeed dead.

Lamphere was sentenced to twenty years in prison. He lasted but one, dying of tuberculosis on December 30, 1909.

Epilogue

As he lay dying, Lamphere reportedly made a deathbed confession. Belle, whom he had assisted with her murderous ways, was still alive. The headless corpse was that of a housekeeper, lured from Chicago shortly before the deed. Belle also killed her own children, started the fire, tossed in her false teeth and fled, a rich woman.

* * *

Theories of Belle's whereabouts abounded. One had her living in California in 1931 as Esther Carlson, who had been charged with poisoning a wealthy man in order to steal his money. Esther supposedly had photos in her possession that resembled the Gunness children. The *La Porte Herald-Argus* published side-by-side photos of Esther and Belle under the headline "Resemblance?" Many readers responded affirmatively, given the striking similarities between the two women. In 1938, former defense attorney and now judge, Wirt Worden agreed that Esther Carlson and Belle Gunness were one and the same. Carlson died of tuberculosis before her trial, however, and her true identity was never ascertained.

Despite these claims, numerous other sightings of Belle filtered in throughout the years from different parts of the country. None proved conclusive.

In November 2007, almost one hundred years after the fire, the headless corpse was exhumed in an effort to learn its true identity. DNA tests were inconclusive, but efforts were ongoing in the hope of finding a reliable source for comparison.

What was true and beyond contradiction, however, were the fates of all of Belle's children and her many other victims.

Tidbits

Lamphere's alibi witness Elizabeth Smith promised to reveal everything she knew about her friend Belle. She never did. Among the numerous items found in Smith's dirty shack when she died in 1916 was a human skull tucked between two mattresses. It was never identified but many suspected that it belonged to the headless corpse.

Part of the extensive folklore in La Porte surrounding Belle Gunness was that she was actually a man. The tales and rumors come from her masculine appearance, large size, and uncommon strength, and also from the rarity of female serial killers.

Belle Gunness for many years has been listed in the Guinness Book of World Records for "Most Prolific Murderers." Many believe her victims numbered forty or so.

Belle's sister Nellie Larson spoke to a La Porte newspaper after the murders were discovered in 1908. "There has been found a lot of dead people on my sister's land," she said. "I don't understand it."

Our Next Tale

In a way Belle must have been somewhat charming given her success in luring so many into her murderous web. In our next tale, we meet the king of charm, the man who dazzled an entire nation and, in so doing, joined the ranks of Bernie Madoff and every other age-old snake oil con artist. This one, though, found immortality.

12

Robbing Peter to Pay Paul

Charlie could not catch a break. As in his words, "Something always happens!" His dream of never having to work a day in his life had died a long time ago. While the gregarious imp was forced into a series of demeaning jobs, far beneath him, he always fancied himself hitting the big time. Every time he tried, though, it seemed to land him in jail. Even when he tried to do right, it came up wrong.

Until he landed in Boston. The tides changed for the first time in 1917, when he met his wife Rose, the love of his life. Then two years later, when he dusted off a scam as old as rocks and set it in motion. The local citizenry hadn't experienced the whirlwind of Charlie and soon grew captivated, if not love-struck. They lined up in droves and begged him to take their money. And then they came to their senses and hurled a very-wealthy Charlie back from whence he came, soon again penniless. In his journey though, he found immortality, for the scheme he had embarked upon would forever bear his name—Ponzi.

$$\star \quad \star \quad \star$$

Carlo Ponzi was born Carlo Pietro Giovanni Guglielmo Tebaldo Ponzi on March 3, 1882 in Lugo, Italy. His family was wealthier in name than in money, and his mother doted on her only child, believing and praying that he would restore the family to its former glory.

Young Ponzi showed promise. An intelligent lad, he gained entrance into the prestigious University of Rome where he quickly grew intoxicated with the charms of money. Adopting the habits and lifestyles of his far wealthier classmates, Ponzi blew through his savings within a year, forcing him to drop out. When employment came in the form of a clerical position, he indignantly refused it, feeling the job beneath him. His family soon decided that the gold-lined streets of America might better suit the large dreams of 5-foot 2-inch Carlo and purchased him a ticket.

Forever claiming that he travelled first class on the SS Vancouver, the reality was that he came to his new home in 1903 courtesy of second class. He also managed to whittle the two hundred dollars his mother had given him to a mere pittance when he landed in Boston two weeks later. As America's newest arrival later put it, "I landed in this country with $2.50 in cash and $1,000,000 in hopes, and those hopes never left me."

Ponzi quickly left Boston for Pittsburgh where he worked a series of menial and unsatisfying jobs to survive. Needless to say, he didn't last long in any of them and soon ventured north, to Montreal where he secured a job as a clerk at a bank.

Banco Zarossi catered to Italian immigrants, and promised to pay unheard of returns to its depositors. The fraudulent scheme, referred to as "robbing Peter to pay Paul," was a simple one, using the money from new investors to pay old ones. Not surprisingly, in time the funds ran dry and the larceny was discovered. The bank collapsed and Ponzi, in an attempt to support his escape, forged a check, for which he was arrested. Sent to jail for nearly two years, he got out early for good behavior.

With the welcoming arms of Montreal now cold, Ponzi decided to head back to the United States. Accompanied on the train by five Italian immigrants, Ponzi, at the border, was arrested for smuggling illegal aliens. Believing a guilty plea would result in a fifty-dollar fine, Ponzi, instead, was whisked back to jail, sentenced to two years in a federal penitentiary in Atlanta and a five-hundred-dollar fine. When he couldn't pay the fine, another month was tacked onto his sentence. He took advantage of his surroundings, speaking with and learning from fellow white-collar criminals.

Upon his release, he settled in a mining town in Alabama where he performed a truly decent feat, giving a total of 122 inches of his skin for a graft for a nurse who had been seriously injured in an explosion. The skin, taken from his thighs and back, landed Ponzi in the hospital for three months. The nurse recovered. Both were scarred for life.

Ponzi's nomadic ways continued. To make ends meet, he often worked as a painter. While so working on a ship, he was tossed ashore after a dispute over pay arose with the ship's

The mughshot of a young Charles Ponzi, 1910.

captain. Stranded in Mobile, he soon found employment as a librarian in a medical college. A good-hearted fellow, well-liked by all, he became a great source of amusement to the school's medical students, who on one occasion snuck a very dead cadaver into his bed. Upon discovering it, the bemused Ponzi exclaimed, "I laid him on the floor of my room. We both slept peacefully, but I woke up first." Soon, however, he found himself embroiled in the politics of the school, which quickly led to his dismissal; another in what he described as "a long circle of bad breaks."

Yet again, Ponzi wandered off, this time landing in Texas where he worked as a clerk in the foreign sales department of the Wichita Falls Motor Company. Here he earned his PhD in financial crime, learning about exchange rates and foreign currencies, tariffs, and postal and telegraph fees, all of which would form the basis of his later larcenous plans.

With World War I raging, Ponzi again tried to act nobly, attempting to return to Italy to join the fight. When he learned that his native nation would not pay for his journey home, however, he jumped ship and soon found himself right back where he had started. After thirteen years of scurrying around, Ponzi landed right back in Boston, where he found work at the J. R. Poole Company, an import-export company. Ponzi was now in his mid-thirties, earning a lowly wage that barely met his needs. "By starving one day and eating a little less the next one," he observed, "we employees always managed, more or less, to keep handsomely in debt." Little did he know that in short order radical change awaited him.

✶ ✶ ✶

On Memorial Day weekend of 1917, Ponzi made a seemingly innocent decision to join his landlady at the evening performance of the Boston Pops. After experiencing a pleasant and enjoyable show, the two trudged to the Boylston Street Transit Station where they waited with others for the next streetcar. As he gazed around the darkened area, his eyes focused upon the lovely Rose Maria Gnecco. Possessing thick brown hair and wide dark eyes, the smooth skinned 4-feet 11-inch beauty captivated him. As fate would have it, his landlady knew the twenty-one-year-old and introduced the couple. Cupid had fired his arrow. "Time, space, the world, and everything else around me, except that girl, had ceased to exist." Love and loyalty followed, as did marriage on February 4, 1918. For Ponzi, he had found paradise.

With a new wife to support, Ponzi decided that the time was ripe for him to venture forth into the business world. After all, the prospect of forever earning meager pay did not afford him the lifestyle he thought a married couple deserved; nor did it quench his everlasting passion of fame and fortune. With his mind racing as to how best achieve his goal, inspiration finally struck when he read about the cost of sending letters overseas. Soon plans were laid to exploit post World War I currency rates through the use of International Reply Coupons issued in post offices throughout the world. The coupons grew out of the need to send letters and packages from one nation to another. The concept was simple. Buy coupons in depressed countries at depressed costs, Ponzi figured, and redeem them in America at higher rates. That he never figured out how his plan, which appeared to be legal, would generate significant cash and profit did not deter him.

A more dapper Ponzi ten years later, in 1920.

He created the Securities Exchange Company and opened up shop on the fifth floor of the Niles Building located on 27 School Street in downtown Boston. Start-up money was needed and initially none was forthcoming. To fill the breach, Ponzi not only stepped over the line, he flew over it. Devising his pyramid scheme, he sold vouchers to a relatively few investors promising exorbitant fifty percent returns in forty-five days.

Through some tantalized early investors, money dribbled in over the coming days and weeks. When the first vouchers became due, sufficient funds existed to make good on Ponzi's promise of a high return. Those pocketing the easy money were ecstatic, bellowing to all within earshot of their good fortune in having found a financial genius. Greedily, many re-invested, unable to resist the lure of money easily made over so short a time. How Ponzi was able to deliver was of no concern. Word exploded of the great profits being effortlessly made and soon the rich and the poor—factory workers, firemen, cops, clerks, food peddlers, waiters, tailors, cleaners, merchants, bankers and even a priest—flooded Ponzi, showering him in money, begging him to do for them what he had done for others. Money came in so quickly that the drawers of his office overflowed and spilled over, forcing the clerks to temporarily store and stuff the cash into every available open receptacle: drawers, wastepaper baskets, whatever served as a short term way station.

With such success came rapid expansion, first locally to nearly a dozen nearby cities, then to offices throughout the area: Vermont, Rhode Island, Connecticut, New Hampshire, Maine and even New Jersey. Ponzi had succeeded. Finally.

Luxury quickly followed. An expensive house in the affluent town of Lexington, purchased mainly with vouchers from Ponzi's company. Fine suits, jewelry, cars, chauffeurs, servants and meals in fancy restaurants followed as did a gold-handled cane brandished as the wishing wand of wealth. Best of all however, respect and admiration, for him and his beloved Rose.

Within seven months, thirty thousand people had ponied up nearly ten million dollars, rocketing Ponzi to the zenith of his fantasies. Little did anyone realize that every dollar invested put Ponzi, and themselves, one step closer to financial calamity.

* * *

The authorities could not figure out how Ponzi was doing what he claimed to be doing, but they didn't really care. No one was complaining, people were making money, so why waste valuable resources? Cops sent to investigate Ponzi were so enthralled by his charm and pitch that they themselves became investors. Eventually, but far too late, it came to light that there were not enough International Reply Coupons in the world to account for the amount of money Ponzi was generating.

As with every such scheme, the number of the previous investors, now large, quickly devoured the incoming money of the newer ones. Upon the realization that time and money were quickly running out, Ponzi struggled to come up with other ways to make good on his promises. He mulled over many ideas—buy the bank into which he was depositing hordes of money; establish a shipping empire by purchasing the no longer needed surplus ships of World War I; or even sell the company outright.

The love of Ponzi's life, the diminutive Rose Gnecco, with attorney Barney Welansky, who would later be imprisoned for his role in the deadly Cocoanut Grove Fire of 1942. (*Courtesy of the Boston Public Library, Leslie Jones Collection*)

Despite his scheming, on July 24, 1920, the teetering world of Ponzi started to crumble when *The Boston Post* began a series of articles on the "wizard of finance." Soon the paper was doing the math and asking questions. The Post's reporting led to a Pulitzer Prize for it, and ruin for Ponzi. Seeking to delay the inevitable, Ponzi contacted the authorities and boldly invited them to investigate his business practices. He even agreed to suspend taking on any new investments until an audit could be performed.

Too late. The public, fearing economic calamity, stampeded to get their money back, overrunning Ponzi's business on School Street. With the lines long, Ponzi provided food for those waiting. Ladies, distressed by the heat, were hustled to the front of the line. Ponzi, in good cheer, returned their monies, initially at least.

In August, though, the house of coupons fluttered down. Ponzi hit bottom, unable to come up with the three million dollars he needed to stay afloat. His accounts were either overdrawn or frozen. Investors rushed to court to sue him. Ponzi turned himself in to the federal authorities, who charged him with fraud. State charges followed close behind. The end had come.

* * *

Under arrest, Ponzi could not make bail pending resolution of the federal charges. On November 30, he realized his options had run dry and pled guilty. His attorney strenuously argued that if left alone Ponzi would've made everyone whole. His words fell on deaf ears. The sentence was a stiff one to five years. While the ruling was applauded by many, Ponzi was nonetheless viewed sympathetically. A *New York Times* editorial called him picturesque and gallant, innocent-like and perhaps as surprised at what occurred as his many investors. As for those who gave money, in the end, the paper concluded, they were unworthy of great empathy given their greed and their search for the easy way out, doing nothing and getting something, none having any of Ponzi's redeeming charms and qualities.

* * *

Despite these feelings and the rarity of the state pursuing charges already addressed in federal court, local officials, embarrassed by the whole affair, jumped in, eager to move against one of their most infamous citizens. Not taking any chances, they proceeded cautiously against Ponzi, splitting up the several criminal charges and going to trial on only a portion of them.

Unable to afford an attorney, Ponzi defended himself. Still able to spin a yarn, he captivated the spellbound jurors, who rewarded his performance, finding him not guilty. Refusing to back off, the state moved to try him on the remaining counts. The prosecution waited though, until November 1924, three months after Ponzi had completed his federal sentence and was free.

Insistent upon sending him back behind bars, the second trial started with an indigent Ponzi again representing himself. Still appealing and persuasive, the jury could not unanimously decide his fate, resulting in a mistrial. Still bent on either justice or revenge, the Commonwealth—now fully aware of Ponzi's trial strategies having twice witnessed them—moved again for trial. The third time, a charm. Ponzi was convicted and given a prison sentence of seven to nine years. He was able to remain free however, pending appeal. He would not sit idly by.

* * *

Business was booming in Florida, thanks to a gush of land speculation. People arrived in herds trying to get in on the action. With the lure proving irresistible to those thirsting for a quick hit, the shark of Ponzi swam south. With people throwing their money at land deals, how could he resist? His plan was a simple one. Buy one hundred acres for forty dollars, split each acre into twenty-three lots, sell them for ten dollars each, and eureka, gold in the form of dirt. That the land was isolated and even swampy in places was a mere speed bump on the road to wealth. To raise the money to launch his scheme, Ponzi perfected his familiar, and simple, pitch. "I'm dealing in land; earn a two hundred percent profit in a mere sixty days; get in now while you can."

Eventually the Florida authorities caught wind of the pitchman and the scam and both were shut down. Convicted of a violation of Florida's securities laws, Ponzi was sentenced to a year in jail. Once again, he was able to win a stay pending appeal. When the powers-that-be in Massachusetts caught wind of the actions of their star convict, they moved to jail him. Ponzi, weary of the certainty of impending imprisonment, had other ideas, finally doing what many were surprised he had not done earlier—he fled.

* * *

Finding manual employment on a ship bound for Italy, Ponzi shaved his head and blended in under an assumed name. Unfortunately, either through braggadocio or inadvertence, he let slip out who he was to a fellow shipmate. Word quickly leaked and in short order Ponzi was apprehended and shipped off to prison, where he served seven long years.

Released in 1934, he had seventy dollars to his name. Despite a strong desire to remain in his adopted land and pleas that he be allowed to do so, he was deported back to Italy. Heartbroken, his still loving wife chose not to join him, hesitant to desert her family and country. As the distance of miles and time weakened their bond, the hope of reuniting slowly dissipated. In 1936, after eighteen years of marriage, Rose reluctantly filed for divorce.

In his early fifties, Ponzi was on the downside of his life, again working an assortment of jobs. Accepting an offer from an Italian airline in 1939, he re-located to Brazil. After three years he left the job but stayed in his new homeland, where he scratched out a living running a rooming house and teaching English.

Shortly before his death in 1949, as he lay as a ward of the state in a hospital bed, he gave his last interview. He confessed the obvious about his scam, "It was the old game of robbing Peter to pay Paul." He died shortly thereafter of a blood clot in his brain, at the age of 66. His worth at death? Not much more than he had when he left prison.

Ponzi being deported in 1934. (*Library of Congress, NYTW&S collection*)

And to the end, remaining totally devoted and hopelessly in love with the woman he left behind.

Epilogue

The attorney, Barney Welansky, who handled Rose's divorce, had an ownership interest in a popular Boston nightclub, The Cocoanut Grove, in which he gave Rose an accounting position. On the evening of Saturday, November 28, 1942, despite the pleas to stay and attend a party there, she left, and by doing so, avoided the second deadliest fire in American history wherein 492 people perished.

When Ponzi heard of the tragedy he wrote his former wife an impassioned letter, noting how he still missed and loved her, concluding, "Here I am, past sixty-one, thousands of miles away from you, physically separated from you these past nine years, legally a stranger to you, and yet feeling toward you the same as I did that night in June when I took you home from the first movies we saw together [on] Somerville Avenue."

In 1956, long after Ponzi's death, she remarried. While her second marriage was a happy one, Rose never gained what she wanted most, children. She died at ninety-seven.

As for Ponzi, he remained to many a loveable rogue. Even his nemesis, *The Boston Post*, recognized the uniqueness of the man that they had helped bring down, writing, at the time of his conviction in Massachusetts, of his "bubbling vivacity, his boundless imagination, his smooth and ready tongue, coupled with a remarkable and winning charm.... Of all the get-rich-quick magnates that have operated, Ponzi is the king."

And remains so to this day.

Tidbits

There are many Ponzi-like schemes. What they have all in common is that the money of new investors is used to pay off the older ones. One fairly recent notorious scheme involved Bernie Madoff, who cheated people out of millions of dollars.

Ponzi was an avid stamp collector.

A lot was going on in 1920 Boston: the fallout from the police strike of 1919; prohibition; women's right to vote; and the actions of foreign subversives and radicals culminating in the sensational Sacco and Vanzetti trial.

The Boston Post's Pulitzer Prize for its Ponzi stories was the first for a Boston newspaper.

Rose was ultimately a key witness in the court proceedings arising out of the Cocoanut Grove inferno.

Our Next Tale

In Chapter 11, we detailed the murderous exploits of Belle Gunness, who somehow figured out a way to murder a lot of people over a long period of time. At the other end of the spectrum—both in intelligence and breeding—stood two young men, who thought that because they were smarter than everyone, they were clever enough to commit the perfect murder. They weren't.

13

As Easy as Impaling a Beetle on a Pin

On May 21, 1924, nineteen-year-old Nathan Leopold was out on a mission with his lover and equally-brilliant partner, Richard Loeb, who was seven months younger. When they spotted Loeb's fourteen-year-old cousin Bobby Franks walking home from an after-school basketball game, they offered him a ride. The Franks family never saw their son alive again.

* * *

Coming from money, it comes as no surprise that Leopold and Loeb heralded from the same wealthy neighborhood in the south side of Chicago—Kenwood. Highly successful in school, both graduated from college at exceedingly young ages; Loeb from the University of Michigan at seventeen, and Leopold, at eighteen, from the University of Chicago, where he stayed, attending law school. Loeb, as a grad student, also entered the University of Chicago where he studied history. Each, as it turned out, filled a void in the other.

Leopold, short and unattractive in his early years, never had many friends; indeed he was often bullied in school. He had also been sexually abused by his nanny. He grew to be an egotistical and unpleasant young man.

At the opposite end of the spectrum stood the charming and attractive Loeb, whose father Albert was vice president of the mammothly successful and ubiquitous Sears and Roebuck. Loeb could be the life of the party so long as he kept a check on an odd behavior trait that people found off-putting. Privately, to relieve himself from the daily strain of study and expectation, he daydreamed of crime, especially committing the perfect one.

Despite their differences, Leopold and Loeb shared some similarities. Both were Jewish—albeit atheists—breezed through school, and followed and adopted the teachings of Nietzsche, who espoused the "superman" theory. Being brilliant, they believed, made them intellectual "supermen," and not subject to the same laws as normal, mentally-inferior men. If they, as superior beings, wished to commit crimes, they could. Even murder. For the thrill; for the experience; to see how easily they could get away with it.

When they became lovers, Leopold was the one far more infatuated. As with many couples, the two bickered. About their relationship, about what crimes to commit. Soon sex became a bargaining chip—Leopold agreeing to commit a crime with Loeb, who in turn agreed to

A serene shot of a murdering
couple, 1924. Loeb is on the left.
(*German Federal Archives*)

have sex with Leopold. In a way each reaching his own personal high. As with all addicts, regardless of the addiction, their compulsion propelled them to new and more intense highs. The ultimate exhilaration—murder—and the promise of getting away with it.

✳ ✳ ✳

The two meticulously plotted the ill-fated kidnap-murder caper for over six months. Plans were made to exact an unneeded $10,000 ransom. As they harkened from rich families, money was never at the center of their plans. Rather, to commit the perfect crime, a ransom had to be a component, leading the authorities down a road dark at its end. But how to collect the ransom without being detected? After mulling it over, brilliance, or so they thought, struck.

The victimized family would receive step-by-step notes and messages the entire way, sending them from one location to the next, ultimately ending on a designated train; the final note instructing them to throw the ransom package from the rear of the train at a specific point. Knowing where it would land, they would be there to pick it up. The police would never be able to anticipate a drop at a specific spot, they reasoned, along the never ending and obscure tracks. That riddle solved, the planning continued.

As Leopold's conspicuous red sports car could not be used, a vehicle would have to be secured. To rent one, a false identity—Morton D. Ballard—was established. A typewriter was stolen to type the ransom note. Their sole spontaneity was who to snatch, who their victim would be. That poor soul was to be chosen totally randomly from an affluent neighborhood.

✳ ✳ ✳

On May 21st, the plot was launched. Cruising the area, the pair scanned the streets for a victim. An unkind irony sent them Bobby Franks. Being the cousin of Loeb made him easy to approach. It also added a certain level of twistedness. After the boy entered the car, he was struck with the taped end of a chisel, the belief being that a single blow would render him unconscious. Then, as per the plan, a rope would be looped around his neck; each killer grasping one end of the rope and together pulling it, chocking the victim until he died. Unexpectedly, and at odds with their well-laid strategy, the child put up a vicious struggle, blood splattering about the car and soaking its interior.

After Bobby was finally subdued, with rags stuffed into his mouth, the duo drove about an hour to a pre-arranged location on the Illinois-Indiana border, stopping en route for hot dogs and root beer, casually eaten while the sun set and their victim lay stuffed dead in the car. Leopold, a seasoned bird watcher, knew of an area in a little traveled section of a state park, Wolf Lake, where the body would be deposited.

Under the black sky, they removed the blood caked body from the car and doused it with acid—soaking Franks' genitals, face and a distinctive mark—a scar—on his body, in the hope of masking the child's identity. Then they picked the small frame up and plunged it head first into a drain pipe. It failed to entirely sink. Try as they might, and after shoving it in as far as they could, the boy's feet still poked out. During the struggle in the dark, while pushing, pumping and exerting, Leopold felt the odd and gentle sensation of something falling and tinkling as it hit the ground. Searching about, he saw nothing. He and his partner then fled, stopping to mail the ransom note and make a chilling call to Mrs. Franks. "This is George Johnson. Your son has been kidnapped. More information to follow."

* * *

The two returned home and played board games. The following morning, Leopold attempted to clean the blood from the murder car, in plain view of a house servant who was struck by the unforgettable sight of his young master actually performing manual labor, an event as common as sighting Halley's Comet.

After notes were placed in a phone booth in a drugstore and on a train, two calls, once again using the false name of George Johnson, were made. The first to a cab company, ordering a cab to the Franks' home. A second to the Franks residence with instructions as to what to do. "This is George Johnson speaking. There will be a yellow cab at your door in ten minutes. Get into it and proceed immediately to the drugstore at 1465 East 63rd Street."

Unknown to the two who had planned the perfect crime, when the Franks received the call, they sadly already knew the fate of their son. They would not be getting into the cab.

* * *

Despite the desolation of the murder site, an employee quietly working in the area was startled at the site of two feet jutting out of the ground. Cautiously moving forward to investigate, he saw that they were connected to a body, a very dead one. He ran to summon help. The police were on their way.

The press followed closely behind. Within hours, the story appeared on the front pages, which boldly told of the macabre finding. As Leopold and Loeb were placing their notes, newspapers

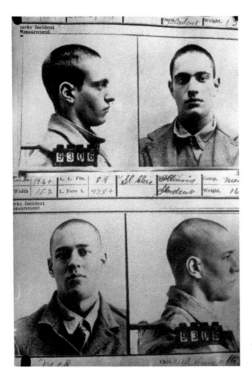

The mugshots of Leopold (on top) and Loeb
(below), 1924. (*German Federal Archives*)

in nearby stands called out to them, smacking them with the news of the discovery of a naked dead boy. Astonished, they could not imagine how the body came to be discovered so quickly.

Against hope and with the knowledge that their scheme was quickly unraveling, they hurriedly called the drugstore to which the Franks had been ordered to travel. The phone rang and rang some more. No answer. Finally someone picked it up. No, there was no one by the name of Franks there.

* * *

As the police combed the crime area to secure evidence, a pair of tortoise shelled glasses shined in the light. Initially thought to belong to the victim, a close look at the spectacles revealed a highly unusual hinge mechanism. When it was soon learned that the glasses did not belong to Bobby, the search was on for its owner. The task was easy. Indeed only three people in all of Chicago had made such a rare purchase. One was named Nathan Leopold.

* * *

It took the police nine days to obtain confessions. While there had been other suspects at first, the glasses pried a hole in the alibis of the two. At first, Leopold claimed that the glasses must have fallen out of his pocket while he was bird watching in the area. As a published author on ornithology, his tale had some validity. Soon, however, when the stolen typewriter, the bloodied rental car, and the false identity all came to light, the reign of the pseudo-Nietzschean Supermen came to a crashing end; they had met their kryptonite.

The master criminal of his own fantasies, Loeb did not take the pressure of real-life interrogation well. His hands shook, and he cried when no one was in the room. It was no surprise that he confessed first. Leopold was the opposite. Convinced that his superior intellect gave him the upper hand, he relished the tête-à-têtes with his interrogator, Robert Crowe, the state's attorney. When Crowe finally asked him how he enjoyed those hot dogs and root beers, Leopold realized that his cohort was talking. Soon so was he, insisting on telling his version of the story.

Both confessions were nearly identical, except that each accused the other of the killing. The two even volunteered to be driven around, providing the police and Crowe with an inside view of the key locations of the plot.

With their cooperation, the brilliant boys buried themselves. There was no doubt in Crowe's mind that that their ultimate outcome would be at the end of a rope. He had a hanging case.

* * *

The services of one attorney were quickly replaced by the hiring of the best trial attorney in the land, Clarence Darrow. Initially a labor lawyer, Darrow, after a falling out with the American Federation of Labor, moved on to criminal law, where he cemented his stellar reputation. He strongly opposed the death penalty, believing that crime was a result of poverty and circumstances, and that to execute someone because they were poor or insane was cruel and unusual. Out of more than a hundred murder cases in Chicago, Darrow lost only one. He was clearly the only hope Leopold and Loeb had for cheating the gallows.

A thorough preparation of the case led Darrow to believe that winning a jury trial was impossible. He thus shocked the prosecutor and court when he announced that both boys would be pleading guilty to the dastardly crime. By so doing, he placed the fate of the boys in the hands of a judge, not a jury. While state attorney Crowe merely assumed that Darrow was placing the rope around the necks of the accused, the wily defense attorney knew that he was entitled to present as much mitigating evidence as he wished at the sentencing stage. He also knew the reputation of Judge John R. Caverly, a liberal who did not outwardly favor the death penalty. Darrow's objective was saving his clients from death, not from jail.

On August 1, 1924, two thousand spectators arrived at the courthouse with the hope of witnessing the proceedings. A much smaller number gained entrance into the packed courtroom, which was dangerously hot due to the heat and humidity of the brutal Midwestern summer.

Both sides presented their witnesses. When the attorneys rested, Darrow waited for the crowd to grow still. When silence finally surrounded him, he slowly rose to give his summation. In time, his impassioned plea came to be considered by many the most brilliant of his long career.

He claimed that the wealth of the defendants and the lack of motive had sensationalized the case. Absent the notoriety, the state's attorney would not have demanded the death penalty for two teenage boys who had pled guilty. Only three people in the history of Chicago had ever been hung after a guilty plea, and each were over the age of 29. There had been no motive

Famed criminal defense attorney Clarence Darrow (1857–1938), whose eloquence saved Leopold and Loeb from a thought-to-be certain death penalty.

for the crime, which Darrow claimed called into question the mental stability of his young clients. To execute two teenagers, he argued, would look to the past, when in fact it was the future that must be considered; to a time when "we can learn by reason and judgment and understanding and faith that all life is worth saving and that mercy is the highest attribute of man." Women in the courtroom wept as the emotional Darrow spoke.

Notwithstanding the strong and emotional argument of the prosecutor that justice demanded death, the judge thought otherwise, basing his decision on the young ages of the defendants. The sentence: life plus ninety-nine years; life for the murder and ninety-nine years for the kidnapping.

The decision was met with great hostility. The crime had been both appalling and vicious, not only because a neighbor, a little boy, a cousin, was killed, but because of the very lack of any motive, other than an intellectual experiment conducted by two privileged and pampered psychopaths who had nothing better to do. Or as Leopold exclaimed, "It was just an experiment. It is as easy for us to justify as an entomologist in impaling a beetle on a pin."

Epilogue

Loeb was killed by a fellow prisoner in 1936. Leopold served thirty-three years—released in 1958—after which he wrote his autobiography, entitled *Life Plus 99 Years*. He moved to Puerto Rico, married a florist, and died in 1971 at the age of 66. In his home he kept, as visitors claimed, a framed photograph of his true life partner, Richard Loeb.

Tidbits

Sausage King Killer Adolph Luetgert, who will be scrutinized in a later chapter, had financial problems with businessman Oscar Foreman, who was squeezing him for the money. Foreman's nephew was Nathan Leopold.

The murder and the strangling of the young boy inspired Alfred Hitchcock's movie *Rope* (1948), which was based on the murder. The film *Compulsion* followed a decade later with Orson Welles starring in the lead role modeled after Clarence Darrow. Traces of the Leopold and Loeb story can still be seen today in one form or another, from the television series *Law & Order*, to the film *Murder by Numbers*, starring Sandra Bullock, and even the young Dumbledore and Grindelwald storyline in J. K. Rowling's final Harry Potter book.

Loeb was the youngest person at the time to ever graduate from the University of Michigan.

To escape the trauma caused by the incident, many family members changed their last names or moved to a different city.

Leopold planned on traveling through Europe later that summer, possibly using the anticipated ransom money. He then planned on transferring to Harvard Law School.

Many of the witnesses who supplied critical evidence were household employees of the Leopold and Loeb families.

President Barack Obama's home in Chicago is only a block from Loeb's former home.

Our Next Tale

Unlike so many depicted in this book, occasionally a criminal, like Ponzi, becomes part of our nation's social consciousness, living on for what seems to be all eternity. One other such person is Al Capone. Such recognition and infamy were not to be, however, for one of Capone's more notable business partners, Fast Eddie O'Hare, whose escapades cost O'Hare his life, but, in a roundabout way, gave America a great hero.

14

Al Capone's Business Partner

No one referred to the popular and outgoing Edward Joseph O'Hare by his first name. The backslapper was always EJ, Easy Eddie, Fast Eddie or just plain Eddie. Large and loud, he was the type of man Jim Fisk and his cohorts, if they had all lived at the same time, would have loved; one who bought the first round at the bar and later picked up the entire tab. More importantly, he also possessed an uncanny ability to make a buck.

* * *

Born in 1893 in St. Louis, Missouri, O'Hare quickly learned the value of hard work and money and worked several jobs. Despite his many ventures, he found time to take business courses at Saint Louis University as well as the bar examination, although he never attended law school (which was permissible at the time). He also found time, at nineteen, to marry Selma Anna Lauth with whom he had three children: two girls and a boy.

As a lawyer and businessman, Easy Eddie focused on how to make his clients, and himself, money. With Prohibition raging, O'Hare recognized the lure liquor held and moved to maximize his financial position. It wasn't easy, however, and in 1925 he and others were indicted for liquor-related violations. A partner, George Remus, was convicted and sentenced to jail for two years. Easy Eddie somehow beat the rap.

With the taste of violating the liquor laws growing sour, O'Hare turned to other money-making schemes. Good fortune had earlier brought O'Hare a new client, Owen P. Smith, who happened to be the Commissioner of the International Greyhound Racing Association. Smith had an idea as to how to revolutionize the potentially highly lucrative dog racing industry. With expenses low and the potential of profit high, all that was needed was gaining and keeping the attention of the dogs that were easily diverted while racing. Smith had the solution—an electric rabbit, which zipped around a track on a rail, always slightly ahead of the raging dogs chasing it. The idea was brilliant. All he needed was an attorney to patent it. O'Hare filled the need.

He also somehow became Smith's partner. And when Smith died in 1927, O'Hare purchased Smith's interest from his widow. And now Easy Eddie was in the driver's seat. That dog racing was illegal was a minor inconvenience to be fought and conquered.

Fighter Pilot and American hero Butch O'Hare, shortly before his death in World War II.

O'Hare opened a dog racing track across the river from St. Louis in Illinois. When the cops shut it down, O'Hare merely moved north, to Cicero, just outside of Chicago and set up the Lawndale Kennel Club. That the Hawthorne Kennel Club already existed in Cicero was yet another minor obstacle for the business acumen of Easy Eddie. O'Hare had the rabbit, the Hawthorne did not. In the perfect world, a track with the rabbit would have put the one lacking it out of business. O'Hare was smart enough to know though that such a strategy could prove fatal when dealing with the owner of the rival club, Al Capone, the nation's #1 criminal, who, when faced with a stiff challenge, resorted to bullets as a resolution. A deal was wisely struck. Merge the tracks, split the profits and everyone makes money.

While dog tracks were also illegal in Illinois, Capone's political connections ensured their success. He even had the mayor of a nearby town as a partner. When the police attempted to close such an enterprise, a judge—the brother of the lawyer representing the tracks—enjoined them from doing so. Soon Capone and Easy Eddie opened other tracks in Boston and Florida. Besides controlling liquor, gambling, prostitution and speakeasies and reaping in millions of dollars a year, Capone now had his hand in the highly lucrative sport of dog racing. Not only did thousands of people attend the races on a daily basis and spend thousands of dollars, but the races were easy to fix. Overfeed seven of the eight racing dogs and the eighth dog wins. Another angle, another racket, another fortune for Capone and his new not-so-silent partner, EJ O'Hare.

* * *

As O'Hare was setting up his professional empire, his personal life was taking a hit. In 1927, the year O'Hare gained sole ownership of the rabbit, he and his wife split after many years of marriage. To be closer to the action and sources of money, Eddie re-located to Chicago, leaving his family behind. It must have been a difficult decision, though, given his strong devotion to his children, especially his teenaged son, Edward Henry whom everyone called Butch. Father and son shared a close bond and mutual love of airplanes and flying. Despite this, the lure of the big city proved too strong for Easy Eddie to resist.

* * *

Surely O'Hare knew the man with whom he was dealing. Capone corrupted all, a fact of which the smart entrepreneur had to be acutely aware. Perhaps O'Hare felt that as long as the relationship was an arms-length business one, he was safe, especially if he distanced himself from Capone's corrupt underbelly. Even with a dirty association, O'Hare managed to stay clean and respected, raking in money from his lucrative law practice and numerous other business dealings.

Still though, O'Hare had to hedge his bets, to protect himself. The decision carried enormous and unforeseen consequences.

* * *

Alphonse Capone was born in Brooklyn in 1899 to Italian immigrants. His father was a barber, and his mother a seamstress, when she wasn't raising a large and growing family. A bright young student, Capone had a temper which exploded when, at fourteen he struck his Catholic parochial school teacher. Expelled from school, he never returned.

In short order, Al joined a criminal gang run by Johnny Torrio, who taught the impressionable youth the importance of balance. Own legitimate businesses, he counseled, and act responsibly in public, with confidence and class. In private, however, engage in any criminal activity which turned a profit: gaming, bookmaking, drugs and prostitution. In a way, Torrio was a criminal visionary, who treated his criminal enterprise as a business.

Fellow criminals around them, however, often acted far differently, striking out violently when confronted with the slightest of insults. Thus, one day when Capone inadvertently insulted a young woman, her brother Frank Gallucio, took out a knife and slashed Capone's face. And forever after, Capone came to be known as Scarface.

In 1920, Capone followed his mentor Torrio to Chicago. Torrio initially went there to assist his uncle, "Diamond Jim" or "Big Jim" Colosimo, who owned a hundred or so brothels in the Windy City, and was experiencing problems from rival gangs. Torrio resolved the dispute

The mugshot of the legendary mobster Al Capone; (1899–1947).

and, after surveying the numerous business opportunities there, especially those born out of Prohibition, decided to stay and join his uncle's syndicate.

When Colosimo failed to share Torrio's views on entering the illegal liquor business, Torrio had him killed. Assuming control of what was now called, in small letters, the outfit, Torrio, like the good businessman he was, expanded it. Within a few years, vast sums of money were flowing in, millions, from gambling, prostitution, and most notably liquor and speakeasies. The ocean of liquor washing over the nation needed a distribution network and Torrio helped establish one—reaching out to gangsters throughout the nation and beyond. The seeds of a national crime organization had been planted.

* * *

With so much money to be easily had and an inefficient and corrupt police force, rival gangs cropped up throughout Chicago. Two main operators reigned above the others. The outfit, led by Torrio, with Capone at his elbow, controlled the Loop (downtown Chicago) and the south and west sides. Irish mobster and flower shop owner Dion O'Banion commanded the north side. Torrio's view that all could live peacefully and make a lot of money gave way to greed, pettiness and a profound lack of wisdom and intelligence. Thus, when O'Banion tried to cheat Torrio out of a sizable amount of money on one of many illegal deals, action had to be swiftly taken. On November 10, 1924, O'Banion found himself at the end of a hail of bullets. The hit caused an all-out war.

Two months later, on January 24, 1925, O'Banion's former henchmen exacted revenge, when they caught up with and shot Torrio, critically wounding him. As he recovered, Torrio reviewed his limited options. Choosing life, he retired, handed the outfit over to Capone, and fled to his native land, Italy. Capone, still in his mid-twenties, was now the CEO of a criminal empire bringing in tens of millions of dollars a year, the majority of it coming from liquor.

And, as Torrio earlier taught him, Capone dressed and acted the part. He dressed impeccably, wore expensive jewelry and ate at the finest restaurants. On the side, despite being married with a child, he carried on with a variety of women. Unlike many criminals who shunned the limelight, Capone reveled in it, ignoring the advice of his mentor to keep a low profile. Highly visible and generous with the press, he exclaimed that he was merely a businessman who gave the public what it wanted. Depicting himself as a modern day Robin Hood, generous and benevolent, he set up soup kitchens for the hungry and gave money to the poor. When the North End gang, now led by Hymie Weiss and Bugs Moran, shot at a lunching Capone, missing him but wounding others, Capone paid the medical bills of those injured.

In stark contrast to his public persona, privately he brutally attacked all those who stood in his way. Rivals who sought to undersell him on the cost of a barrel of liquor paid with their lives. When minor hood Joe Howard publicly smacked around and embarrassed the outfit's accountant, Jack "Greasy Thumb" Guzik, Capone hunted Howard down and blew his brains out.

On Thursday, February 14, 1929, Capone's two identities merged, with fatal results for all.

✳ ✳ ✳

When two "police officers," aided by two or three others, raided the garage at 2122 North Clark Street on Chicago's North Side, the seven men inside thought it was merely an attempt to harass and shakedown their boss, the dim-witted Bugs Moran. When they were told to line up against the wall, ostensibly to be frisked, they obeyed. With their faces to the wall, they didn't see those barking out the orders, raise their machine guns and blast the seven into premature death.

The savagery of the St. Valentine's Day Massacre shocked Chicago and the nation. And spelled the end of Al Capone, who while in Florida at the time, was believed to have orchestrated the murders, using hit men dressed in stolen police uniforms.

✳ ✳ ✳

Capone's notoriety was now so widespread that even the President of the United States, Herbert Hoover, was calling for his head. And soon federal taskforces were set up to catch public enemy #1. Eliot Ness from the Bureau of Prohibition and tenacious treasury agent, Frank J. Wilson, led the assault. Knowing that Capone was leading a lifestyle light years beyond his reported income, Wilson followed the money.

What Wilson needed, however, was inside information and turned to a well-connected and knowledgeable newspaper reporter, John Rogers, from the highly regarded *St. Louis Post Dispatch* for help. Rogers, in turn, introduced Wilson to O'Hare.

It is perhaps ironic that Capone's downfall came neither from the violence he perpetrated nor the many people he brutalized, but for tax evasion. To build its case, Wilson relied on O'Hare, who provided a treasure trove of invaluable materials; so much so that Wilson later revealed that O'Hare was the most significant factor in prosecuting Capone and sending him to Alcatraz.

✳ ✳ ✳

Knowing he might be signing his own death warrant, why did O'Hare agree to help the government? Many theories abound. Did he cooperate out of fear of prosecution himself? Was it due to a falling out with Capone? Did he wish to get Capone out of the way for business reasons? (As it turned out, with Capone out of the way, O'Hare made a lot of money.) Was he, albeit unlikely, merely doing his duty as a stand-up citizen? Or perhaps as many think, did he strike a deal with the government to help his beloved son, to whom he remained deeply committed? Butch desperately wished to become a flyer and enter the Naval Academy. In exchange for his cooperation, EJ's son would be admitted; or in the alternative, if there were no cooperation, Butch, a talented individual in his own right, would be given no consideration.

Faced with the choice of helping his son or saving his life, O'Hare opted for the former. Capone was convicted and sent to prison. O'Hare was murdered.

Epilogue

Butch O'Hare graduated from the Naval Academy in 1937. On February 20, 1942 he almost singlehandedly saved his ship, the USS *Lexington*, which was being threatened by Japanese aircraft. In so doing, Butch shot down numerous enemy airplanes. For his great bravery, he became the first naval aviator to receive the Congressional Medal of Honor, presented to him by President Franklin Roosevelt. A wartime hero, he toured a grateful nation, whose citizens turned out in the tens of thousands to cheer him. He promoted war bonds and the military before returning to active duty, a group leader. He was a universally beloved and charismatic commander. On November 26, 1943, during a nighttime battle, his plane was shot down. Neither his body nor his plane was ever recovered.

Posthumously he received additional medals and accolades. In 1949, an airport in Chicago was named for him.

Tidbits

Unfortunately for the USS *Lexington*, O'Hare wasn't around to save it from enemy attack on May 8, 1942, which resulted in the ship's sinking.

Capone and his fellow criminal cronies from around the nation met in Atlantic City on May 13, 1929 to discuss business. A similar meeting in upstate New York in 1957, discussed in a later chapter, had a vastly different ending.

Judge James H. Wilkerson presided over Capone's trial. Wilkerson had replaced Kenesaw Mountain Landis, who left the bench to become the commissioner of baseball. Capone earlier pled guilty to the charges and, with the agreement of the prosecutor, was to be sentenced, at a later date, to two-and-a-half years. At sentencing, allegedly after interference from the highest levels in Washington, Wilkerson refused to accept the agreed-upon sentence. The plea was withdrawn and Capone later went to trial. Many of his former associates and employees, under great pressure from the prosecution, testified against Capone.

O'Hare tipped off Wilson that Capone had secured a list of potential jurors and bribed some. At the last minute, Capone's jury pool was switched with another group of jurors, thus thwarting Capone's efforts. The new jury pool consisted entirely of those who would be unfriendly to Capone; they lived outside of the city, were older, conservative, non-Italian, and non-drinkers. It appears thus that the government was far more successful in tainting the jury than Capone.

Of the twenty-two charges against him, Capone was found guilty of only five. His sentence of eleven years was the harshest ever given on a tax case.

Capone was released on November 16, 1939, after serving seven-and-a-half years in prison, including a stint in Alcatraz. A week or so earlier, on November 8, Easy Eddie was murdered. It is unclear who did it. Was it Capone seeking revenge? Was it someone else with a grudge? Was it due to his being an informant? Or perhaps, Capone's muscle, Frank "The Enforcer" Nitti, wanted O'Hare out of the picture so that he could easily marry, a few years after O'Hare's murder in 1939, O'Hare's former secretary, Annette Caravetta. Capone, in a state of dementia, died in Florida at the age of forty-eight in 1947 due to the advanced stages of syphilis.

For three hundred dollars, Eliot Ness sold his life story to Oscar Fraley, who highly fictionalized it and turned Eliot Ness and his Untouchables into a national sensation, television show and movie. In fact, Frank Wilson was far more worthy of accolades. Like the unrecognized William Dawes who rode with the celebrated Paul Revere, Wilson today lives in anonymity.

Our Next Tale

Easy Eddie wasn't the first insider to become an informant. One of the great early mob snitches was killer Abe "Kid Twist" Reles, whose testimony resulted in dozens of murders being solved. Reles was placed, with a few others, in an around-the-clock, tight protective custody in a highly guarded hotel. To this day, no one quite knows how he came to die in a sensational fashion while there.

Kid Twist Goes Flying

Abe "Kid Twist" Reles sat in jail and mulled over his options. Charged with murder, he faced the electric chair. Deciding he'd rather sing than fry, he cut a deal. As he flew out the sixth floor window of his police-protected hotel on Coney Island, he might have been wiser to risk the chair.

* * *

Reles was born in 1906 to Sam Reles—a tailor—and Rose Schulman, two immigrants from Austria who settled, like millions of other Jewish immigrants, in Manhattan's Lower East Side. Hoping to perhaps escape their crime-ridden neighborhood, the Reles family regretfully relocated to Brownsville, a lawless section of Brooklyn. There young Abe found his calling— stealing, beating and robbing. While he did serve time, most of his cases were dismissed for a lack of evidence, the police quickly discovering that witnesses against Reles tended to disappear or suffer from sudden losses of memory.

How he came to be known as Kid Twist is unclear. Some say he was named after an earlier gangster he admired, Max "Kid Twist" Zweibach, a leader of the Monk Eastman Lower East Side Gang, who was murdered in 1908; others opine it either emanated from his uncanny strength and unique ability to strangle his victims, or, far more innocently, out of his sweet- toothed appreciation of a similarly named candy. What is clear is that he was cheap, crude, violent and widely disliked.

* * *

Even a thug like Reles realized that the true money and prestige were in organized crime. Aligning himself with other equally brutal and ambitious criminals—Martin "Buggsy" Goldstein and Harry "Pittsburgh Phil" Strauss—he set his sights on taking over all of Brownsville. Standing in his way were the Shapiro brothers—Meyer, Irving and Willie. Soon Reles cut a deal with a rival gang, run by the gloomy and dour Harry "Happy" Maione and his second in command, Frank "Dasher" Abbandando, and together they sought approval for taking out the Shapiros with the head of all Brooklyn crime, Umberto Albert Anastasia.

Anastasia ran the docks of Brooklyn through which one-third of America's foreign trade passed. Anastasia got a piece of all the property passing through.

Anastasia gave his blessing and in 1934 Reles eliminated the Shapiros. Now in control of Brownsville, he expanded his gang, bringing in, among others, the 420-pound loan shark Louis "Tiny" Benson; car thief Sholem Bernstein; Oscar "the Poet" Friedman, who, when he wasn't dealing stolen goods, was reading classical poetry; and Orthodox Jew Samuel "Red" Levine, a hit man who refused to kill on the Sabbath.

* * *

As powerful as Anastasia was, he paled in comparison with the man J. Edgar Hoover dubbed the most dangerous criminal in all of America, Louis "Lepke" Buchalter. Born, in 1897, the youngest of seven children to loving parents, he was called Lepkeleh, Yiddish for Little Louis, by his devoted mother. In time, members of his family grew to be law-abiding and highly-successful citizens, working as a rabbi/college professor, school teacher, pharmacist and dentist. One studied psychology at Columbia.

Like them, Lepke also achieved great success, albeit on the wrong side of the law. In 1932, at the age of thirty-five, Lepke made millions of dollars, controlling all of the rackets, most notably the garment, food and trucking industries, in New York City. Among fellow gangsters, Lepke was considered a great intellect, due in no small part to his educational achievements, having graduated elementary school. A dedicated family man, Lepke didn't drink, smoke, gamble or cheat on his adored wife, Betty. Quiet and almost deferential, the 5 feet 7inches Buchalter looked the part of a modest and successful business executive in charge of a large empire. Even his warm, soft brown eyes were misleading. His outgoing appearance, however, masked a far more sinister being. Looking for muscle to break a labor strike or handle other matters that required brute force, Lepke turned to Anastasia and Reles, men with whom he worked but didn't socialize. More often than not, the victims of the mob were fellow lowlifes. Take John "Spider" Murtha, whose resume consisted of gouging out the eyeball of a rival and committing five murders, one of which involved killing a woman who innocently declined an offer of a drink. His plan to take on Reles was met with two shots in the head and three in the chest, administered on March 3, 1935 by Abbandando, thought by many to be a moron, and Max "the Jerk" Golob.

Or two years later, when their business associate and friend Walter Sage, who controlled all gambling in the Catskills, was suspected of dipping into the profits. Stealing from fellow thieves was frowned upon and resulted in Sage being stabbed thirty-two times with an ice pick. Dropped into a lake, Sage quickly sank, thanks to the slot machine tied to his body.

If anyone saw or knew anything that could prove troublesome, Lepke's motto was "No witnesses, no indictments." And with that, killings soared, many at the hands of Kid Twist and the notorious organization for which he was a leader, Murder Incorporated.

* * *

As organized crime does not keep corporate records and record minutes of meetings, it is somewhat difficult to pinpoint exactly when Murder Incorporated first came into being. What is known is that Lepke, Anastasia and Reles were all major luminaries who took, what they called, the Combination to the next level during the 1930s.

Their operating procedure was simple, depending upon the situation. If the one to be hit was an associate of theirs, standard procedure called for recruiting one of the intended victim's close friends, who undoubtedly was also in the rackets, to lure the unsuspecting mark to a certain location where the hit would occur. Such was the fate of Walter Sage, killed by his best friends and former roommates, Harry "Pittsburgh Phil" Strauss and the 230-pound goon, Irving "Big Gangi" Cohen. Fellow Brooklyn mug, Jacob "Jack" Drucker, assisted in the killing. Sage himself had a few years earlier set up his own close friend, Red Albert. The message from a higher up to Sage was simple. "It's your hit. You're a good friend of Alpert. He won't get suspicious if you come around."

Conversely, if the mark was not an associate or lived outside of New York, a crew, typically consisting of a finger man to point out the victim, the killer and the getaway driver, was assembled to meticulously plan the killing. A car was stolen, onto which stolen license plates were affixed, and hidden at a secure location until the last minute. If a gun was to be used, it was untraceable; inevitably, it was also ditched immediately after the hit. Every contract went through "The Lord High Executioner," Albert Anastasia, who relied heavily on Reles and others. The killers received a straight salary plus a commission depending upon the circumstances of the murder. Some jobs were more intricate than others, requiring greater planning and manpower. Often, the killers had no knowledge why the victims had been targeted. Their only concerns were getting paid and not getting caught.

The territory covered by Murder Incorporated extended throughout America. Whenever a crime boss needed a problem to go away, a call was made to the Combination. The assignment landed on Anastasia's desk and he selected the crew, which might have to travel hundreds of miles, to carry out the job.

To cover their tracks, once the foul deed was consummated, those responsible immediately left the area. Often, by the time the body was discovered, the killers were long gone. Local foes who had a motive to kill the victim were given sufficient advance notice to allow them to establish airtight alibis.

So competent the crews that they became a key and highly respected component of organized crime. In the end, it's thought that the Combination carried out over a thousand killings. And they would have continued but for two unforeseen events, one of which directly involved Kid Twist.

* * *

The first occurred on July 25, 1939 and involved Irving Penn, a forty-two-year-old, short heavy-set fellow, who was married with two daughters. Employed by a classical music publisher, he had no enemies and was well liked. Sadly, he also resembled Philip Orlovsky, who lived in his same Bronx apartment building. Unbeknownst to Penn, the mob had a contract out on

Orlovsky, a crooked union official, who decided to cooperate with the authorities who were building yet another case against Lepke. The hunters had shadowed Orlovsky for days and knew his routine. On the 25th, he mindlessly changed it, leaving his apartment atypically early that morning to grab a shave at a local barbershop. Penn wasn't so lucky. He left for the subway at 7:55 a.m. Mistaking Penn for Orlovsky, the Murder Incorporated killers blasted away. They hit the wrong guy.

One dirt ball killing another dirt ball garners little public outrage. When decent citizens get shot down in broad daylight, however, it's a different story. The rare bungled hit brought additional heat on organized crime, which was already reeling from the manhunt for a hiding Lepke, who had been on the lam for nearly two years after learning that pending indictments and arrest were imminent.

The police reacted to the Penn killing by arresting anyone connected with the rackets and cracking down on all illicit moneymaking operations. Newspapers called for action and justice. Lepke, being shuttled from one safe house to another throughout the metropolitan area, ordered Anastasia to take out anyone who could be a witness against him. In some cases, terrified gangsters, knowing that their time was limited, voluntarily turned themselves in and became witnesses against the man trying to do them in.

In the orgy of death, scores were killed. Orlovsky was on the hit list. Penn got it instead. Lepke was Public Enemy #1. With the heat now boiling, even Lepke's friends were pressuring him to surrender to the authorities. When he resisted, the mob set him up, telling him that a deal had been struck in which he would plea to federal charges, go to prison, and not be subject to Dewey and state prosecution. Believing that, Lepke, on August 24, 1939, with the assistance of nationally-syndicated columnist Walter Winchell, turned himself into J. Edgar Hoover. It was his last act as a free man.

* * *

Things were also starting to go rapidly downhill for Kid Twist. 1940 proved to be the end of his tumultuous criminal career. It was then that Harry Rudolph, a gravely ill convict, decided to exact both vengeance and justice by telling the police the story of the 1933 gangland murder of his friend, nineteen-year-old Alex "Red" Albert, who had gotten into an argument with Phil Strauss over jewelry Red stole and wanted Strauss to fence. The disagreement was settled when Sage lured his friend Albert to a location where Reles and others shot and killed him. Soon a case was developed, murder indictments were secured and Abe was looking at the electric chair.

He didn't like what he saw and on Good Friday sent his pregnant wife Rose to the district attorney, William O'Dwyer. Abe wanted to make a deal. And what a deal he made.

* * *

In exchange for Reles' cooperation, District Attorney William O'Dwyer agreed to let the man he believed to be "the most effective informer in the annals of criminal justice" walk.

Abe Reles, the New York mobster and killer galore, whose cooperation with the authorities solved scores of crimes and landed him in the morgue.

A pass for every murder and crime committed. The price was exorbitant, but Abe kept his end of the bargain.

Over the course of two weeks, Reles proved to be not only a gifted killer but one possessing an astounding memory, able to recall in minute detail the scores of crimes in which he was involved. In short order he solved eighty-five murders. Soon he was in court testifying, first against former close associates "Happy" Maione and "Dasher" Abbandando and, in a second trial, "Buggsy" Goldstein and "Pittsburgh Phil" Strauss. All four were found guilty of murder and sent to the chair. The crime world was in a tizzy with mobsters diving for cover. Even Anastasia dropped out of sight.

Reles knew he was a marked man and greatly feared for his safety. District Attorney O'Dwyer seemingly shared those fears and, with the police, devised a seemingly foolproof protection plan. Reles and three other turncoats—Allie "Tick Tock" Tannenbaum, Sholem Bernstein and Mickey Sycoff—were sequestered in Coney Island's majestic Half Moon Hotel, comprised of four hundred rooms spread over a sixteen-story center section sandwiched by two eleven-story side wings. The east wing of the sixth floor was sealed off with a bulletproof door, which served as the sole entrance and exit to the ten-room fortress. Handpicked officers provided twenty-four hour security, five in the suite and others in the lobby. Reles, guarded "like the gold pile at Fort Knox," was alone in Room 623, safe and secure.

* * *

November 12, 1941 was a Wednesday. Inside the hotel lobby and away from the cold and dark 4:30 morning, a bellhop chatted with two cops. A second hotel employee snoozed nearby. Suddenly a loud thud shook him awake. The four, not anxious to venture out into the elements, theorized that a car had jumped the curb and struck the building. No one was particularly interested and nothing was done.

Two-and-a-half hours later, around 7:00, an employee of the Coney Island draft board, housed in Room 123 of the hotel, arrived at work and glanced out of his window. A lifeless body sprawled out on the kitchen extension roof greeted him. Trembling, he called the assistant manager, who rushed down. The police on the sixth floor were alerted and hustled over to Reles' room. Their report exploded throughout the city: "Abe went out the window!"

* * *

The respected police Captain John McGowan quickly took charge of the investigation. Inexplicably, he failed to seal off the crime scene, secure the physical evidence or interview hotel guests and employees; he severely limited the police photographer, who took a single photo of Reles, who had already been slightly moved. He failed to sequester the five guards, who, within earshot of each other, told a similar tale—Reles was routinely checked, the last time being around seven.

By evening, the case was "solved." Reles died trying to escape. He had tied a bed sheet from his room, flung it out the window, attempted to climb down to an empty room below, and somehow lost his grip, falling fifty-two feet to his death.

Questions burst forth from the press and public. They went unanswered. Why would Reles, who was petrified of the mob, try to escape? How did he know the room below, #523, was empty? Even if he had gained entrance there, how was he going to waltz past the guards in the lobby? Why did he only have $2.35 in his pockets? Why was no one else identified as being outside, waiting to whisk him away? If Reles had been checked and seen in his room around seven, why would he then try to escape in broad daylight? Why didn't any of the cops

The window Abe flew out of on November 12, 1941. (*Brooklyn Public Library*)

guarding him see anything? How did he have the stamina to climb out and shimmy down when he had been released just three days before from a nine day hospital stay due to chronic lung disease? What was that thud heard at 4:30? Why did he land so far from the building if he merely fell? Why were no forensic tests conducted?

To the police the case was closed. "We were well rid of him. Brooklyn didn't shed any tears when they buried Reles. We lifted a toast."

And so the end of a man who only shortly before had been crowned the greatest informer in history.

Epilogue

Although Reles was listed as a witness in the Lepke trial, which was going on when Reles died, his testimony was not crucial. Lepke was convicted and ultimately sent to the chair, becoming the first mob chief to suffer such an outcome. Albert Anastasia, on the other hand, who was in hiding, came out when the key witness against him went out the window. Anastasia benefitted greatly when Reles died and went on to lead a long criminal life, until he himself met a violent ending in 1957.

We'll never know who killed Abe. Clearly, many wanted him dead, from mobsters to crooked politicians and police on the take, about whom Reles was never questioned. Was it the guards who did it? If so, why didn't any of them show any signs of financial prosperity? Or was it the three other turncoats, upset for any variety of petty reasons or perhaps pulling off what surely would have been the ultimate inside job?

Tidbits

Another theory had Reles, a jokester, shimming down and out with the idea of immediately returning and surprising his flummoxed guards. The premise is probably even more ridiculous than the escape theory.

Lepke's negotiated surrender, with Walter Winchell acting as the go-between, took weeks. It culminated with Anastasia driving Lepke to Winchell, who in turn drove Lepke to Manhattan's 23rd Street and Fifth Avenue and pulled in behind FBI Director Hoover's parked car. It was shortly after 10 p.m. when Winchell walked Lepke over to Hoover.

The district attorney at the time, William O'Dwyer, mysteriously never charged Anastasia—against whom a strong case existed—so long as Reles was alive. O'Dwyer went on to become the embattled and scandal-ridden Mayor of New York City. Forced to leave office prematurely, he was later named ambassador to Mexico—a position which he subsequently resigned—after being nationally skewered before the Kefauver Committee, which was investigating organized crime and the Reles killing.

Charles "Lucky" Luciano, Frank Costello and Lepke all indicated, at various times, that the cops, led by Captain Frank Bals, who was instrumental in setting up Reles' protection, were responsible for the killing.

Reles also solved the 1935 murder of Dutch Schultz and three of his associates, who happened to be in the way. With Prosecutor Thomas E. Dewey investigating the mob, Schultz, who was also feeling the sting, went to Lepke, Luciano, Anastasia and others and asked permission to kill Dewey. Knowing the heat it would bring upon them, the proposal was vetoed. When Schultz indicated he was going forward anyway, the order went out to hit Schultz, which was carried out. Ironically, in the end, Lepke helped spare the life of Dewey, who in turn prosecuted Lepke and sent him to the chair.

Lepke's wife Betty was no shrinking violet. She enjoyed partying, nightclubs and played both cards and the horses.

Sidney Hillman, who helped to economically lead the nation through the Depression and later during World War II, as a trusted advisor to President Franklin Delano Roosevelt, had earlier headed a garment union which used the violent services of Lepke. Many claim that Hillman had strong ties to the murderous underworld and refused to cooperate with Dewey's efforts to prosecute the mob.

Lepke was serving federal time at the time of the state death sentence. Some opined that the FDR Administration was afraid that Lepke, in a bid for clemency, might start naming names of mob connected labor leaders who were strong backers of the Democratic Party. The feds finally turned Lepke over to the state on the condition that the state sentence be carried out. In the end, Lepke died without implicating anyone.

Our Next Tale

As demonstrated in the last chapter about Al Capone, organized crime, much like many legitimate businesses, had periodic meetings to discuss topics of concern. In 1929 Capone met with crime bosses from throughout the nation in Atlantic City. Nearly thirty later, the next generation of mobsters again met. And Albert Anastasia, who survived nearly two decades after Kid Twist drifted down from his sixth floor hotel room, was a major reason why they were meeting. This time, though, their get together did not go as planned, with dramatic and long-lasting repercussions.

16

There is No Mafia

While in a local hotel investigating a bad check, State Trooper Edgar Croswell's ears perked up when he overheard Joe Barbara Jr. reserving three rooms for three unnamed people. Barbara explained to the hotel manager that his father, who ran a soft drink bottling plant, was conducting a meeting for some out-of-town businessmen in the soda industry.

Croswell knew that Joseph Barbara Sr. owned such a business. Indeed, he owned several businesses, even securing a coveted license to distribute beer. Croswell also knew that Barbara was a Mafia chieftain, up to no good.

* * *

If the town of Apalachin were any quieter, it'd be dead. Located in upstate New York about 170 miles from New York City, it had a population of 280 people. Barbara moved there in 1944 to escape the increasing pressure from the police that he was receiving in Pennsylvania. The authorities had good reason to follow him given his long history of criminal activities, including prostitution, larceny and murder.

* * *

In the 1950s, under the closed eyes of the Federal Bureau of Investigation and its stern leader, J. Edgar Hoover, there was, in his view, no such thing as organized crime or as he succinctly put it, "There is no Mafia." Hoover believed in branding different criminals, whether they be John Dillinger or Louis Lepke Buchalter, a public enemy and bringing them to justice. As for crime being organized, Hoover thought the notion speculative and unworthy of any commitment of manpower and resources. Without the involvement of the federal government, the states were thus left to their own meager and underfunded police forces, wholly unable to investigate wide-ranging crimes committed across state lines; a menace recognized by all except Hoover.

Many have guessed the reasons for Hoover's denial. Some have said he had his own connections to the Mafia, and consequently, could not risk exposing himself. Others have claimed he was being blackmailed by the Mafia, which had proof of Hoover's homosexuality and threatened to out him if he interfered.

It took a freshman Democratic Senator from Tennessee, Estes Kefauver, to unmask the threat. From 1950 through 1951, the "Special Committee to Investigate Organized Crime in Interstate Commerce" went on tour, holding hearings in fourteen cities and calling over six hundred witnesses. Initially, the hearings drew little attention, until they landed in New York City. Over nine days, the major networks televised the hearings and the American people were spellbound, witnessing a parade of shady characters often pleading the Fifth about their various activities. As the NYPD monitored these gangsters, police detectives were able to outline how the mob functioned.

Of all of those appearing, Frank "The Prime Minister" Costello was the highlight. A leader of the Lucky Luciano crime family and prominent mob leader, Costello wished to maintain an aura of respectability. Consequently, unlike many of his peers, he refused to take full advantage of his constitutional right not to answer questions that might tend to incriminate him, choosing instead to answer, albeit evasively, queries put to him. Costello made a request, however, that his face not be televised. The committee obliged, resulting in the viewer only seeing Costello's hands, which when not nervously tapping his stubby fingers, were wrapped tightly around a handkerchief running over and through his clenched fists. In addition to this highly dramatic sight, Costello recently had undergone throat surgery, giving him a raspy voice which made his appearance even more sinister.

After hearing from all of the witnesses, the Committee concluded that "There is a sinister criminal organization known as the Mafia operating throughout the country with ties in other nations. [...] The Mafia is a loose-knit organization specializing in the sale and distribution of narcotics, the conduct of various gambling enterprises, prostitution, and other rackets based on extortion and violence."

Despite the clarity of the conclusions, few tangible results came about. Nationally, no legislation was passed; locally the committee's findings were minimized. Only Frank Costello suffered. He brought the charges on himself when, in response to a question about what he had done for his country that allowed him to grow rich, he responded that he paid his taxes.

New York mobster and crime family boss Frank Costello appearing before the Kefauver Committee in 1951. (*Library of Congress*)

The IRS got involved and determined that he hadn't. Jail followed, which didn't deter him from running his criminal enterprise.

✳ ✳ ✳

Set up like a corporation, the mob consisted of a ruling body, the Commission, which functioned like a Board of Trustees or Directors. The five families of New York City were represented as were those from Buffalo and Chicago. With the Kefauver hearing behind them, and having suffered no real damage, organized crime hummed along, making a mountain of money without any significant law enforcement concerns. Until 1957.

✳ ✳ ✳

1957 was a seminal one for the mob, an organization in flux. The conservative faction, led by an alliance between bosses Frank Costello and Albert Anastasia, was being challenged by a newer one, emerging under the tutelage of crime boss Vito Genovese, who had been plotting the overthrow of the old guard. Genovese recruited Anastasia's underbosses—Tommy Lucchese and Carlo Gambino—to aid in the battle.

In early May of that year, Costello was hit, the target of an assassination attempt widely believed to have been ordered by Genovese. At eleven in the evening, Vincent "The Chin" Gigante waited for Costello to arrive home to his posh Manhattan apartment. When Costello came, after dinner with some friends and acquaintances, Gigante greeted Costello with a gun and a shout, "This is for you Frank!" He fired. The bullet missed its mark, barely grazing Costello's head. Costello got the message though. His days were numbered. He retired and ceded control of his crime family—the Charlie "Lucky" Luciano family—to Genovese. Meanwhile, Costello refused to cooperate with the authorities investigating the shooting, insisting that "I didn't see nothing!"

Fearing he was next to be targeted, Albert Anastasia, who by now had moved beyond Murder Incorporated but was still having people killed, sought permission from the Commission to take out Genovese. Instead, wishing to avoid an all-out war, Joseph Bonanno, the head of the Bonanno crime family, negotiated a peace. It was short-lived. On October 25th, with Anastasia casually reclined in a barber's chair in Manhattan's Park Sheraton Hotel on 56th and Seventh, two masked gunmen wandered in and started blasting him. Thanks to a classic photograph of the dead mobster sprawled out on the floor, the murder became instant folklore. With his power consolidated, Genovese soon became a Commission member, ruling over one of the most powerful families in the nation.

✳ ✳ ✳

Given the turmoil swirling around, it was unsurprising that a decision was made by the mob to gather to discuss a number of issues. First, the in-fighting surrounding Costello's retirement and Anastasia's assassination had to be resolved. Second, was how to make even more money

Fellow mobster and crime family boss, Vito Genovese, 1959. (*Library of Congress*)

by exploiting the growing and highly-profitable drug trade; soaking even more money out of the garment industry; and expanding their loansharking business. Lastly, a strategy had to be put in place to counter the rumblings of federal intrusion led by Robert Kennedy.

With the decision made to meet, the next one was where. Why not the cozy and comfortable confines of small-town America, where they could meet far away from the prying eyes of law enforcement? After all, they had successfully met there just a year prior. Joseph Barbara, the boss of the northeastern Pennsylvania family, once again offered his locale of Apalachin. Soon the invitations went out to about a hundred mobsters from around the nation: New York, Pennsylvania, Buffalo, Cleveland, Illinois, Dallas, Colorado and Los Angeles.

* * *

After Croswell heard Barbara Jr. reserving the hotel rooms, the state trooper conducted a brief investigation, and soon learned that Barbara had ordered over two hundred pounds of meat that was being specially delivered from Chicago. With his suspicions sizzling on the morning of November 15, 1957, Croswell checked both Barbara's bottling plant, where he found nothing, and then Barbara's home on McCall Road. Once there, he immediately observed an area overrun by luxury cars and limousines. Croswell left his vehicle and, joined by fellow State Trooper Vincent Vasisko and two agents from the Federal Bureau of Alcohol,

Tobacco, and Firearms, started recording the license plates numbers, which later revealed registrations to known criminals.

When Barbara's well-heeled visitors caught wind of what was occurring, they panicked, yelling "It's the staties" and took off into the woods like jack rabbits at the sound of a shotgun blast. Seeing the mayhem, police reinforcements were called to the scene. A roadblock was quickly assembled. Although seemingly no laws were being broken, arrests were nonetheless being made. If they ran, they must be guilty of something.

Cons stopped at the roadblock were taken into custody. The countryside was scoured, looking for those who fled. Unprepared and unable to stay in the woods for any length of time, they soon took to the roads, where their glittery silk suits, wing-tipped shoes and fedoras screamed out for attention. "One by one we rounded them up," Croswell explained, "bedraggled, soaking wet, and tired."

By shortly after five o'clock in the afternoon, fifty-eight men had been taken into custody, overrunning the small police facility. In all, those arrested had $300,000 in cash, much of it bunched up in large wads. Others, who had little money, were suspected of dumping it in the woods.

When questioned, most insisted that they were there to visit their old, sick friend, Joe Barbara, who suffered from a heart ailment, and that it was merely a coincidence that they all converged at the same time. Another claimed he was looking for someone to help fix the brakes of his new car. In his memoir, Joe Bonanno denied even being there, claiming someone had falsely used his driver's license, which he had left with his brother-in-law to be renewed.

With no evidence of a crime, the men were released. Ironically, Barbara's house was never searched and served as a safe haven for those who had kept their wits and patiently waited out the storm.

* * *

The news from the quiet town rocked the nation, which learned conclusively that organized crime existed. No longer could the FBI ignore what was now obvious. Steps, giant ones, were in the process of being taken.

It started with twenty of those who attended the Apalachin meeting being dubiously charged with conspiring to obstruct justice by lying about the nature of their meeting. And convicted. Thirteen were fined $10,000 each and given hefty prison sentences ranging from three to five years.

Not surprisingly, in November 1960, their convictions were overturned, the Court observing that "Since the Government had not tried to prove that the meeting, in and of itself, violated any state or federal law, how could it prove that the defendants had conspired to lie about their presence there? . . . Bad as many of these alleged conspirators may be, their conviction for a crime which the Government could not prove ... and on evidence which a jury could not properly assess, cannot be permitted to stand."

Epilogue

Despite their attempts of secrecy, the mob had been exposed. The federal government, which had long ignored the cancer, was now forced to confront it. A greatly embarrassed FBI Director, J. Edgar Hoover, quickly set up the "Top Hoodlum Program," with the aim of rounding up Mafia leaders. The Apalachin Meeting served as a starting point, providing many names to investigate—often those of businessmen who ran legitimate businesses as fronts for their involvement in organized crime. The battle the government launched would be a long one, still being fought today.

Tidbits

Another freshman senator, Republican Joseph McCarthy of Wisconsin, competed for the position that was obtained by Kefauver, whose party was in power. McCarthy in turn went on to investigate the "threat" of Communism, turning our country upside down, and ruining many innocent people in his unrelenting fervor to root out communists and subversives.

Costello's tax evasion conviction arose out of his wife's outrageous shopping sprees whenever she discovered yet another illicit affair of her husband. Over six years, she spent over a half a million dollars, far in excess of Costello's reported income.

Marlon Brando's character's voice in the movie *The Godfather* is said to have been based on Costello's testimony.

Joe Barbara was indicted for not revealing what happened at his home in Apalachin and later, in 1959, was charged with tax evasion. He never made it to trial, dying of a heart attack that June. His home became a tourist attraction.

Vito Genovese loved a married woman. He had her husband killed so that he could marry her. He died in prison in 1969 while serving ten years of a fifteen-year sentence for heroin trafficking.

Paul Castellano ("Big Paul", "The Pope") was one of those picked up in Apalachin. He later became boss of the Gambino family before he was killed in 1985 on the orders of John Gotti.

III

Damsels in Dastardly Distress

S ADLY, WOMEN OFTEN FIND THEMSELVES in precarious positions, frequently it is no fault of their own; the classic wrong place at the wrong time, or the equally common tragic association with an evil man up to no good.

Helen Jewett and Mary Rogers were loved and admired by many. Both were killed. Edgar Allen Poe was so enthralled with Mary that he wrote a short story about her unsolved murder. Everyone knew who killed Helen, including the jury that nonetheless acquitted him.

A doctor and a handyman killed many, while an ambitious young man—a sausage king—killed only the girlfriend and wife with whom he had grown tired.

Of course, not all women are so innocent, as evidenced by our next tale; circumstances sometimes propel them to do things that they ordinarily might not do. Such was Bathsheba Spooner, the well-bred, intelligent and attractive woman from a noteworthy family. In a scenario as old as humans, she was married to the wrong man. With her young lover, and others, the problem was solved.

17

A Cold Blooded Murder with an Asterisk

As Joshua Spooner stumbled home on March 1, 1778, he could barely make out his feet hitting the rut-gutted, frozen ground. Whether it was due to his inebriated state or, more likely, the moonless night, was of no consequence. The businessman-farmer trudged up the four stone steps leading to the solid front door of a secluded house buttoned shut against the cold. Little did the curmudgeon know that he had but a few minutes to live.

As Spooner went to open the door, he was pounced upon, savagely beaten and strangled. It took but a short time to render him dead. Out of the shadows, the killer's two partners rushed in, stripping the corpse of its valuables, before hurling the lifeless mass head first down a nearby well.

Surely Spooner's wife who had been sitting on the other side of the door, heard the commotion, heard her husband's screams of agony and horror. In response to his cries, she did nothing. Why would she? She had orchestrated the murder.

* * *

Bathsheba Spooner was born on February 15, 1746 into a prominent family. Her birth in Sandwich, Massachusetts, marked the sixth generation of her family's residence in the colonies. Her father Timothy was a mountain of a man, who stood over six feet tall and towered over the much smaller, average-sized men of his day. He graduated from Harvard in 1732, was a vegetarian and rarely drank. Within short order he became a lawyer and a long-term member of the state legislature.

Bathsheba was named for her fiery mother, Bathsheba Bourne, who also came from a socially prominent family. Indeed, the town of Bourne as well as the Bourne Bridge, which connects the mainland to Cape Cod, bears the family name. Bourne married William Newcomb and proceeded to have seven children. Newcomb died in his early thirties and five months later, on September 18, 1736, his wealthy headstrong thirty-two-year-old widow married twenty-five-year-old Timothy Ruggles.

The Ruggles lived for seventeen years on the Cape and had seven children. In 1753, Ruggles decided to move his large family to Hardwick, twenty miles from Worcester, where he built a mansion set upon lush and lovely grounds. Unfortunately, the French and Indian Wars interrupted their tranquility and Ruggles answered the call to duty, serving until 1759. As with everything he did in life, he achieved great success, rising to the rank of brigadier general.

Upon his return from service, Ruggles re-entered his world of civilian accomplishments. In 1762, he was named Chief Justice of Worcester's highest trial court. In another era, Timothy Ruggles would have continued his rise, possibly becoming governor of Massachusetts or even president of the United States. But these were revolutionary times and Ruggles sat on the wrong side of history. A staunch loyalist, he lived in a land teeming with radicals. As times worsened, circumstances compelled his fleeing the state, never to return. His wife meanwhile remained behind, perhaps relieved by her regained freedom.

In an ironic sense, Judge Ruggles, as before, had again climbed above all others, achieving the status as one of the most reviled men in all the colonies. The hatred hurled at him would have a devastating effect on his favorite child, Bathsheba.

* * *

Given the personalities of her parents, it is easy to conclude that the blood that flowed through the veins of Bathsheba Ruggles ran hot and passionate. Accompanying what had to be a forceful personality, were brains and radiance. Why then would she settle and marry the weak-kneed Joshua Spooner in 1766? While wealthy and well connected, he was timid, if not cowardly. He was also a mean drunk. Whether he slept with the help is an allegation lost to history. Perhaps Bathsheba's father, in an attempt to help his cherished daughter, arranged the marriage.

After giving birth to four children, one of whom died at an early age, Bathsheba found herself financially well-off but emotionally bereft. She had clearly lost all respect for Spooner, a man she perhaps never loved. It was clear she wanted nothing to do with him. Unfortunately, given the times, divorce was out of the question. She was in a quandary, fretting, miserable and praying for guidance. It came in the form of a light knock on her door.

* * *

Although seemingly a mere child, sixteen-year-old Ezra Ross was a battle-weary and seasoned veteran of the Revolutionary War. Discharged from the military, he was left to his wits to make the 240-mile trek home in the dead of a brutal winter. Worse, he was ill. He had either picked up one of the various rampant diseases crawling around his infested hell hole of a camp or something equally nasty along the way.

In dire need of food, lodging and rest, the frostbitten, undernourished and desperate youth stumbled to the door of the Spooners. There, he found all that he needed and far more.

Immediately drawn to the handsome features peeking out from the sickly youth, Bathsheba slowly nursed him back to health. In long talks, he told her of his background and his large and very patriotic family. He was one of seventeen children, seven of whom had died young. At the outset of the war with England, four of his brothers enthusiastically enlisted. They followed the tradition of an older brother Abner, who fought and died before Ezra was even born, during the French and Indian War. Although Ezra did not know it, Abner's commanding officer at the time had been Timothy Ruggles, Bathsheba's father.

Fourteen-year-old Ezra could only watch as his brothers marched off to battle the British. He yearned to join them and anxiously waited his turn. It came quickly. At fifteen, he enlisted. Soon he found action, and the misery and brutality of war.

After a year in the military, his enlistment expired and Ezra was discharged. His arduous trip home would have been a tragic one, but for his chance meeting at a welcoming home along the way, offering refuge and help. Ever so thankful for Bathsheba's care, he grew saddened upon the realization that with the welcome gaining of his health, home beckoned. The bittersweet feeling of impending departure was mutual, for Ezra had also provided much comfort to Bathsheba as evidenced by their passionate love affair.

⋆　⋆　⋆

As Ezra departed, he surely thought that he would not be soon returning to his lover. Once again, however, fate, in the continuing form of the lasting war, intervened. When the call went out for additional manpower, Ezra re-joined the army. En route to his new assignment, he again passed through the heaven of Brookfield, Bathsheba's home town. He stayed for what must have been a blissful reunion during a hot and sultry August.

And as summer turned to fall, he marched off again, to fight in other long and bloody battles. With the survival gods smiling down upon him, he managed to avoid serious injury. When his time for yet another release from the military arrived, Ross traveled to his new home, that of his lover in Brookfield. Bathsheba was ecstatic to see him; so too Joshua, who took the lad under wing, making Ezra his traveling business assistant. And when Joshua traveled alone, Ezra satisfied the needs of a very grateful and happy Bathsheba. An unforeseen event awaited, the resolution of which carried fatal consequences.

⋆　⋆　⋆

Bathsheba's joyous affair with a man half her age was balanced by her hatred of her husband, a man she daily prayed to be out of her life. At first it was a fanciful dream. Divorce was out of the question as was the likelihood of her thirty-seven-year-old husband dying anytime soon. Fantasy turned to reality, if not horror, however, when Bathsheba discovered she was pregnant.

The punishment for adultery was harsh: being stripped half-naked and whipped; then often tarred and feathered and paraded throughout the town. Given the added hostility toward her loyalist father, no mercy would be shown; indeed the punishment might be intensified. Well aware of her dire straits, and with the need to do something quickly, she reviewed her limited options.

She thought of joining her father. But with war raging and patrols rampant, travel, especially in colder weather, was hazardous. And what of her three young children? Would she desert them? How could she? Trapped, her thoughts turned more sinister. Get rid of the man who caused her so much angst.

Turning to Ezra, she besieged him to poison her husband. He reluctantly agreed and half-heartedly made an attempt. The toxic potion he slipped into Joshua's drink was so pungent, however, that Joshua immediately spit the liquid out. Bathsheba told Ezra to try again, this time on their next business trip. Along with his travel articles, Ezra packed the poison but never gave it to his intended victim. Instead he jumped on a horse and rode to his parents' home in an effort perhaps to distance himself from the madness engulfing him.

In the face of a growing pregnancy and the subsequent ruin that would follow, Bathsheba grew more and more desperate. Intent on carrying out her foolhardy plan, she imprudently turned to others. Glancing out of her window one day, she happened to spot two nefarious characters. Steadying her gaze, she saw them to be British soldiers and obviously on their own. Bathsheba yelled for her servant, who was sent scurrying out to fetch them.

Sheepishly and suspiciously, thirty-year-old Sergeant James Buchanan and his illiterate dunce of a partner, Private William Brooks, aged twenty-seven, followed the maid back to the Spooner home. Like many of their fellow British soldiers, they were trapped in America, hungry and anxious. Initially captured, they escaped, wandering aimlessly around the countryside, doing whatever it took to survive.

Bathsheba invited the two misfits in, and with Joshua and Ezra still away, treated them to warmth, food, wine and friendship. Soon she was confiding her "utter aversion" to her despised husband and her plans to kill him. With Joshua out of the way, she spoke of her freedom and availability, hinting to Buchanan of sexual favors in return for assistance. The two soldiers jumped at the opportunity to aid their benevolent seductress.

* * *

Strangely, Bathsheba continued on, enlisting others. So bizarre and half-baked her actions—there were no plans to either conceal the murder or escape—that her attorney later at trial would characterize her as insane. Bathsheba sought out two locals and yet another British soldier whom she drunkenly wooed at a tavern. Plans were developed and abandoned, often due to the "faint heartedness" of those recruited. She even wrote Ezra, who unwisely decided to return the day of the murder. Whether he did so out of jealousy, bravado, youthful indiscretion or just poor judgment, his presence commanded tragic results. He decided to join the plot, acting with two enemy combatants—Brooks and Buchanan—whom he likely only recently fought against.

Time continued to pass. Action was needed. Now. When finally taken, it came without wisdom, planning or common sense.

* * *

Plied with liquor, Brooks did the awful deed. Ross and Buchanan rushed in. The body was stripped of valuables and tossed into a well, the only source of drinking water for those in the household. As inept the murder plan and implementation, the escape was even more incompetent. The three assailants fled to Worcester, whereupon Buchanan and Brooks entered a tavern, drank and showed off the easily identifiable valuables they had stolen. They also had some of Joshua's money, given to them by a grateful Bathsheba after the murder. Ross, feeling remorse, attempted to hide at a nearby boarding house.

Within a day, Joshua's lifeless body was discovered and the three arrested. They quickly confessed and fully implicated Bathsheba.

* * *

Approximately seven weeks after the crime, the trial—the very first of its kind in the new republic—commenced, on April 24, 1778. It took place in the same courthouse in which Bathsheba's father earlier presided. Starting at eight in the morning, it ended at midnight. A guilty verdict, by a jury of all white men, followed shortly thereafter. The sentence—death.

But there was a wrinkle. Bathsheba was pregnant. And according to the law, a pregnant woman could not be executed.

To those bent upon carrying out the verdict against the "evil and detestable adulterer," however, there was a way out. If the fetus hadn't "quickened" (moved) as of yet, the sentence could be imposed.

Midwives and experts were called in to perform, what turned out to be a painful and even cruel examination. Their determination—the fetus had not as yet quickened. Shocked, those few who supported the condemned Spooner, protested, forcing, shortly before her scheduled execution, a second examination. Even more intrusive and heartless than the first one, the result remained the same.

* * *

The date of the execution, July 2, 1778, proved to be a festive one, except for those being put to death, much like ballgames today. Souvenir and refreshment stands were set up to accommodate the large crowd. Although 2,500 people lived in the immediate vicinity, 5,000 showed up, attesting both to the notoriety and show of the event. Not even a brief violent and sudden storm, which turned the sky black as thunder and lightning ripped through it, dampened the spectacle. As the air returned to normalcy, the three men were marched to the scaffold. Bathsheba needed assistance, still feeling the effects of her painful physical examination. Despite her pain and discomfort, she came to her execution in style, smartly dressed, including an ostrich-plumed hat.

After the speeches and ceremonies, the sentences were imposed in what at the time was thought to be "the most extraordinary crime ever perpetuated in New England." The four were hanged. Bathsheba was thirty-two, Ezra seventeen.

* * *

An autopsy indicated that Bathsheba was carrying a five-month-old male fetus. There is no question that a fetus that far along would have quickened. Perhaps the contrary medical determination had less to do with medicine and more to do with vengeance and hatred toward Bathsheba and her father. Or perhaps it was due to the role of John Avery Jr., the Deputy Secretary of the ruling Council, appointed by the legislature to preside over the

The talented and alluring Bathsheba Spooner, who was trapped in a loveless marriage. (*Worcester County Law Library Trust*)

Commonwealth when the British left. Avery was the most radical of radicals at the time and surely came into great conflict with Bathsheba's father. He was also the beloved step-brother of the man she murdered.

Epilogue

At the time, Bathsheba was judged by all to be a cold-blooded killer, who solicited many, including a mere child half her age, to execute her well-respected and successful husband. With the passage of time, while many still hold that original judgment, others now view her more sympathetically; as an intelligent woman tragically living in the wrong century. Today, Bathsheba would have merely divorced a man she didn't love and moved on to live a successful, creative and rich life. In 1778, she had no such options. Through murder, Bathsheba created her own way out.

Tidbits

Palpable animosity existed between Bathsheba's parents, which might have begun during Timothy's prolonged absences during the French and Indian War campaigns. During that time, his wife would have been the head of the household and may have been reluctant to hand it back to one thought to be a controlling and obstinate spouse. When Timothy left Hardwick in 1774 to join the Loyalist camp in Boston, his wife did not join him. Both died at eighty-three, Ruggles in Canada, his wife still in Hardwick.

Bathsheba's trial, the first capital case under the new American government, featured several significant national figures. Robert Treat Paine, signer of the Declaration of Independence, was the prosecutor. Levi Lincoln, who defended the four perpetrators, would later become Attorney General under President Thomas Jefferson. William Cushing, one of the three presiding judges in the case, subsequently became the Chief Justice of the United States Supreme Court.

The site of the Spooners' house can still be seen today, about sixty-five miles outside of Boston in Brookfield; so too, remains of the narrow stone well into which Joshua was thrown.

Legend holds that grass has never grown on the grave plot of Joshua Spooner, who is buried in the Brookfield Cemetery. His tombstone reads, "Joshua Spooner Murdered Mar. 1 1778 by three soldiers of the Revolution, Ross, Brooks and Buchanan at the instigation of his wife Bathsheba. They were all executed at Worcester, July 2, 1778."

Abortion at the time was legally and morally acceptable since a fetus wasn't considered alive until it "quickened," which was usually four months into the pregnancy. Why Bathsheba did not attempt to secure one is unknown but it may have been due to the unreliability and unavailability of the procedure during that period.

Prominent women's suffrage leader Elizabeth Cady Stanton wrote of the Spooner affair in the 1899 *New York World*, titled "The Fatal Mistake that Stopped the Hanging of Women in Massachusetts."

Our Next Tale

She heralded from a small New England town in the early 1800s and was so charismatic that a traveling author, upon meeting her as a young girl, wrote glowingly about her. She was also smart and ambitious. Learning of the greater prospects that cities offered, she quickly moved to take full advantage of them, first to Boston and then New York. And the profession she chose to move up the ladder of opportunity was the oldest one the world has known. Like Bathsheba Spooner, another woman trapped in an uncompromising time, she too would suffer a similar fate—death. But in her case, she was murdered. And her killer went free.

18

A Girl on the Town

Rosina Townsend jerked awake at the knocking on her first-floor bedroom door. A voice on the other side meekly muttered that he wished to depart the locked premises. Rosina grunted, "Get the woman to let you out!" Upset that she was being bothered by the customer of one of her girls, whose duty among others was to escort their hourly lovers out of the house dubbed The Palace of Passions, she nonetheless quickly fell back to sleep.

Loud knocking at the front door of her mansion put a second sudden halt to her slumber. Rosina stumbled out of bed and answered it, allowing in a very late-arriving client. As the john trudged up the stairs to meet his paramour Elizabeth Salters, Rosina glanced at the clock on the mantel. It read 3 a.m. Anxious to return to bed, something out of the corner of her eye caught her attention. A globe lamp, ordinarily in the upstairs room of Helen Jewett, was instead glowing on a small table in the back parlor.

As Rosina slowly walked over to check it out, she noticed that the rear door had been opened and remained ajar. Outside, the sixty-foot-deep backyard stood barricaded as usual, guarded by a white fence, ranging from eight to twelve feet high, to keep all unwanted visitors at bay. Perhaps, Rosina surmised, a resident or guest had gone out to use the privy.

Returning to her bedroom, she remained uneasy. Raw weather and inside chamber pots augured against anyone venturing outside to relieve themselves; nor did she hear anyone returning to the warmth of the house. Again leaving her cushy surroundings, she cautiously returned to the rear entrance, peered out and yelled out into the darkness, "Who's out there?"

Hearing no response, she deemed it wise to survey the premises. Retrieving the globe light, she cautiously walked upstairs, heading for Helen's bedroom. With its lock unlatched, Rosina gently pushed the door open. Smoke billowed out. Fire! Was Helen okay? Was her guest, Frank Rivers? Would they suffocate?

With smoke and terror filling the hallway, Rosina pounded on the adjoining door. Screams of fire rang out, awakening all. Everyone scrambled—the prostitutes for safety, their customers for anonymity. A nearby watchmen heard the commotion and called for help. Rosina and a fellow housemate, Maria Stevens, braved the perilous conditions and rushed into Helen's room to rescue her. Unexpectedly, neither a fire nor even a blaze greeted them. Rather, Helen's once luxurious double mahogany bed smoldered, spitting out noxious fumes. On it lay Helen, dead in a pool of blood, her nightclothes reduced to ashes and one half of her body charred,

Helen Jewett, a cultured and charismatic woman who catered to the sexual tastes of the upper class.

like a roasted marshmallow, to a crusty brown. As they crept closer, they spotted three deep, bloody gashes on Helen's battered forehead. Helen had been murdered. Her appointed lover gone. Rosina stiffened at the thought that the person who had earlier knocked on her bedroom door was the person who had killed one of her most desirable workers, the vivacious twenty-three-year-old Helen Jewett.

* * *

The real Helen Jewett will never be known. When one, especially one who stirred up grossly mixed feelings, dies in 1836, there is often precious little to mark their existence. In Helen's case, however, some letters she wrote and received survived, as did the many newspaper accounts that documented her tragic story. While some disagreed about who she was and how she appeared, no one denied her strong, if not overwhelming, attraction to men, many of them rich and powerful.

* * *

Dorcas Doyen was born in Maine on October 18, 1813, to poor parents. When her mother died, she, as an early teenager, became a house servant, in 1826, to Judge Nathan Weston and his wife and their six children. Judge Weston was a highly respected citizen and jurist, serving as Chief Justice of Maine's Supreme Court. While living with the Weston family, Dorcas was exposed to books, knowledge and style.

On one occasion, author Anne Royall, one of the first female journalists to travel the nation in search of stories for her books, visited Augusta to write about its residents. Quickly she was directed to one of the state's foremost figures, Judge Weston. While struck by the soft-spoken, dignified and youthful judge and his clan, which she dubbed "[t]he only truly worthy family in Augusta," she was even more taken by his young servant. The fourteen-year-old Dorcas moved the veteran writer, who was now in her fifties, with her grace and sweetness and charismatic appearance. With the subsequent publication of Royall's book about her Maine experiences, she wrote about, and in a sense conferred fame upon, the young child. Now when Dorcas traveled to the town bookstore, in addition to being exposed to a variety of books, one volume even had her as a character, albeit a minor one.

At eighteen or so, Doyne left her employer, apparently anxious to break away from whatever restraints she imagined on herself. Moving to Portland, she both changed her name, first to Maria Stanley and then to Maria Benson, and her profession, to that of a girl on the town, a euphemism for prostitute. Soon, perhaps to find a wider range of affluent clientele, or just out of boredom, she departed, plying her trade briefly in different locations under different names before landing in Boston, as Helen Mar (the surname of a character in a famous novel at the time), and then New York City, as Helen Jewett.

In the big, bustling metropolis, she made her mark, cavorting and sleeping with the rich and well-to-do. Many willingly listened to the stories of an obviously bright, attractive and sexually-active young woman. She regaled them with tales, often false or exaggerated, of how she grew up an orphan and attended a private and exclusive school, thanks to a wealthy and generous benefactor. In fact, she was neither an orphan nor the recipient of a private education although Judge Weston, being a benevolent man, sent the young family servant to the local school.

The question which will forever remain unanswered is her sexualization. Did she go into it willingly, generally unheard of at the time, or was she the victim of the advances of a nefarious young man, whose seduction drove her into a life of defiled debasement?

Regardless, in New York, where she would live for four years, she quickly became popular with the males of high society. She continued to read voraciously and even subscribed to some of the leading literary journals of the day. Working in various houses, Helen occasionally left to live as a kept mistress, before finally landing in 41 Thomas Street, the stylish well-respected brothel of Rosina Townsend in lower Manhattan. There she typically saw two well-paying clients a day. A personal maid tended her room. Squired around by, and sleeping with, politicians, lawyers, businessmen and writers, she easily held her own, bedazzling them in dress, jewelry, style and intellect. Each felt a special connection with Helen, who fostered an active correspondence, using the finest of stationaries. To one paramour she ended a missive, in French, "Goodbye until the delicious moments." Clearly she had captivated a city.

And then she met Richard Robinson, who used the alias Frank Rivers when consorting with prostitutes.

* * *

Richard P. Robinson was eighteen, good looking and from a large respectable Connecticut family. His father, a farmer and dabbler in real estate, came to own much land over the course of his life. Evident of his standing in the small town of Durham, he was elected eight times to the state legislature. He married twice and had twelve children. Richard was the eighth and the first son.

Little is known of the young man other than he attended school and left as a young teenager, moving to New York, like so many of his generation, seeking to stake out a career. He worked as a clerk in a dry goods store for Joseph Hoxie at 101 Maiden Lane.

Helen and Richard met in June 1835. As with many of her lovers, a lively correspondence soon sprang up between the two. In her room, at her death, were forty-three letters she sent him and the fifteen he sent her. Their literacy was often striking; smart letters, poetic and loving with rich imagery. At eighteen, he was four years younger than Helen, who seemingly, given her experience, should have been light years ahead of him. Apparently this was not so, both in savvy and passion. It is clear that, at the outset anyway, a deep and mutual affection between the two existed.

In one early letter, Helen wrote, in part,

> I anticipate a further acquaintance with you will
> throw an additional charm over my time, and make the
> sands of life run more gaily than before. There is
> so much sweetness in that voice, so much intelligence
> in that eye, and so much luxuriance in that form,
> I cannot fail to love you. The pleasure I feel in
> your presence and smile, speak of hours and nights
> of joy; I long to see you, to hear your conversation
> animate your features once again, but I must defer
> that pleasure until your next visit. I must now bid
> you an affectionate adieu.

His posts to her, in turn, were also plush in language and romance. Soon, he started presenting her with gifts, a major one being his portrait miniature, a significant gesture in pre-photographic America. She, in turn, was also generous, providing him with symbols of her strong affections.

That she was a prostitute seeing other lovers was seemingly an accepted aspect of their relationship. When he strayed, however, it brought harsh rebukes from Helen. And soon the romance, perhaps due to the youth and circumstances of the parties, started, ever so slowly, to crumble. Their visits became tense, with Robinson admittedly acting inappropriately. "You must think it very strange that I profess to love you so much and yet always treat you so harshly."

As the strains increased, Robinson finally suggested that perhaps it was time for them to go their separate ways. He also thought it wise for them to return to the other their many love letters, which he did. Given that they were all ultimately found in Helen's room on the night of her death, indicates that, for whatever reason, she moved more slowly. Perhaps, she hadn't gotten around to it, or maybe she was hoping for a reconciliation. Or, maybe blackmail, either real or imagined, figured into the equation.

* * *

Despite Robinson's belief that it was time to end the relationship, it limped along, like a small rickety boat on the windswept shoals of a rocky shoreline. As the months moved on, the rancor grew. Robinson's letters became increasingly bitter and hostile, accusing Helen of debasing and betraying him. "[A]nd if you can convince yourself that you are acting a noble part in cutting my throat, go on, is all I have to say. My course will be short and sweet! No bitter, bitter as well you know."

How Helen was betraying him was unclear although a faint whiff of criminality, perhaps embezzlement or larceny, lingered. Robinson was a poorly paid store clerk with an affection for high style. Helen cost money. Robinson brought her presents and had to pay for her favors as well as for his assignations with other similarly situated young ladies.

In the face of Robinson's hostility, Helen vacillated, from trying to pacify him to demanding to see him. When he was slow in responding, she unleashed a furious response. "Do you think I will endure this. [...] [Y]ou drive me to madness. [...] Come and see me and tell me how we may renew the sweetness of our earlier acquaintance, and forget all our past unhappiness in future joy."

Robinson's response was toxic. "I have read your note with pain, I ought to say displeasure; nay, anger. Women are never so foolish as when they threaten."

As these missives were flying back and forth, Helen moved into different brothels. In the end, she returned, on March 18, 1836, back to Rosina Townsend's house. That she didn't tell Robinson of her wanderings added to his anger.

In the final three weeks of Helen's life, Robinson visited her frequently, from six to eight times. To Rosina and the other working girls, nothing appeared amiss between the two. Indeed, it seemed that it was business as usual for Helen, seeing others in addition to Richard; oddly, including his roommate, James Tew.

On the day before her murder, Helen casually chatted with the maid, Sarah Dunscombe, cleaning her room. As she dusted the bureau, Sarah noticed a lovely piece of jewelry that she had seen Helen wearing around her neck in the past. When she inquired of it, Jewett told her that it was a miniature, a portrait of Richard Robinson. What she didn't tell Sarah is that Robinson had been asking for it back for months.

* * *

Saturday, April 9, 1836, coincidentally Robinson's nineteenth birthday, was an unseasonably cold night, coming at the end of the coldest and longest winter of the early nineteenth century. Helen was expecting Richard that evening, as she innocently mentioned to some of her fellow residents over tea in the early evening, around seven. Thus when he arrived a few hours later, no one at the brothel was surprised. Helen greeted him by name and the two went up to her room where they remained for a few hours. Around eleven, Helen, now in her nightclothes, came downstairs in search of some champagne, which Rosina volunteered to get. A few minutes later Rosina, having retrieved the liquor, walked up the stairs and into Helen's cozy and well-furnished room, where Richard was under the covers in Helen's lush French bed, leaning on his left side, reading something. Rosina, having never really seen Robinson without his hat, was struck by a noticeable bald spot, which she had never seen before. After a short and pleasant chat with Helen, Rosina left. Within a few hours, Helen was dead and Rivers, nee Robinson, in custody.

* * *

The authorities quickly assembled the many pieces of the puzzle. When it all came together, the picture was one of now nineteen-year-old Robinson committing murder.

The suspect was with Jewett; after he killed her, he lit a small fire, knowing it would soon blow out of control and burn all of the evidence. Needing someone to unlock the front door to allow him to get out, he grabbed the lamp in Jewett's room and went down the darkened staircase and knocked on Rosina's door. When she refused to help, he went out the back door, leaving the lamp in the parlor, and jumped over the fence. In his haste, the murder weapon—a hatchet—dropped, the twine holding it ripping from his cloak, which was also discarded and recovered in a nearby yard. The hatchet came from the store in which he worked, as did the twine which held the hatchet to the cloak. When arrested at his apartment, his pants contained a white stain that matched that of the white fence in Townsend's backyard. A miniature was also found in his possession; the very one seen the day before in Helen's room. It was a hanging case.

Until the newspapers and Robinson's clever attorneys got involved.

* * *

Many today trace the birth of the tabloids to the Jewett affair. While "unseemly" crimes ordinarily went unreported, here one sat big and bold, front and center. The brutality of a crime involving a young boy from a good family and a beautiful prostitute captivated the city mesmerized with the unexpected glimpse behind the mysterious closed curtains of sexual impropriety. Recognizing the great hunger for the story, newspaper editors tossed aside past practices and sensibilities and watered a story that grew exponentially.

James Gordon Bennett, the ambitious and bright editor of *The New York Herald*, broke new ground by personally rushing over to the murder scene and viewing the dead body. He gushed in his description of the victim. "What a sight burst upon me! I could scarcely look at it for a second or two. [...] It was the most remarkable sight I ever beheld. [...] The perfect figure, the exquisite limbs, the fine face, the full arms, the beautiful bust, all, all surpassed in every respect the Venus de Medici."

Along with the newspapers, prints, many of them highly erotic, of Jewett, skyrocketed in popularity. Business was booming. And to feed that thirst, if a shift in focus became necessary, so be it. And soon papers were reporting the flip side of the tale. Whether they caused, or merely reported, it, slowly public sympathy started to shift in favor of the alleged killer, who was portrayed as a well-liked and earnest young store clerk.

At the same time, condemnation started raining down from the many pulpits throughout the city, accusing the victim of engaging in ungodly and highly sinful activities and receiving, in the end, a richly deserved fate. To many, Robinson had done society a favor, ridding the city of a cancer. A newspaper in upstate New York invited Robinson to visit its polluted neighborhoods and whack out justice there. Moral societies used the offense as fuel for their crusade against lust and immorality.

Townsend and those who worked for her found themselves harassed, causing the brothel to be shuttered and its contents sold. Out in public they were followed and insulted. Sympathizers of Robinson started wearing his dandified style of dress—colorful clothing and caps—popular with the city's modish young men. Robinson was depicted as an innocent youth led astray by temptation in the form of a "miserable, execrable being [...] leprous in soul and body." As the police often allowed such filth to fester, the logic followed, they too were part of the problem. And perhaps they were framing a poor innocent boy to cover their dirty dealings.

Against this volatile backdrop, the trial started in early June. And not only New York, but the nation watched.

✳ ✳ ✳

Despite the continuing horrific weather of the first six months of 1836, thousands rushed to view the pageant, loudly jostling with each other and the guards trying to maintain order. A large number—a thousand—ultimately gained entrance. Trials at the time were like sporting events, noisy entertainment, with the audience cheering those with whom they liked and jeering the others.

Despite the overwhelming circumstantial case against Robinson, the stars started to align for the young defendant, who entered the courtroom located on the second floor of City Hall neatly attired and with his head shaved, perhaps to counter any identification by Rosina based upon his bald spot. Behind him sat his father, who as a state legislator in Connecticut was close to its governor, the brother of the presiding judge, Ogden Edwards. Judge Edwards, a highly respected jurist, heralded from a well-established family, much like the defendant.

Robinson, thanks to the support of his boss Joseph Hoxie, had three attorneys representing him. Leading the defense, Ogden Hoffman, shared both a first name with the judge and a high regard in the legal community. At forty-three, he enthralled all with his sharp wit and superb eloquence delivered in a honeyed voice worthy of the stage. Having recently been the district attorney, he knew the courts and cops and how to try a case. His compatriots, High Maxwell and William Price, both having gone to Columbia, added firepower to an already powerful arsenal. Ironically, author Anne Royall, who nearly a decade earlier had written so glowingly about the future victim, also wrote about Maxwell and Price, viewing them as "pettifoggers." Her assessment, however, stood in sharp contrast with those familiar with the legal acuity of the duo.

Across the ring sat the vastly overmatched district attorney, Thomas Phoenix, and his associate, Robert Morris. Neither measured up to their opponents in style, intellect and courtroom agility. As if these shortcomings were not crippling enough, the judge provided further obstacles, sustaining nearly every objection raised by the defense and not allowing the prosecution to introduce powerful evidence such as the many threatening letters, save one, the defendant sent the victim, ruling, almost incomprehensibly, that they were too old in time to establish what had happened that fatal night. When the prosecution tried to introduce testimony that Robinson tried to purchase arsenic, ostensibly to kill rats, a week before the murder, the judge ruled the testimony inadmissible as the victim was killed by a hatchet not poison. Still, however, damning circumstances were produced—the hatchet, the cloak, the paint stain on Robinson's pants, and the miniature taken from Jewett's room and found in Robinsons'.

To counter these allegations, the defense showed that many similar hatchets were manufactured, that the cloak was similar to, but not definitively the same as, Robinsons', and that the white paint stain came from the store, which had been recently painted, in which Robinson worked. As for the other damaging testimony, the defense savagely attacked the character of the witnesses, arguing that the words of low-life prostitutes could never be believed. Many in the courtroom shouted their approval. The hammer for the defense, however, came from the surprise testimony of Robert Furlong, a small grocery store owner who placed Robinson, a frequent shopper of cigars, in his store on the night in question. How that night was any different from any of the other nights Robinson came in was never established. It also helped that Furlong was friendly with some of the twelve all-male jurors, a few of whom were grocers. Robinson's roommate, James Tew, added to the alibi, placing Robinson in their shared room at the time Rosina had him on her premises.

When the testimony closed, after nearly an unconscionable week of eleven to twelve hour court days with only brief breaks in the later afternoon, the highlight the masses so eagerly awaited commenced—closing arguments. While the five attorneys spoke collectively for over ten hours, the room belonged to Hoffman, who took three hours to spellbind his captured audience. Like a spider spinning its web, Hoffman ever so slowly drew the jurors in, ensnaring them.

In the end, however, the comments of the judge compelled the outcome. In the guise of jury instructions, he added a fourth summation for the defense. Words of a prostitute could not be believed; nor words from those like Sarah Dunscombe, who cleaned Helen's room and saw the miniature. Disregard their testimony the judge told the jurors. As for the hatchet, it was understandable why one would bring it to a hellhole of a brothel. After visiting, Robinson, if he even owned it, probably left it behind where another could use it. The hardworking grocer Furlong was a credible witness, worthy of belief, the judge further opined. And on it went.

Finally, after a fourteen-hour day, and despite it being after midnight, the jury was sent out to deliberate. Within a few minutes, less than fifteen at most, a verdict returned. Not guilty.

Epilogue

In the end, the case was more about class and its protection rather than murder. Young, privileged boys played. Prostitutes were a commodity, to be used and discarded. Despite this, the verdict stunned the public and press. Soon, calls, which went nowhere, were made for the dismissal of both the judge and DA Phoenix for participating in a mockery of justice.

Meanwhile defense attorney Hoffman's career continued to fly upward, holding both prestigious federal and state posts, most notably, as a member of Congress. Years later he was heard to remark that winning a case for one who was guilty was not necessarily a victory. Living an elaborate lifestyle, he died penniless.

Ten years after the trial, co-counsel Price committed suicide. So too, Robert Furlong, who provided the key alibi testimony for Robinson. Shortly after the trial, his store failed and he fell into despondency and liquor. In 1838, in a drunken stupor, he fell off of a ship.

As for Robinson, he left New York for Texas, eventually settling in Nacogdoches, where he dropped his last name in favor of his middle one, and became known as Richard Parmalee. Many of his Connecticut siblings eventually joined him there. He married a young widow with two children and a host of slaves and became a successful and wealthy businessman and civil servant serving, among other positions, as a clerk in the district court. The Nacogdoches Courthouse today sits on the land that once held his large house. He also donated hundreds of acres for a college.

On a business trip in August 1855, Robinson fell fatally ill in Louisville, Kentucky. In his last highly feverish hours, he was tended to by an elderly African-American caretaker who didn't quite understand his delirious ravings about some woman named Helen Jewett.

Tidbits

Four days after she was buried, Helen's corpse was stolen and used for medical purposes—dissection—at a local medical school. *The Herald* reported that her skeleton was "elegant and classic."

Helen was also repeatedly referred to as Ellen. Given that she signed her name with an H, she obviously preferred the former. Perhaps at the time, the two names were basically synonymous.

Helen used a variety of names, including Helen Mar, from a famous novel at the time. So popular the work, that two boats were also so named. In 1836, Jewett was murdered and the two boats sank.

Jewett was in effect a relatively well-known celebrity in the city. Even the Mayor visited the murder scene. After the crime, Robinson also became a minor celebrity, of which he quickly grew tired.

Shortly after the trial, letters written by Robinson to a friend surfaced. Their content placed him in a highly negative light. In one, he offered to seduce the wife of a friend who was tired of her, explaining his experience and comfort with sleeping with married women who have "felt my persuasive powers." Whatever positive views some held about him were dispelled.

At the turn of the century, sex outside of marriage was rampant. Around 1800, approximately 30–40% of women were pregnant at the time they married.

Premeditated murder was relatively rare in 1830s New York. In 1835, when its population was over a quarter of a million people, there were only seven official homicide cases. In 1836 only two capital murder cases reached trial. This perhaps explains why at the time NYC did not have an organized police force.

Judge Nathan Weston's grandson, Melville Weston Fuller, served as the eighth Chief Justice of the United States Supreme Court from 1888–1910.

In the zest to stamp out houses of ill repute, moralists published pamphlets decrying the shame of prostitutes and those who frequented them. As the locations of the brothels were included, the brochures ironically had the opposite effect for many, providing addresses for those seeking such services.

One wonders if the trial would have had a different result if the district attorney had been Ogden Hoffman, who held that post from 1829–1835, leaving just prior to Helen's murder.

At the time of the murder, the competition between the dailies was sizzling, leading to fights for readership and circulation. The reporting of Jewett's murder greatly aided business and forever changed the way papers operated and covered crime.

Our Next Tale

A few years after Helen's death, the striking and vivacious Mary Rogers ruled New York. Her employer thought that business would improve at his cigar store if he hired the best looking female he could find. His plan could not have worked out better as men, rich and poor, old and young, respectable and loutish, from throughout the city ran to admire the beautiful cigar girl. One killed her. But who?

19

The Beautiful Cigar Girl Got Snuffed

Wednesday, July 28, 1841 was another scorcher in New York City. The tenth straight day with temperatures soaring over 90 degrees. To find relief from the stifling heat, thousands ferried across the Hudson River to Hoboken, which promised at least a semblance of fresh air. Little did anyone suspect that they would find far more than a gentle breeze.

* * *

Much like Paris Hilton and all of the Kardashians, Mary Cecilia Roger's notoriety was unburdened by either talent or achievement. What Mary had was uncommon beauty and charisma, both of which served as lightning rods for the attention and affection of men. Her greatest asset perhaps was her ability to "fan the flames of ardor without giving false hope."

Born in 1820, she lived comfortably in Connecticut until several tragedies struck. Her mother Phoebe had married Ezra Mather, a descendant of legendary Puritan leaders Increase and Cotton Mather, and together Phoebe and Ezra parented five children. Ezra suddenly died of illness. After waiting a respectful time, Phoebe remarried. Her new husband was Daniel Rogers, to whom Mary was born. Daniel sadly also died, the victim of a steamship explosion. Shortly thereafter, three of Mary's siblings joined Daniel's fate, all dying prematurely. Then came the bank panic of 1837. Forced to sell their property, a nearly impoverished sixty-year-old Phoebe and Mary moved to New York City, where they hoped to find greener and lusher pastures.

Within a short time of their arriving there, Mary met the entrepreneurial John Anderson, the owner of Anderson's Tobacco Emporium in lower Manhattan. The store catered to writers, reporters and those working in the city's nearby government offices. Unfortunately the notorious, crime-ridden Five Points section of the city was also in the vicinity, bringing in its often unsavory crowd.

In the hopes of improving business, Anderson enlisted the services of the very attractive seventeen-year-old Mary to serve as a saleslady. Little did he realize the explosion of her presence. Word of mouth quickly blanketed the immediate area while enthralled newspapermen fanned the city with tales of "the beautiful Seegar Girl." Soon she was featured in poems. One proclaimed her smile as being a glimpse of heaven.

And then suddenly, one year after arriving in NYC, Mary went missing. The papers leaped, tumbling over one another to explain the mystery. A suicide? A runaway? A failed love affair? And then, as quickly as she disappeared, she resurfaced, explaining she had simply visited a friend. Rather than calm the waters, the turbulence continued, some papers accusing Anderson of orchestrating a gigantic hoax to garner publicity.

As comfortable Mary as had been working in the store, the dynamic had now changed as even more customers appeared to experience the even greater celebrated beauty. She grew uncomfortable with the attention. Thus, when the chance to leave Anderson's Emporium presented itself, Mary leaped. One of her surviving half-brothers had found riches on the high seas and upon coming to the city opened a boarding house for his mother and Mary to run. Within a year, that brother too would die, drowning after accidently falling overboard. Ensconced in her new surroundings, Mary continued to have a bevy of suitors. Two stood out. Alfred Crommelin, a boarder at her house, was tall and courtly with a polite manner. While initially encouraging his attention, Mary soon turned hers to Daniel Payne, the friendly maker of bottle corks used to cap medical, chemical and alcoholic containers. Unfortunately Daniel also liked to imbibe and drank excessively. Soon they were engaged, however, despite the misgivings of Phoebe. With the battle of the hearts lost, Crommelin departed the boarding house.

On Sunday, July 25th, at 10 in the morning, Mary went to Daniel's apartment and told him she was taking the omnibus—public transit at the time in the form of a horse-drawn carriage—to visit her aunt, with whom she would go to church and for Daniel to meet her upon her return early that evening.

Mary never made it to her aunt, who had no inkling of the intended visit. Indeed the aunt wasn't even home that morning. And what of the note Crommelin received two days earlier, written by Mary, but signed Phoebe, inviting him to call at the boarding house? Was any of

Mary Rogers was so beautiful that legions of men, rich and poor, flooded the tobacco store in which she worked.

this related to a heated argument between Phoebe and Mary, which ended with Mary telling her mother she would break off her relationship with Payne? And what of the reaction of Mary's mother to her daughter's disappearance, "We'll never see her again!"?

These questions all needed answering because on Wednesday Mary was found dead.

* * *

To escape the oppressive heat, Henry Mallin and two of his friends made the ferry trip from New York City to Hoboken. It was shortly after 3 in the afternoon. As they leisurely strolled the scenic shores of the river, an unusual object floating on the waters caught their attention. Upon looking more closely, to their horror they realized it was a body. They jumped into a boat, rowed out the few hundred yards and came upon the beaten, battered and waterlogged body of a dead young woman. With some difficulty they guided the body to shore, where it roasted in the hot sun for an hour until Dr. Richard Cook, the New Jersey coroner, arrived. Alfred Crommelin, Mary's former suitor, heard of the discovery and rushed over. Viewing a figure with a nearly obliterated face, he made his identification from her cloths and a unique patch of hair on her arm.

That evening Dr. Cook, wishing to discern the cause of death, performed an autopsy. Did Mary Rogers innocently, albeit tragically, drown or were more sinister forces at work? The question was quickly answered.

In addition to Mary's brutalized face, bruising in the form of a man's hand and fingers around her neck indicated that she had been choked. Examining the area more closely, Cook discovered a garrote of lace submerged in her skin. The lace had come from the trimming of Mary's underskirt. She had been thus strangled twice Cook concluded. First, the hands of her killer rendered her unconscious, at which point he ripped away part of her clothing, placed it around her neck and strangled her. Burn marks on her wrists indicated that her hands had been tied together and that she had tried to escape her bondage. Raw skin on her back and shoulders indicated she both struggled and had been dragged for some distance. More fabric from her clothing had been ripped away and used in different manners; one section as a gag; another as a handle to drag her. Lastly, bruises and abrasions covered her "feminine regions." Dr. Cook concluded that Mary had been abducted, brutally violated and murdered by at least three assailants.

All that remained was the identity of the killers. And leading the charge was not the fragmented, corrupt, understaffed and inept police force, but the press, hell-bent on sensationalism and writing whatever sold papers, which often rendered the truth invisible. A large reward was also offered in the hope of loosening some tongues.

* * *

The vicious murder of arguably the most beautiful woman in all of New York galvanized the city and nation. While the papers trumpeted that a gang of ruffians killed Mary, others were more circumspect. If killed by a gang, why the need to restrain her wrists? Why the need to drag her when a group could merely have carried her away?

Suspects were brought in, often arrested and grilled. One clue centered on a particular type of knot, commonly utilized by sailors, used to bind her. Twenty-two-year-old navy man William Kiekuck had stayed in Mary's boardinghouse and had come back to his ship on the day of her disappearance highly agitated. Luckily for him, he had an alibi. Another suspect, the mutton-chopped Joseph Morse, who ran an engraving shop near where Mary lived and worked, was seen in Hoboken on the Sunday she disappeared, arguing with a woman who fit Mary's description. That night he did not return home. When he finally did return, he explained to his wife that a sudden storm had forced him to spend the night in Jersey. Given his reputation of running with the ladies, Mrs. Morse was convinced he was lying; so also thought Constable Hilliker, especially when Morse skipped town. Tracked down and arrested, Morse protested his innocence, despite being caught in a series of lies. To his ultimate relief and exoneration, the woman with whom he in fact did have designs and spent the night with in New Jersey ventured forward. With yet another suspect scratched off of the suspect list, the police turned to others—Payne, Crommelin and even her former employer, John Anderson.

With no arrests and no leads, frustration started to set in. And then Frederica Loss, the owner of Nick Moore's Tavern in Weehawken, New Jersey, just north of where Mary's body was discovered, sent two of her sons on an errand. Deciding to take a quiet path that led them by an isolated thicket, the two stumbled upon a woman's undergarment of clothing. As they examined their find, they noticed other garments—a silk scarf on a nearby boulder and strips of torn white fabric hanging on some branches. Suddenly, something white wedged between a rock and a tree trunk caught their attention. They retrieved what turned out to be a handkerchief. On it were initials. MR.

They gathered the clothing and gave them to their mother, who neatly folded them up and put them in a drawer. Inexplicably she waited seven days before contacting the authorities, who immediately pounced on the scene. It was clear what they thought they were viewing—where Mary had been murdered.

A new witness placed Mary in the company of a "swarthy" man at the tavern. Another tale told of a dark, well-dressed tall gentlemen travelling with Mary from New York and going with her to the Loss' establishment. Visitors swarmed to the inn and area where the beautiful cigar girl was last seen alive. One such person was a now morose and suicidal Daniel Payne, who to the chagrin of the police and press did not meet the description of the swarthy man. Payne had a drink at the tavern and traveled to where his fiancée met her demise. He slowly surveyed the area and then reached into his jacket to retrieve a vial of poison he had earlier purchased in New York. He took a swig. His body started to quiver. Soon he was dead. He wasn't the only one.

* * *

As Loss repeated what she knew, suspicions arose. She repeatedly changed her accounts of the events in question. Originally, she told of hearing blood-curdling screams; now that violence of sound became whimpers, neither particularly loud nor distinctive. She initially indicated that Mary and the swarthy man had left alone; now perhaps they left with a group. With the onslaught of questions seeking to clear up the inconsistencies, Loss surely felt discomfort. True pain, however, lurked. First, it was discovered that her tavern served a far different purpose then serving refreshment and shelter. Abortions were being performed there. As if this wasn't enough, Loss got herself shot.

* * *

The victim of an errant blast from the shotgun being negligently cleaned by one of her sons, Loss slowly died over the course of a week. One son was overheard telling another that with her death "The great secret will come out." When she died, the magistrate proclaimed that Loss and her three sons, all "profligate and worthless characters," were responsible for Mary's death. Her murder was a cover-up for a botched abortion.

The charges went nowhere as nothing could be proved. Indeed, the evidence pointed in other directions. If Loss were involved, why would she have brought a world of attention upon herself by revealing the victim's clothes? Why hadn't the autopsy revealed evidence of the abortion? And what of the physical evidence—the strangulation marks on Mary's neck, the burns marks on her wrists?

Epilogue

The murder of Mary Rogers was never solved. Theories abounded. In a sensational fictionalization of the homicide, "The Mystery of Marie Roget," Edgar Allen Poe wrote his story as the real one was being played out. So unsolvable the crime, however, that even in fiction a culprit could not be named. Poe did however have a particular interest in the event—he too was a customer of Anderson's Tobacco Emporium and a great fan of the very beautiful Mary Rogers.

Tidbits

Mary's story about visiting her aunt via omnibus was the similar to the one she used to explain her strange disappearance three years earlier. Some opine that both times Mary dropped out of sight to procure an abortion. Other noteworthy abortionists at the time included New York's Madame Restell and perhaps someone who worked for her in New Jersey, Madame Costello. A mob gathered in front of Restell's house, shouting, among others things, that Restell murdered Rogers.

Daniel Payne left a suicide note. It read, "Here I am on the very spot. God forgive me for my misspent life."

Some believe that the discovered clothes had been planted. In the "murder scene" a pair of Mary's gloves were discovered. Yet when she was fished out of the water, she was wearing gloves.

The notorious abortionist, Madame Restell who many thought had some role in Mary's death.

Mary's ghost apparently paid visits to her boarding house, to a quickly mentally deteriorating Daniel Payne, to a dying Frederica Loss, and, years later, to her former employer, John Anderson.

In his 1842 short story, which was the sequel to "The Murders in the Rue Morgue," considered the first modern detective story, Edgar Allen Poe changed both Mary Rogers' name to Marie Roget and the location, from New York to Paris.

Legal reforms as a result of Mary's death included improving the City's police force and passing restrictive abortion laws.

Like William Desmond Taylor, featured in Chapter 3, a bevy of suspects existed in yet another unsolved murder mystery.

In a story similar to that of Bathsheba Spooner, a different woman named Mary Rogers conspired, in 1902, with a lover, Leon Perham, to murder her husband. Both teenagers were caught. To save himself from the death penalty, Leon testified against her. Rogers was the last woman legally executed in the state of Vermont. A year before the murder, Mary "accidentally" dropped her six-month-old daughter who subsequently died of a skull fracture.

Our Next Tale

He was a dashing young doctor, to whom many young ladies came calling. They all left dead.

20

Dr. Slice, Dice and Sauté

He was a catch. Handsome, of medium height and build, dapper in appearance and dress, exuding wealth. A doctor no less, and young, in his later twenties. And with an affable manner that no one, neither man nor woman, could resist. When he focused his attention upon you it was as if you were the only person in the room. At least that's what his wives and innumerable murder victims thought.

* * *

Herman Webster Mudgett grew up in a joyless environment with a brother and sister on a farm in New Hampshire. His parents were strict religious disciplinarians, harshly meting out punishments for even the slightest of offenses. His one close friend, Thomas, fell and died while playing in an abandoned house with Herman.

Mudgett was a good student and upon graduation became a schoolteacher. Soon he met Clara Lovering and on their nation's birthday, July 4, 1878, they wed. The union would never, legally at least, end. Quickly bored, Herman left, never to return and never seeking a divorce, leaving her and a child behind. Deciding to become a doctor, he attended a few schools, before finally settling in Ann Arbor in 1882, where he went to the well-regarded medical school at the University of Michigan. A mediocre student, he graduated two years later, whereupon he traveled around and about, ultimately opening a practice in Mooers Forks, New York. Although he ultimately failed, as people didn't have the wherewithal to pay his bills, he was held in high regard. That a young boy in his company mysteriously disappeared was of no moment, especially given Mudgett's innocent explanation that the boy merely returned to his native Massachusetts.

In need of money, Mudgett hatched an elaborate life insurance scam in which he conspired with others to take out policies on their lives, fake their deaths and collect the proceeds. That the plot required decomposed and basically unidentifiable corpses resembling those who were insured was a task easily met by the wily doctor and con artist.

With money in his pocket, Mudgett skipped town late one evening, stiffing his landlord. He ultimately landed in a pharmacy in Philadelphia, left when a child died after taking medicine from that establishment and headed to Chicago, a city he grew to love upon earlier visits while attending medical school. It was around this time that Mudgett read about a fellow doctor, one in England, Sir Arthur Conan Doyle, who was writing about a grand detective, Sherlock Holmes.

* * *

It was a hot day in August 1886 when the nattily dressed H. H. Holmes, formerly Herman Mudgett, stepped off his train and arrived in his new home, Englewood, a city just south of and touching Chicago. As with all those who ventured in the area, Holmes was smacked by the putrid odors of horse excrement, thick black train exhaust and the repugnancy rippling through the air from the nearby Union Stock Yards, where tightly penned-in pigs with no room to move were delivered in a succession of never-ending truckloads. They were thrown onto conveyor belts, chained by their hind legs and violently hoisted upward and propelled, squealing wildly, into the bowels of the darkened and blood-soaked factory where a brutal slaughter greeted them. Holmes must have thought he was in Nirvana.

Ambling down 63rd and Wallace, he noticed a pharmacy, Holton Drugs, across from a large empty lot. Walking in, he was wearily greeted by its elderly proprietor. Soon she was telling him of her dying husband and the burdens of tending to both him and the store. Holmes listened in great sympathy and at the end of her tearful story offered to assist her. He was after all a doctor. Soon he was working there. When Mr. Holton died, probably of natural causes, Mrs. Holton, overcome by the charm of her new friend, sold the pharmacy to Holmes, who purchased the property by mortgaging its fixtures and merchandise. He allowed her to live upstairs. And then one day she disappeared. Holmes said she was visiting relatives in California. As time moved on, he indicated that she so liked it there that she decided to stay. While surprised she should do such a thing, everyone in the end believed the convincing doctor.

* * *

The handsome and glib Dr. H. H. Holmes (1861–1896), who commanded and killed a host of female admirers.

The H. H. Holmes Pharmacy ran swimmingly. Patrons, especially younger women hoping to catch the eye of the handsome young proprietor, swarmed the store. They not only purchased tonics and lotions that they did not need, but never realized that what they were buying were often useless concoctions of Holmes.

As the money started to flow in Holmes made two fateful decisions. The first was to court the blond-haired, blue-eyed Myrta Belknap, a woman he had earlier met while traveling in Minneapolis. Over the months he traveled back and forth from Chicago to woo her and her parents. In short order, they all were quickly swept over by his numerous charms and jumped when he proposed. The two were married on January 28, 1887. That he was already married was a detail not shared with his newly betrothed.

Initially all went well, Myrta joining her husband in running the pharmacy. While she loved the kind manner in which she was treated and that he neither drank, nor gambled nor ever uttered an unkind word, she soon grew resentful over the attention of the various women who frequented the store. Holmes convinced her that perhaps she would be happier handling the financial end of the business, which could be done in the quiet of the second floor. Soon, she grew lonely and bored, exasperated further when she envisioned the female attention paid to her husband a mere floor below. She also noticed his strong ambition to succeed and make money. Even a pregnancy did not relieve her feelings and when her parents relocated to Illinois, Holmes suggested that perhaps it would be best that she move in with them, which she did, giving birth to a daughter, Lucy in 1888. In time, the dutiful husband became less so. He, at first, visited often; soon, however, his visits dwindled.

With his wife out of the way, Holmes moved onto his next major project, the purchase and development of the large vacant lot across the street from his pharmacy. It was here that his most diabolical dreams sprang to life. He purchased the property using a false name, H. S. Campbell, as a shield from the many creditors whom he had no intention of ever paying. He didn't hire an architect as he didn't wish anyone to know precisely what he was planning; nor did he pay the many workers he came to employ, which both saved money and kept anyone from knowing too much for they all quit when they realized they would not be compensated for their work. Holmes did however take a liking to a few of his laborers, including Benjamin Pitezel, who was married with five children, including Alice, Nellie, and Howard. An alcoholic ne'er-do-well with bad teeth, Pitezel served his master well as did another worker, Charlie Chappell, who was handy with a knife.

The structure, which took over two years to build, was so large and all-encompassing that it swallowed the whole block. The locals dubbed it The Castle. A more accurate name would have been the Holmes House of Horrors.

Its first floor housed many retail establishments including a barbershop, restaurant and gift shop; its third floor, with thirty-six rooms, came to be a hotel. Both would serve to bring in the many young women he craved. It was the forbidding second floor where many would meet their end. Other than innocently housing his own expansive living quarters, including a bedroom and office, the remainder was an amalgam of oddly twisted, mysterious and hidden rooms, thirty-five in all, snaking throughout six corridors. One room was sealed and bricked-in, with a trap door leading to a hidden chamber. There were dark rooms, rooms with five doors leading to other rooms, a hanging room and a death room. The pièce de résistance, however, was an airtight bank vault turned into a gas chamber, devoid of light and sound, next to a shaft, greased to quiet its movements, in which bodies were sent hurtling to the basement. Once there, an assortment of devices lay in wait; Holmes deciding the manner in which to dispose of his latest victim. Would he cremate her? Slowly and meticulously dissect her? Or merely chop her up and causally toss the remains, like those from the pig slaughter house, into the lime pit. Perhaps, he would store some of the remains in yet another covert room in a sub-basement.

The Castle opened in 1890. With the Chicago World's Fair opening in a few years, bringing with it the promise of young women flocking to Chicago, Holmes waited in anticipation. But first, he had more pressing matters.

✶ ✶ ✶

When Ned Conner, his wife Julia and their eight-year-old daughter Pearl moved to Chicago, good fortune followed, or so they thought, as they quickly found work in the Holmes Pharmacy. Holmes even allowed them to live in the building. As proof that opposites attract, Ned and Julia were mismatched, she being the far more comely and intelligent of the two. They shared, however, a common respect for their charismatic boss. Ned admired Holmes for being so successful at such a young age, while Julia, like so many woman, simply wanted him. Soon she succeeded and Ned was out of the picture. Prior to his leaving however, his sympathetic boss offered to sell him the pharmacy at a very reasonable price in the hope it might help him reconcile with Julia. Ned jumped at the opportunity. Soon when the store's many creditors swarmed over him, Ned realized that not only had he lost his wife but the pharmacy as well. Holmes remained sympathetic.

With Ned divorced and out of the picture, Julia pressured Holmes to marry her. While he initially deflected her desires, soon she announced she was pregnant and they would have to marry. Holmes appeared overjoyed with the news and happily agreed to her proposal. However,

Holmes Castle of Horrors.

he declared, having a child now and under these circumstances was scandalous and simply out of the question. An abortion, at his hands, a well-respected doctor, was their only option.

On Christmas Eve, on the second floor of the Castle, Dr. Holmes administered the chloroform that he always kept in large quantities. Soon Julia drifted off, reassured by the soothing words of her soon-to-be-husband that all was well and together they and young Pearl would joyfully celebrate Christmas.

* * *

When Julia and her daughter failed to appear for a holiday party, questions were asked. No one had seen them, at least not since the 24th. When asked, Holmes calmly explained that mother and daughter had left earlier than expected for a wedding in Iowa. While the tale appeared unlikely, how could one doubt the earnest and sincere manner in which it was told?

As Holmes was weaving his story, he was awaiting the arrival of Charlie Chappell, his former laborer, whom he had summoned. Chappell had mastered the art of articulation, the ability to strip flesh from bones, a skill Holmes put to good use.

Holmes led Chappell to the basement, where an unidentifiable body of a female on a table greeted him. Holmes had earlier started the dissection "by splitting the skin down the face and rolling it back off the entire body" taking large chunks of flesh with it. The blood was drained from the body, which was gutted, like a fisherman to his catch. Chappell so masterly completed the task that a local medical school jumped at the opportunity to purchase the pristine skeleton of what had once been Julia Conner.

As for Julia's young daughter Pearl, Holmes had earlier tossed her chloroformed remains into the lime pit where they slowly decayed and rotted.

* * *

With Benjamin Pitezel in a bad way, suffering greatly from his alcoholism, Holmes sent his valuable assistant to a clinic in Illinois. There the hapless drunkard met and became enamored with Emeline Cigrand, a lovely twenty-four-year-old, blond employee of the institute. Pitezel wrote Holmes of her great beauty and shortly thereafter, Emeline was working for Holmes in Chicago. Soon she was in love with her charming boss with the time spent together sheer bliss.

But there were warning signs. Being his bookkeeper she learned of troubles with creditors. She had also lent him money with no sign of it ever being repaid. And then one day, a Ned Conner wandered by, looking for Holmes. Not finding him, Ned spoke ominously of her boss.

Perhaps Holmes was also tiring of Emeline for on one day she too simply disappeared. Holmes explained that she had run off to get married. And, once again, Holmes sold another clean skeleton to another medical school.

And on it went. He met Minnie Williams, who unlike his past adult victims, was atypically unattractive, being short, plump and bland. Her crowning attribute, however, was her being an heir to a fortune. Holmes wooed and "married" her, in a sham marriage, all the while successfully angling to have her fortune transferred to him. When Minnie's sister Anna became suspicious, Holmes charmed the doubt out of her. He also one afternoon innocently asked her to grab some papers in his vault. She went in and never came out. Minnie met a similar fate.

While the Williams sisters were slowly advancing to their deaths, the magnificent Chicago World's Fair opened on May 1, 1893. Many guests, female mainly, stayed in the conveniently located nearby hotel, owned by H. H. Holmes. Many never returned home.

*   *   *

In the end, the pressures mounted. There were now far too many creditors asking far too many questions and making far too many demands. Relatives of the missing, too, were arriving, as were private detectives acting on their behalf. All asking questions and demanding answers. It was only a matter of time before those asking the questions of Holmes would meet and compare notes amongst themselves. With the threat of confrontation and discovery advancing, Holmes fled, taking Pitezel with him.

While Holmes didn't want for money, having accumulated a mass of it throughout all of his fraudulent dealings, he nonetheless craved it. Like an addict hungering for heroin, Holmes lived for cash, in ever-increasing dosages, seeking an even higher high than the one before. So he dug deep and returned to his earlier insurance scam. They'd insure Pitezel and then fake his death and collect the insurance proceeds. Even Pitezel's wife was brought on board. In the end, however, Holmes added a fatal twist. Why get a body that looked like Pitezel's when he could merely kill Pitezel and use his? And—to add to his pleasure and depravity—why not kill three of Pitezel's young children along the way?

*   *   *

In 1891 there were nearly six thousand murders in America. Most went unsolved. Indeed, most police departments were not only understaffed, but simply incapable of handling the most basic of cases. With so many dead people, with so many people who simply disappeared, especially in Chicago which was overflowing with those attending the World's Fair (indeed on a single day, nearly 750,000 people attended), the police, both in the Windy city and beyond, were simply overwhelmed and outmatched. There were exceptions, however, to the national rule of ineptitude. At the head of that line stood Detective Frank Geyer, of the Philadelphia Police Department.

*   *   *

With detectives from the famed Pinkerton National Detective Agency, hired by the insurance company, on Holmes' tail, it was only a matter of time before he was apprehended. Planning on boarding a ship out of America, Holmes was arrested in Boston on suspicion of insurance fraud. As the scheme emanated from a ten thousand dollar policy the Fidelity Mutual Life Association of Philadelphia had issued, Holmes was shipped to the City of Brotherly Love, where trial awaited.

Not being particularly concerned with a measly fraud case, Holmes spoke freely, often implicating himself but always trying to casually explain his way out of the mess in which he found himself. Detective Geyer, who shared Holmes' indifference with the fraud charge, was far more focused on the three missing Pitezel offspring—fifteen-year-old Alice, eleven-year-old Nellie and eight-year-old Howard—who had last been seen traveling with Holmes.

With Holmes arrest, a packet of letters was taken from him. Written by Alice and Nellie and addressed to their mother, the missives outlined their travels with Holmes, who neither mailed, nor discarded, them. The correspondence provided an invaluable roadmap to Geyer in his search for the missing children. First to Cincinnati, then Indianapolis, Chicago and Detroit. At each locale, Geyer made startling discoveries. In Chicago, for instance, the police had never even heard of Holmes despite the high number of inquiries being made concerning missing women who had stayed in his hotel. In Indianapolis, Geyer discovered that Holmes had the three children in one hotel, Mrs. Pitezel and her two other children in another hotel, and yet another wife, Georgiana Yoke, who he had picked up along the way, staying in a third location, all within blocks of one another. Geyer's greatest jolt came, however, upon reading one of the children's later letters. "Howard is not with us now."

Once the newspapers caught wind of America's tenacious detective, its readers stood transfixed. Geyer meanwhile painstakingly followed up the hundreds of leads streaming in. From a faraway source, his tenacity finally paid off.

∗   ∗   ∗

Thomas Ryves lived in Toronto. He remembered the odd man who had briefly rented a house next to his and who had asked to borrow a shovel. When Ryves identified Holmes' picture, Geyer's heart skipped a beat. Grabbing the very shovel earlier lent to Holmes, Geyer and another officer raced over to the rental house and quickly squirmed into its claustrophobic, dark and dank basement. A loose patch of dirt in the corner caught their attention. They dug for but a few seconds before the ground opened up. Geyer was hit with the overpowering stench he knew only too well, that of death.

The two girls were naked, packed neatly next to each other. Nellie's feet had been sliced off. She had also been partially scalped.

Three months later, following up on yet another tip, Geyer traveled to a small town outside of Indianapolis. There he discovered Howard's chopped-up and burned body parts stuffed tightly in the stove and chimney flue of yet another rental house.

Epilogue

When Holmes was in the midst of his killing spree in 1888, the world was being mesmerized by the atrocities of Jack the Ripper, whose antics surely served as an inspiration to the very warped Dr. Holmes. Unlike the Ripper though, whose notoriety is still with us, Holmes in time was quickly forgotten, notwithstanding the grip his tale and trial held on the nation.

On May 7, 1896, Holmes was hanged, paying society for his transgressions. In one of his many confessions, he admitted to having killed twenty-seven people. In reality, the number was far in excess.

Reviled and repulsed by all, he was, however, missed by a few—the prison guards in fact, who found the chatty and model prisoner to be irresistibly charming.

Tidbits

An apocryphal tale holds that an English nobleman visiting the Chicago World's Fair had a tryst with a woman who subsequently became pregnant. The child of that liaison, featured in the second chapter of this book about Fatty Arbuckle, was Virginia Rapp. As she was apparently born a few years prior to the opening of the Fair, the story is questionable.

After Alice, and Holmes, identified Pitezel's body, the insurance company paid $10,000. Holmes then persuaded Mrs. Pitezel to allow Alice, Nellie and Howard to travel with him to visit her husband, who allegedly missed the kids. In fact, by that time, Holmes had already killed Pitezel. Soon, Holmes had all of the parties travelling throughout the Midwest.

Pitezel's wife, Carrie, was a not-so-innocent dupe, agreeing to the insurance scam, but unaware of the homicides. She grieved the murder of her three children.

For a portion of his trial, Holmes represented himself, a hitherto unknown practice occurring during a capital case.

As Holmes' trial of the century was unfolding, his "Horror Castle" became a tourist destination. It shortly burned down.

Our Next Tale

From mass murder to ordinary murder. Like Bathsheba Spooner, Adolph Luetgert was tired of his spouse. That he had vats of acid at his disposal made the perverse and gruesome episode especially attractive to a voracious public, riveted by the shocking details.

21

The Sausage King Sizzles His Wife

Perhaps Louise should have been more suspicious when her husband Adolph explained that their maid was needed to make up his bed at the factory where he spent most nights. Perhaps, though, Louise thought little of it as Mary the maid was her cousin. She had every right to be concerned for, as it turned out, Mary was making both the bed and the man in it. In the end, however, this would be the very least of Louise's problems.

* * *

Adolph was the King—King Luetgert, the King of Sausages. He even looked the role. A large man, broad and stocky, he commanded the respect of all those with whom he came in contact, not only for his foreboding physical appearance but for his business acumen. He was, after all, the preeminent maker of sausages, a scrumptious item of which the population of Chicago could not get enough. That he discovered a method to manufacture the wildly-popular, cylindrical-cased, minced meat during the stifling and oppressive summer months set him apart from, and above all of, his competitors. His factory commanded the street where it was located while he and his family lived in a nearby mansion.

In many ways, he was the epitome of the successful immigrant experience. Born in Germany in 1845, he came to America twenty-four years later with only thirty dollars in his pocket. He settled in Chicago and worked a variety of jobs, always saving and always looking to move his way up. The alcohol he sold out of his basement soon moved to his successful saloon and liquor store.

In contrast to his flourishing businesses, his personal life was marked by tragedy. His first wife and one of their two young children died at young ages. Within two months, in 1878, he re-married, this time to the slightly built, but attractive, Louise Bicknese, who had also emigrated from Germany. They had four children, two of whom also sadly died in infancy. Luetgert sold his saloon in favor of a butcher shop in yet another move to economically better himself, or so it seemed. Perhaps the dead body of Hugh McGowen which had been discovered in Luetgert's barn motivated the change. McGowen had been drinking in Luetgert's saloon and somehow wound up in the barn, oddly sitting upward on the floor, his head split wide open and two ounces of chewing tobacco, which his family never knew him to use, jammed

Adolph Luetgert, the Sausage King, who grew tired of his shrewish wife.

down his throat. A coroner's jury consisting of the King's friends and neighbors heard the evidence and rendered a verdict. Suicide.

After yet another change of scenery and jobs, Luetgert had amassed enough money, credit and knowledge to open a sausage factory, located on North and Sheffield Avenues in Chicago. Within a year, his fifty employees were ringing up over $100,000 annually in sales. Indicative of his wealth, status and ambition, he soon purchased five acres at Hermitage and Diversey for $30,000 and then spent the ungodly sum of $140,000 on a new house and another factory, for which he borrowed $50,000 to build. The remainder of the property was further developed into "Luetgert's Subdivision," which consisted of eighteen house lots.

With the opening of the World's Fair in 1893, business was booming, masking a recession that had gripped the nation. And although Luetgert never once visited the wildly popular fair, his sausages became a culinary favorite.

When the fair closed, the hidden recession burst out with a shattering effect. Luetgert, like all businessmen, felt the wallop, which quickly blossomed into an all-out catastrophe. Unable to pay the bank, he sought investors. Soon a smooth-talking English businessman and all world con-man, Robert Davey, swindled him out of what little money he had, and skipped town.

The factory was shuttered in part and most of the employees let go. Louise, who never wanted to buy the property in the first place, loudly vented her frustration with the turn of events. And now the other sore spots—masked in the past by wealth and success—were fed with the fertilizer of stress and financial ruination; before long, the wounds were open and festering. The arguments grew worse, Louise now also angry at the attentions Adolph paid various women. For his part, a despairing Adolph battled daily against an onslaught of debt and destruction.

And then came yet another illness to one of their children. Two of their little baby girls had already died of cholera, one at eleven months and the other at thirteen. Now five-year-old Elmer also fell ill. Louise, nudged closer to the edge, started acting more and more oddly and out of sorts. On the final days of April 1897, between crying and laughing fits, she told various people of her despair and need to just leave, to get out of the cage of the king and Chicago.

✳ ✳ ✳

Louise was last seen on the late evening of May 1st when she had a brief conversation with her eleven-year-old son Louis, who had gone to the circus earlier that day. After her disappearance, Adolph seemed singularly nonchalant, being far more concerned with the impending foreclosure of his factory. In conversations with his attorneys and others he barely mentioned that his wife of nearly two decades was gone. When confronted by Louise's siblings, he merely shrugged it off with an, "isn't she with you?" response, explaining that she had been threatening to leave for a long time and now finally did. He merely assumed that she was with relatives.

When Louise's brother Diedrich reported her missing to the police, a manhunt ensued. Their big tip came two weeks later when Frank Bialk told of the highly suspicious actions of his boss Adolph. Of how Frank and another employee were ordered to haul two heavy barrels of caustic potash to the boiler room and empty the acid-like contents into the 3' x 11' x 3' middle vat, which was then uncharacteristically fired up and kept boiling throughout the night; of the door to the basement being locked; of being asked to run an errand to buy something Adolph already had; of Frank seeing a woman resembling Louise enter the factory late that night with Adolph; and of the next day being ordered to clean the foul-smelling vat with its gooey, reddish contents.

Louise Luetgert, the victim.

With their focus narrowing, the police traveled to the factory. Outside, they found a pile of ashes. Raking through it turned up bone fragments and a piece of corset-steel. Inside, they went to the vat, half full with a brownish-red liquid. It stunk. The water was drained. On the bottom was a sticky mess, peppered by, like chips in a cookie, additional tiny bits of bone, an upper false tooth and two rings. One of them contained the initials "L.L." Louise Luetgert. They had their man.

* * *

The first trial lasted months, with over a hundred witnesses called. As in the Webster-Parkman murder case a half century before, there was no body. Like that case, the prosecution here also explored the volatile relationship between the couple while its experts testified to the pea-like remains having belonged to a female; a dentist even favorably compared the false tooth discovered to one he had earlier made for Louise. Most damning though was the L.L. ring.

The defense countered with its own experts who opined that it was impossible to discern anything about the traces recovered, including whether they even came from a human being. Unlike the Webster-Parkman case, which had chunks of a body to work with, here there were merely fragments. The defense also insisted that Mrs. Luetgert had a mental imbalance and had merely run away, calling a litany of witnesses to whom Louise had made the threat. They also called people who claimed to have seen the disheveled Mrs. Luetgert in various locales. Indeed sightings had been coming in from all over the world, from Wisconsin to New York, California, Paris and London. As for the ring, the defense argued that the police had planted it there, acting in conformity with the past practices of a highly suspect and corrupt police force, which also served to intimidate and harass anyone saying anything favorable for the defense. Many spectators, fully aware of that perception, nodded in agreement.

The trial morphed into a media sensation, covered throughout the nation. Hundreds fought to see it in person. Those who could not get in lined the roofs of nearby buildings in the hope of seeing something, anything. The atmosphere resembled more an unruly mob, jockeying for position, than an orderly court proceeding. Noticeably, many in the crowd were female, young and old, poor and rich, drawn to the display. Some indeed came dressed as going to the theater, even toting opera glasses to get a better view. A few corresponded with the accused, some going so far as to propose marriage. For his part, Luetgert often appeared disinterested during the trial, even reading newspapers while witnesses testified. Undoubtedly he was reading about himself as while in jail he whittled away the hours by granting interviews, particularly to those journalists who provided him with cigars. Throughout, he remained confident of the outcome.

Meanwhile, the sale of sausages plummeted, the rumor being that Luetgert not only murdered his wife, but stuffed her remains into his tasty product.

The trial lasted for months. Witnesses testified. Experts testified, some telling of their experiments of attempting to replicate the crime by throwing cadavers into acid laden vats. A sequestered jury, which had been away from family and friends for what had to seem like an eternity, heard six days of closing arguments from the four attorneys—two for each side—who summed up their case. During the long days and nights of deliberations that followed, the public had ears in the jury room, courtesy of some mischievous, *Chicago Journal* daredevil reporters, who had lowered one of their brethren 150 feet down a narrow shaft to eavesdrop on the jury and report what was overheard.

It thus came as little surprise when the jury publicly stated what they had privately decided. They could not unanimously decide upon the guilt or innocence of the man who stood before them. A mistrial was declared.

* * *

A do-over. With one glaring difference. Luetgert's lead attorney, William Vincent, a former chief justice of the New Mexico Supreme Court and one time law partner of the legendary Clarence Darrow, withdrew from the case, replaced by the far less competent Lawrence Harmon.

Whether it was a different jury hearing the same facts and arriving at a different verdict or a jury repulsed by a savage murder, an unsympathetic defendant and his bombastic attorney will never be known. Luetgert was found guilty and sentenced to life in prison. He lasted but fourteen months, dying of heart disease. To the end, he maintained his innocence. Louise was never seen again.

Epilogue

In 1904, a major fire destroyed the inside of the Luetgert sausage factory. Over time, it was erroneously reported that the entire building had been destroyed. It wasn't. Today, it houses upscale condominiums whose residents have no clue that they are living in the very same building in which the sausage king unceremoniously sizzled his unsuspecting wife.

Tidbits

The diminutive Louise, under five feet tall, stood in marked contrast to her husky, 5'10", over two hundred pound, husband.

Ghostly sightings of the murdered Louise, in her former home, the factory and the neighborhood, were commonplace.

In prison, Luetgert was a model prisoner. When he died, though, his former paramour, Mary the maid, exclaimed, "I for one will weep no tears."

A huge crowd attended his funeral, at which his second attorney, a highly emotional Lawrence Harmon, spoke, dramatically calling upon Louise to come forward. She didn't.

Harmon, convinced of his client's innocence, continued investigating the case, in pursuit of Louise, whom he never found. Ultimately, and probably not due to this case, he went insane and died in an institution for the mentally ill.

The prosecutor on the case, Charles Deneen, ultimately was elected governor of Illinois and later to the US Senate. While in the Senate, he nominated Howard Luetgert, Adolph's grandson, to West Point. Howard decided not to accept the appointment.

Our Next Tale

Chester no longer loved Grace. When she got pregnant, he decided, like others in this book, that murder was the only way out. So infamous the deed that Hollywood latched onto it, making a movie, which won six Oscars and is considered by many to be a classic, starring the very beautiful and alluring Elizabeth Taylor.

22

A Place in the Sun

Chester Gillette had it all worked out. Cashing in on his uncle's lofty position in town, Chester mingled with some of its loveliest ladies. He was also seeing Grace Brown on the side. Everything was perfect. Until Grace got pregnant.

* * *

Born on March 20, 1886 to a farm couple in the bucolic town of South Otselic of Chenango County, New York, Grace Brown was a simple and respectful young lady. After attending school, she sought the greener pastures away from a subdued country home and moved to Cortland, New York, in 1904. Living with her married sister, Grace soon found employment in the Gillette skirt factory where she eventually came into contact with Chester. One mythical tale has them romantically meeting when a ring fell from Grace's finger, rolled slowly across the floor and stopped when it came into contact with the shoe of a very handsome and attentive Chester Gillette.

* * *

Harkening from Montana, Gillette—born three years prior to Grace—came from a devout middle-class family. His parents joined the Salvation Army, renounced all worldly possessions and set about spreading the gospel as missionaries throughout the Pacific Northwest. Chester eventually left his touring family and, with the financial assistance of another wealthy uncle, attended school at Oberlin College in Ohio. Whether it was due to a lack of effort or excessive partying or general disinterest, Chester left his junior year, whereupon he worked a series of odd jobs including that of a railroad brakeman. He soon found himself in Cortland, working at his uncle's skirt factory.

Utilizing his good looks and charm, as well as playing upon his uncle's strong reputation, Chester in short time was partying with the town's most desirable wealthy young women. On the side, he was clandestinely also seeing Grace, behind closed doors at her new residence, a boarding house.

Chester Gillette, who had many attributes but choose not to take advantage of any of them.

∗ ∗ ∗

When Grace announced in mid-May that she was pregnant, a shocked Chester convinced her to leave town and return to the family farm to live with her parents. Upon arriving back home, she kept her pregnancy a secret. She also started writing Chester a series of daily letters, expressing her love and beseeching him to take responsibility for his actions. For months, her pleadings went generally unanswered. Until the day Chester wrote and announced that they should meet and travel to the romantic and lush Adirondacks. She was intoxicated at the thought of being with her beloved Chester. Her prayers had finally been answered.

She packed her entire wardrobe. Chester, meanwhile, packed but a small suitcase. He knew his stay with her would be a short one.

∗ ∗ ∗

They departed on Monday, July 9, the year being 1906, travelling by train. To avoid even the semblance of scandal, or perhaps because Chester simply did not wish to be seen with a woman who had become a major inconvenience in his life, they sat in separate railway cars. En route, Chester unexpectedly ran into two female acquaintances from Cortland, who he promised to join near Eagle Bay by the end of the week.

The journey was a long one. As the train was not a sleeper, Grace and Chester got off and stayed at local hotels, where Chester registered them under false names as husband and wife, before boarding other trains to continue on their journey. Finally they arrived at their destination, registering as Grace Brown of South Otselic and, ominously, Carl Grahm of Albany.

That same day—July 11, a Wednesday—they sauntered down to the scenic, and aptly named, Big Moose Lake and rented a rowboat for a casual cruise on its gentle waters. Oddly, Chester brought along his suitcase with a tennis racket attached to its side, which numerous people would later recall seeing. Even though Chester had little money, he was not concerned with having to pay the boat's rental fee upon his return as he had no intention of coming back.

* * *

Although no one is exactly sure what happened on the lake that day, prosecutors would claim that Chester rowed to a secluded cove, retrieved his tennis racket, smashed Grace over the head with it and tossed her overboard. It was of little concern to him whether she was rendered unconscious or merely stunned as he knew she could not swim. Either way, once she went in, she wasn't coming out.

The deed done, Chester rowed the boat to land near a main road, jumped ashore and hustled through the woods, joyful at the notion that he was now a free man, no longer burdened by Grace and the misery she had brought him. On his short journey, he had not anticipated encountering three hikers, who distinctly remembered him due to the rarity of seeing a man walking in the wilderness hauling luggage.

* * *

Within a day, Grace's body was found in the lake. Her forehead and mouth had unsightly slashes and cuts. When the police could not locate her companion, "Carl Grahm of Albany," they feared that what they had was far more sinister than an accidental and tragic drowning. Three days later, Chester was arrested near Eagle Bay where he had joined his two female vacationing friends, who were staying at a nearby hotel. In addition to Chester, the police

Grace Brown, the kindly and romantic country girl
who fell in love with the wrong man.

retrieved his tennis racket, Grace's letters to him and scores of witnesses placing the victim and suspect together. They also had a suspect who denied even knowing the deceased. When confronted with contrary evidence, he explained that a tragic accident had occurred. Later the story became a suicide.

* * *

The charges brought a firestorm of attention. A handsome young man accused of murdering his pregnant girlfriend, who had written him a fistful of love letters. Chester's rich relatives, now disgraced, abandoned him, forcing him to request a court-appointed attorney for legal representation.

In contrast to the flesh and bones of Chester sitting all alone in court, the spirit of Grace permeated the trial through the presence of her supporters and strong family, who sat front and center during the proceedings, reacting, often understandably grief-stricken, to the testimony of the one hundred witnesses and the introduction of a like number of exhibits.

The prosecutor methodically laid out the evidence before the jury. He even read many of the letters Grace had sent him, which showcased the full range of human emotions—devotion, love, doubt, anger, fear and shame. Many in the court were brought to tears as her portrait slowly came into view; that of a sad and simple twenty-year-old girl, who disastrously fell in love with a cad of a man.

Countering the cry of murder, Gillette's attorney argued that a highly distraught Grace, unable to cope with her fragile condition, had committed suicide. When Chester told her marriage was out of the question, she jumped from the boat, hysterical, and quickly sunk to the lake's murky bottom. Some of her missives supported the premise. In one, written on July 5th, just six days prior to her death, she penned, "You will never know what you have made me suffer, dear. I miss you and want to see you, but I wish I could die."

The jury didn't buy it. Neither did the judge. Gillette was found guilty and given the death penalty.

Epilogue

Gillette's mother, who arrived from Denver in a trip paid for by a newspaper, just in time for the sentence, launched a speaking tour throughout upstate New York to churn up support for her son and raise money for his appeal. Despite her tireless efforts, his conviction was affirmed and Governor Charles Evan Hughes refused to reduce the sentence. Prior to his electrocution at 6:14 a.m. on March 30, 1908, Chester met with his mother and a priest. While the contents of that conversation were never revealed, both later expressed that the jury had spoken correctly. Indeed, some of Chester's last letters indicated the same.

Tidbits

Books, movies and even an opera have been written based on the murder. Theodore Dreiser, a magazine editor from New York City who had followed the trial, wrote what is now considered a classic novel, *An American Tragedy* (1925). In the fictional work, he added a wealthy, "other woman" to the cast of characters, giving Gillette an even greater incentive to kill a poor and pregnant Grace who was holding him back. This other woman would later be played by Elizabeth Taylor in the highly regarded 1951 film, *A Place In the Sun*, which also starred Montgomery Clift (as a rather sympathetic protagonist) and Shelley Winters as Grace. Ironically, the prosecutor was played by Raymond Burr, who would later go on to star on television as the famed defense attorney Perry Mason.

Like the spirit of Louise Luetgert, through the years, many people have reported seeing Grace Brown's ghost on and around Big Moose Lake. Indeed, the Lifetime Channel featured her story on an episode of *Unsolved Mysteries*.

Grace's nickname was Billy, from her love of the contemporary song "Won't You Come Home Bill Bailey." She also fancied Billy the Kid and signed many of her love letters "The Kid."

Gillette's diary and letters were donated to Hamilton College. He is buried an unmarked grave in Soule Cemetery, outside of the town of Auburn, New York.

The governor, Charles Evan Hughes, who upheld the death sentence, had an illustrious career. Two years after Gillette's execution, Hughes was appointed to the United States Supreme Court, from which he resigned to run for president in 1916. He narrowly lost to Woodrow Wilson. After serving as Secretary of State under President Harding, Hughes was re-appointed to the Supreme Court, this time as its Chief Justice. He served until his retirement in 1941. As Chief Justice, he resisted President Roosevelt's unsuccessful attempt to pack the Court.

Our Next Tale

In Chapter 20, we discussed mass killer Dr. H. H. Holmes. In our next tale, we talk about another serial killer. Although he was featured in national newspapers and magazines, including *Life*, and served as the inspiration for countless horror movies, no one remembers him today.

23

The Mad Butcher of Plainfield

Elmo Ueeck and the unassuming, but odd, Ed Gein chatted about the mysterious disappearance of tavern owner, Mary Hogan. Older and unattractive, the nearly two hundred pound Hogan had served the needs of those residing in the nondescript sleepy town of Plainfield, Wisconsin. She provided the town's residents with some alcohol and a place to drink it, albeit in surroundings much like the town itself, small, quiet and somewhat rundown. "If you had spent more time courting Mary," Elmo told Ed, "she'd be cooking for you instead of missing."

"Eddie merely rolled his eyes," Elmo later recalled, "and wiggled his nose like a dog sniffing a skunk and said, 'She's not missing. She's down at the house now.' But Eddie was always talking crazy like that."

But this time though he wasn't. Mary was indeed at his house, all neatly gutted, carved and chopped up, with her most intimate body parts already added to Ed's already extensive and gruesome collection.

* * *

Eddie Gein very much loved his best friend in the entire world, his mother, Augusta, notwithstanding her harsh ways and her intense dislike of nearly everyone, especially women. The way they flaunted their bodies, flirted with men, wore indecent clothing and make-up, all immoral and evil. It was all against God's supreme will and all deserved to be punished for disobeying His word. The large-boned, coarse-faced Augusta was not shy about her beliefs, which were instilled harshly upon her by a brutal father who used beatings to ensure that she did not stray.

Augusta in turn became her father—rigid, humorless, unloving, and domineering. Unattractive in mind, spirit and body, she unsurprisingly had few males who exhibited any interest whatsoever in her. Until George wandered into her sphere. Notwithstanding the tragedy of being orphaned at a young age when his parents and young sister tragically perished in the unexpected rising waters of the Mighty Mississippi, George appeared straight-laced, laidback and strong. In fact, he was the opposite, not reserved but weak, with inner demons that haunted him, soothed only by a growing dependence on alcohol.

The unlikely and ill-fated pair was wed in their hometown of La Crosse, Wisconsin, on December 4, 1899 and within short order Augusta loudly ruled the roost, openly disgusted and berating her listless husband. Sex, she believed, was a disgraceful abomination, to be engaged in solely for procreation and no other reason. George for his part withdrew, descending even more deeply into his private world, spending more and more time, and what little money he had, at the local tavern, which only further infuriated his unforgiving wife. On one occasion, he returned home intoxicated. Augusta exploded, spitting out a string of insults. Losing control, George repeatedly struck her. Knocked to her knees, she screeched even more loudly and venomously. Finally she raised her hands to the skies, imploring God to do the just thing and take her useless husband.

And to these cockeyed parents first Henry and then Ed were born.

* * *

Augusta wanted a child, but only a female. Men after all were, like her husband, of no value and undependable, all lustful, sin-seeking, loud, malodorous and offensive.

So when Henry came along, on January 17, 1902, she was determined to right that horrible wrong by gritting her teeth and trying once more for a female. Ed's birth on August 27, 1906 caused further outrage and heartache. Through her anger and resentment she vowed that this one would be different. She would see to that. And Ed became her favorite.

George, meanwhile, tried to right himself, opening, thanks to the financial assistance of two of Augusta's successful brothers, a small grocery store. Soon, however, rough patches were encountered and Augusta jumped in, taking control of the business and relegating George to working as a clerk in the very store he originally owned.

* * *

Ed loved his mother deeply and without reservation despite his always, in his view, failing her. When as a young child he lost a few cents she had given him, he cried uncontrollably at how he had let his mother down. When he worked up the nerve to tell her, she castigated him, yet again reminding him of his worthlessness. She would never, she reminded him, make such a mistake; she was the only one upon whom the family could count. As she yelled, he peered over to his defeated father, meekly shuffling about in the corner of the store.

In 1913, with some money saved, Augusta unilaterally decided that the family she totally dominated needed to take a new direction, that of farming. A small dairy farm was purchased forty miles from La Crosse. A year later, with visions of even more land and greater wealth, a second, and final, move was made—to a 195-acre farm in Plainfield. While deeds at the time almost always stood in the name of the male of the family, the deed for this plot listed but one owner, Augusta Gein. Perhaps most attractive to Augusta was that their new home existed in the middle of nowhere, six miles from the center of the small town. She and her family were now nearly totally isolated, far away from temptation and evil.

* * *

Augusta kept the tidy home, which had neither indoor plumbing nor electricity, in tiptop shape. While others might have more money, no one would keep a cleaner residence. Very quickly, however, she discovered that while her home might be a gem to behold she did not want any of the townsfolk visiting for they, like all others, were people of low moral standards, to be avoided.

To her chagrin though, while she was content living in a sealed atmosphere, she could not keep as tight a leash on her sons as she had hoped. Having to attend school, they were exposed to the frailties of others.

While Ed did well in his studies, he was in reality a social leper. Meek and somewhat effeminate, slight of build, easily brought to tears and unable to take a joke, he quickly became an outcast. A droopy left eyelid and an odd grin served as ammunition for those who teased them. He was now painfully experiencing his mother's teachings about the wickedness of the outside world. Whenever he made a rare friend, Augusta immediately raised whatever moralistic objections she could muster about the boy and his lowlife family and ensured that her young son would have nothing to do with him.

As the Gein family soon discovered, farming was difficult and a living was barely eked out. Ed's existence soon fell into one of melancholy and loneliness, with his mother serving as his beacon. As he aged, the repeated lesson she pressed upon him and his older brother was the evilness of the modern woman, who flaunted her body and ways, all in violation of the order of the universe. Rocking back and forth and gesticulating as she read the Bible, she spoke of the greatest of all sins, fornication and made her sons promise that they would obey her every command and admonition. Henry got the message first and quickly shrunk from approaching any female. He would become, like many of Augusta's brothers, a lifelong bachelor.

* * *

In 1940, father George, at the age of sixty-six, left this world for one in which he surely prayed was a better one. The family barely missed him. Indeed, with his failing health he became an even greater inconvenience to those forced to support him. With the outbreak of World War II, Ed took the longest trip of his life, to a recruitment center 130 miles away. He was rejected due to his vision. Given Henry's age, he too did not serve. Both did handy work around the town to make some money and, being dependable and hardworking, found employment. While Henry was the better worker, Ed, while odd, was nonetheless likable. Indeed, Ed was a good neighbor, always quickly agreeing to help out and lend a hand whatever the situation and however inconvenient. Although it was often difficult to discern what went on behind his vacant grin, neighbors by and large had no problems with him.

To many, Henry and Ed were a team. Certainly Ed felt that way towards his big brother whom he looked up to. It thus came as a shock when Henry questioned his younger brother's dependence and unwavering support for their mother. The criticism jolted Ed for he believed that Henry shared all of his strong beliefs and love for their saintly mother.

To those investigating Henry's untimely death on May 16, 1944, nothing seemed amiss. A brush fire had spun wildly out of control. The two brothers fought it. Henry died. A terrible

Ed Gein, (1906–1984), the inspiration for horror and slasher movies which rarely do him justice. (*Library of Congress*)

accident. That Henry didn't appear to be burned, indeed his only physical marks seemed to be some strange bruises on his head, did not deter the authorities from quickly marking the death as one caused by smoke inhalation, not even requiring an inquest. After all, who would want to do Henry any harm?

And now, with George and Henry both dead, Ed had only his best friend to rely upon, his mother. But not for long.

Augusta's first stroke came, necessitating a hospital stay, at which her remaining son sat dutifully. Certainly the shock of harm to his impenetrable mother rocked Ed, but he quickly recovered, tending to her every need upon her return home and seemingly nursed her back to health.

In late 1945, with Augusta now able to move around, she and Ed travelled a short distance to the farm of an ornery and mean neighbor to buy some hay for what little livestock they owned. As they slowly came into view, they saw farmer Smith brutally beating a young dog, whose yelps of pain pierced the still air. On the porch of the farm house, an older woman screamed out and cursed the brute, besieging him, to no avail, to stop the onslaught. As the poor dog breathed his last breath, Augusta bitterly turned to her son and spat out her strong disdain, not for the senseless violence, but for "Smith's harlot," an unmarried female living in sin.

Within a week, a second stroke hit Augusta and she died. Ed, who believed that "Smith's harlot" was responsible for his mother's fatal woes, wept uncontrollably at her funeral. Entering his fortieth year, he was now all alone.

* * *

To those who saw him, Ed seemed to adjust to the death of his beloved mother and for the next ten years remained nicely settled with his fellow six hundred residents of Plainfield. He remained the same withdrawn, shy and meek man with the droopy left eyelid and the sly ever-present mysterious smile, they had always known. Always considerate of others, he always went out of his way to help when asked. Given his odd demeanor, he served as the inevitable butt of many a joke, all the while seemingly enjoying the company of those who teased him. That he sorely needed a bath and a shave and dressed the same with his plaid flannel jacket and hunters cap didn't detract from the affection many held for him. His peculiarities, however, often bubbled to the surface. For one, he had an aversion to blood, despite his life on the farm where the hunting, capture and gutting of animals was the norm. Secondly, he was forever, when in the company of men, talking about the latest true crime magazines he had read. In the 1950s, such magazines bordered on the lurid, featuring well-endowed woman in the clutches of some fiendish and violent predicament, either barely escaping or succumbing to the advances of venal villains.

Little did the townspeople know or suspect what his private life held, when he wasn't around them. The most innocent of his activities centered on additional readings, about Nazi medical atrocities, cannibalism and sexual perversion and mutilation. And the obituary pages.

* * *

In the quiet of his dark ever-dilapidating house, which was falling apart—it appeared—by the hour, Ed took no heed to cleanliness. In short order, his surroundings became an utter pigsty with garbage thrown about. Soon much of the house was closed off, Gein living in but a few rooms, inhabited by filth. The interior hadn't changed much in the decades he had lived there. It still lacked the basic necessities of indoor plumbing and electricity. He still had no phone. The constants in his dark world were loneliness and thoughts of evil women, the townspeople who had abused him, and his mother, who he missed greatly.

In the times he ventured forth, it was either to his kindly nearby neighbors, the Hill family, who offered him a hot meal and idle chatter, or to Mary Hogan's tavern, located in Pine Grove, seven miles from Plainfield. The bar itself was inhospitable, a ramshackle concrete blocked structure serving the need to grab a drink and some small talk. Middle-aged Mary, at fifty-four, was large, loud and overweight, weighing nearly two hundred pounds. She spoke with a German accent, mirroring Augusta's German heritage. While alcohol was, like sex, evil, as Augusta drummed into her impressionable son, Gein nonetheless occasionally imbibed. After all, he couldn't go to the bar and not drink, which would incur the wrath of the innkeeper and bring unwanted attention upon him. Having a rare beer masked the real reason he went, to focus on Mary. In her, Gein saw a great enigma. A woman who resembled his saintly mother but who was no saint herself, indeed the very type of woman Augusta had railed against.

Mary vanished on December 8, 1954.

* * *

For a decade, starting in the late 1940s, people in the area started slowly disappearing. It was as if one giant hand had silently swooped down from the sky and grabbed the victims. It started on May 1, 1947, when little eight-year-old Georgia Weckler was dropped off by her farm after school and was never seen again. On October 24, 1953, Evelyn Hartley, a fifteen-year-old honor roll student, walked off to babysit and never returned. Clues turned up: a discarded shoe; bloodstains leading away from the house; the victim's panties and bra off Highway 14; but, no Evelyn. On November 1, 1952, two hunters entered the woods and never exited.

Like the others, the crime involving Mary again rocked the area. But there was an additional irritant in this one. Able to handle herself, Hogan had obviously been shot and dragged away, as evidenced by the blood smears on the floor. By who though, and when, what with people coming and going in the bar at various times during the day? For two years the local paper on the anniversary of her abduction reflected the feelings of many in asking, "What Happened to Mary Hogan?" and calling it "a complete and deep, dark mystery."

The answer eventually came. On November 16, 1957. In the brutalized dead carcass of Bernice Worden, who at fifty-eight, had the same stout-like body features as Mary Hogan and Augusta Gein.

* * *

Hunting season in Wisconsin lasted but nine short days during mid-November 1957. In that brief span, forty thousand deer would be killed along with thirteen hunters, making it deadly for both animal and man. Nearly all of the men of Plainfield partook in the festive tradition. Except for one.

On late Friday the 15th, Gein traveled into town and inquired of Bernice Worden, the very capable proprietress of Worden's all-purpose farm store, the price of antifreeze. Ed had recently started hanging around the store which caused some discomfort to Bernice although she, like so many others, considered Gein the village nitwit, someone to be tolerated, not feared. As he and his family had been good customers over the years, she bit her tongue and treated him cordially, as did her son Frank. When Gein innocently inquired of Frank his plans the following day, Frank responded that he, like nearly everyone else, would be hunting.

When Ed returned to the store the following morning, it was thus, as expected, empty. Except for Bernice, who filled Ed's order for antifreeze, took his money and wrote out the final receipt of her life. Ed took the jug and departed, returning seconds later, inquiring of a rifle on the wall of the store. Bernice retrieved it and handed it to him. As he looked the weapon over, Bernice aimlessly wandered to the window, gazed out and commented about a car which came into view. What she didn't see was Gein silently removing a bullet from the pocket of his overalls and placing it into the chamber of the rifle.

* * *

Late that afternoon, Frank returned. Despite having failed in his efforts to bag a buck, he stopped by the filling station, the official gathering spot for the hunters, to see how the others had fared. While chatting, the station attendant asked Frank whether Bernice had joined him in the fields, given that the store had been closed since early morning.

Alarmed, Frank bolted over to the locked store. After retrieving the key, he gained entrance. A jolt of electricity shot through him. The cash register was gone and the floor was covered with blood. A receipt by the counter revealed a sale, for antifreeze.

When the sheriff arrived, Frank greeted him with the horrific news and his strong belief as to who had committed the crime—the little man who had been hanging around the store, who had just yesterday inquired about the price of antifreeze and who had asked whether he would be around that day. Ed Gein.

* * *

The police hustled over to Gein's ramshackle farm and quickly ascertained he wasn't there. They sped off to the Hills, a neighbor with whom Gein was known to associate. When they found him there they asked whether they could speak with him. Ed, as always, quickly cooperated.

After a few minutes, Ed blurted out that someone was framing him. For what? the officers inquired. For Mrs. Worden, Gein replied. What about her? Well, she's dead, ain't she? How could he know that? The police had their man.

All that remained was searching his house, a task that fell upon Sheriff Arthur Schley, who had been on the job for only six short weeks, and Captain Schoephoerster, who while from another county, assisted when called upon. What they soon saw sent them both retreating, puking their guts out. Soon, the entire nation would join in the retching agony.

* * *

Gein's forbidding home sat in utter darkness and desolation as the outside winds howled. When the two officers arrived, they braced themselves for the eerie and surreal world that awaited them.

Guided by the dim hue of the beams of their service flashlights, the officers gingerly entered what was known as the summer kitchen, a structure attached to the house. Try as they might, they had difficulty sidestepping the rot festering all about them. The decaying food, ripped boxes, rusted and broken farm utensils, piles of papers and discarded cans made for an impenetrable minefield of junk. As Schoephoerster navigated his way to the far side of the room, to a door leading to the main part of the house, Schley, still waiting for his eyes to adjust to his surroundings, gently brushed up against something. As he turned, he focused his light on the intrusion.

At first he thought it was the dead carcass of a deer, hanging by its hind legs and split and gutted. In the brief seconds it took for the picture to come more sharply into focus, he realized that what he saw was not an animal at all, but a human, with no head, strung up by its heels, a gaping black hole oozing slime where it had been recently eviscerated. He had found Bernice Worden.

Screaming out in disbelief and shock, he fled, vomiting. His partner quickly joined.

* * *

As officers, alerted by a frantic radio transmission, rushed to and entered the house of hell, they were stunned into silence as they viewed the mutilation, having never before witnessed so galling a violation. It got worse.

In the kitchen sat a soup bowl, formerly one half of someone's head; on the stove Bernice's heart in a stew pan. In the bedroom, bedposts adorned by human skulls. Chairs with seats of human skin, used also to fashion bracelets, lampshades, a small garbage can, a drum and the cover for a hunting knife. A window shade handle made of a woman's lips. A belt festooned with female nipples. A tattered shoebox housing female genitalia, one of which painted silver with a red ribbon. A container of noses. A human mask collection. And the severed heads of Mary Hogan and Bernice Worden. Into each of the ears of Bernice, Gein had shoved a bent nail, to which he attached some loose fitting twine, making a handle for what was to be either a trophy hung on the wall or a basket to be paraded throughout the house.

One last horrid and blood curdling revulsion awaited discovery—a human body suit, made from the body parts of his female victims, neatly sewed together into a vest, complete with breasts and female genitalia and leggings. An outfit into which Gein could submerge himself, prancing around, his mother reincarnated.

As for Augusta's upstairs bedroom, it was spotless, as neat as a pin. In what would have made her proud, Ed had kept it in immaculate condition.

Epilogue

The insane brutality grabbed the staid 1950s nation, which became fixated on the man dubbed the Mad Butcher of Plainfield. Soon unfamiliar and strange words such as necrophilia, transvestite, fetish, voyeurism, sexual deviant, cannibalism and Oedipus complex entered everyday lexicon. Psychiatrists fell over one another trying to describe "one of the most dramatic human beings ever to confront society" who had a mental condition "unparalleled in modern history"; of Gein consciously loving his mother and hating other women, but subconsciously the reverse; of Gein in one instance raising his mother and bringing her back to life when he donned the homemade body suit while at other times killing her off; of becoming his mother and murderously striking out at all evil and promiscuous women.

As always, Ed was friendly and cooperative with his interrogators and volunteered what he could remember, which—at times—was not much, due to his acting as though he were in a complete daze. He spoke, without remorse or appreciation of the enormity of his actions, and related dark tales as if he were talking about an innocent trip into town or visit with a neighbor. The vast number of body parts, he revealed, came from recently deceased older women who he dug up at three local cemeteries and hauled back to his house. Sometimes he came out of his trances, at which point he returned the stolen bodies to their initial resting places. While initially reticent to talk about Mary and Bernice, he finally admitted to killing both, although he insisted that Bernice had been shot accidentally. As for the young female children and hunters who disappeared, he insisted that he had nothing to do with them. Lie detector tests verified his many tales as did the empty graves to which he directed the police.

Determined to be incompetent to stand trial, he sat in a secure hospital for the mentally insane. After a decade, he was finally found fit and, in a jury-waived trial, was found not guilty by reason of insanity. The townspeople, some who thought him crazy while others believed him cunning, could hardly believe how much he had changed, from a hollow-faced shabbily attired sad sack of a man to one who had grown old and hardy, if not plump, eating three square meals a day in the confines of the state institution. He still, though, had that look.

Shortly after the discovery of the bodies, an inspired author, Robert Bloch, wrote a novel, basing his mother-obsessed madman on Gein. The character was named Norman Bates; the book *Psycho*. Alfred Hitchcock bought the story and made the movie, considered one of the classics of all time.

Tidbits

Gein died an ill and decrepit old man at seventy-eight on July 26, 1984, having never been released from the insane asylum.

While it appeared that Gein had killed two and collected the remains of approximately thirteen others, the total number is unknown. Some of the body parts came from young females, none of whom having been buried in local cemeteries.

In a way all slasher movies—*The Texas Chain Saw Massacre, Friday the 13th, Halloween, A Nightmare on Elm Street, The Silence of the Lambs* and all others—have Gein as their inspiration.

The authorities seized Gein's house, land and property, planning to auction them off. Sightseers by the thousands travelled to the farm hoping to catch a glimpse of the now infamous locale. Shortly before the sale, a mysterious fire burned the house down. A huckster purchased the death car in which Gein carried his victims and turned it into a carnival sensation.

Mary Hogan abandoned her ten-year-old daughter Christine decades earlier. For years, Christine attempted without success to locate her mother. Along with the rest of the nation, she finally found Mary.

Some locals were outraged by portions of the press coverage, viewed as inaccurate, sensationalistic, and manipulative of the facts.

Very often in the face of such tragedy, black humor serves as an outlet to a distressed population. Such was the case here. Such jokes included: Why did they keep up the heat in Ed Gein's house? So the furniture wouldn't get goose bumps; Why did Ed Gein's girlfriend stop dating him? Because he was such a cut-up; They could never keep him in jail. He'd just draw a picture of a woman on the wall and eat his way out; Why do people go to Plainfield? To get a head.

Our Next Tale

Hot and sassy, she backed down to no one, including the police. When detectives came to her house to search it, they encountered more than they could handle. What next happened would come to affect nearly every criminal case forever after in America.

24

Good Golly Miss Dolly

The call to the police came in at three in the morning. An explosion had obliterated the front porch and door of a gangster simply known as The Kid. When Dolly heard about it she knew she had problems. When the police came looking for one of the bombers at her house, the severity of her problems quickly escalated. What happened next was monumental.

* * *

Dollree "Dolly" Mapp was born in Austin, Texas on October 31, 1924 to a racially-mixed couple. Her childhood years are somewhat unclear. It appears that she was one of seven children and did not share a good relationship with her father, Sam, whom she described as overbearing and strict. At one point, when she was around ten, she decided she had had enough and ran away, traveling to an aunt who lived over two hundred miles away. When her parents were notified, they arranged for Dolly's return, where, she reports, she was severely beaten.

Things grew worse. At sixteen she became pregnant. Refusing to give in to the pressure to give the baby up for adoption, she was kicked out of the house as her father felt that she had disgraced the family. She turned to friends, who provided money and support.

Still a teenager and already a mother, Dolly found herself in Cleveland, which at the time, unlike today, was an exciting town. With a rocketing and vibrant nightlife, gamblers and conmen added a touch of sin and glamor to a Runyonesque atmosphere.

And Dolly fit right in. Despite being a young mother, she had developed into a head-turning, traffic-stopping beauty with allure, style and street savvy. Men coveted the opportunity to be with her. With the fast crowd, Dolly kept up, partying, working the numbers racket, and running with boxers who lived in the limelight. She married one of her early benefactors—the highly regarded boxer Jimmy Bivins, who in his career would defeat eight world champions, although he himself would never be one. The abusive Bivins unfortunately could not turn off his in-ring brutality and Dolly, not one to take his flak, left the man she described as "a bastard and a brute."

Not alone for long, she soon took up with the highly-respected, former light-heavyweight boxing champion of the world, Archie Moore, to whom she was briefly engaged. When he broke it off, she did not go meekly into the night. Instead, she sued him for $750,000. Dolly

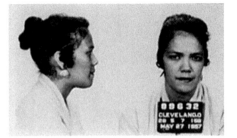

The sexy and street wise Dolly Mapp who never let anyone take advantage of her, 1957.

ultimately dropped the case. Her incentive for so doing is unknown. One imagines it was either due to threats or a payoff.

Despite those in the boxing world letting her down, she was not finished dealing with them. Indeed, The Kid, himself a future boxing impresario, would propel her to the legal heavens.

* * *

The bombing on May 20, 1957 sent a message—if you run an illegal gambling operation make sure you pay off the local crime boss. The Kid didn't, the result of which was violence. It came compliments of the very colorful Shondor Birns, who—when he wasn't charming people—was killing them. A sharp dresser with a fondness for large cigars and seeing his name in the newspapers, Birns organized the numbers game in Cleveland to ensure that everyone made money and no one tried to undercut the other. Of course, he was paid handsomely for the arrangement. When one balked, trouble followed; usually in the preferred form of communication, a bomb, of which its use was succinctly explained by one veteran police detective as "Either it's to make someone start doing something, make someone stop doing something, or to kill someone."

In The Kid's case, it was to get him to pony up the money he owed. When the bomb went off in the wee hours of the morning, the twenty-five-year-old terrified target called a cop he knew, Sergeant Carl Delau, and complained that part of his house had been blown away. Rather than being cowed, The Kid told Delau, as well as the press who eagerly jumped on the story, who he suspected of trying to silence him—Shondor Birns and a small gang of others. Within hours Birns was in custody as the police built its case. In three days, they hit the jackpot when an anonymous tip came in—search the house on Milverton Road in the Shaker Heights section of Cleveland; there you'll find Virgil Ogletree, one of those responsible for the bombing, as well as a large amount of gaming materials. The owner of the home—Dolly Mapp.

* * *

Delau was familiar with both. Ogletree assisted Birns in the gaming business and sometimes added muscle when it was needed. As for the "foxy" Mapp, Delau, like all men, respected her beauty and brains. He also knew her to occasionally work for both The Kid and Shondor, picking up or dropping off bets and even keeping the books when needed. On one occasion three

The low level thug called The Kid who took umbrage when the mob blew up his porch.

years earlier, Delau spotted Dolly and decided to tail her. Obviously aware that the police were following, Dolly started tossing betting slips by the hundreds out of the window of her speeding car. After being pulled over and confronted with the gathered gambling papers, Dolly professed shock and disbelief. She did however willingly pay the court costs and hundred dollar fine.

Her future encounter with the police sergeant involved far higher stakes.

* * *

In response to Delau and his partner Michael Haney knocking on her front door, Mapp called down from her second floor window and asked what they wanted. When they replied that they'd like to come in, she had them wait as she called her attorney, the same one who was handling her civil suit against former boyfriend Archie Moore. Told not to let the police in unless they had a warrant, Dolly relayed that information to Delau and Haney, who left to secure one.

While search warrants today are commonplace with police departments informed and educated as to their intricacies, the scene was radically different in 1957, when warrants were a rarity. Not only were they time-consuming and cumbersome to prepare, but the police legitimately feared that the target would be tipped off by a police or court insider on the payroll of a mobster.

Delau called for assistance, told a warrant would be written and applied for and to wait for its arrival. When it did, the police acted, gaining entrance through Dolly's back door. How this was effectuated was subject to some discrepancy. While the police insisted they merely pried the door open, Dolly insisted that they violently smashed it. Regardless, Dolly demanded to see the warrant. When they showed it to her, she quickly snatched it, shoving it into her bra. After a brief struggle, the document was retrieved, as were Ogletree, gambling material and "four little pamphlets, a couple of photographs and a little pencil doodle—all of which [were] alleged to be pornographic." Most of the materials were found in the basement of the single-family dwelling that contained two separate apartments. Dolly lived on the second floor; another tenant, Minerva Tate, resided on the first.

Mapp was charged with possession of both gambling paraphernalia, and lewd and lascivious books, pictures and photographs. As her case was proceeding through the legal system, so were those against Shondor and four others. Given the state of the evidence, they were charged with blackmail in that they were forcing their victim to pay to participate in the gaming racket. When he balked, his house was bombed.

* * *

For one involved in the criminal underworld, The Kid surprisingly willingly cooperated with the authorities, despite threats against him not to do so. Just one month prior, upon walking to his garaged car, he heard some movement in the nearby bushes. Immediately sensing danger, he turned and ran. A shotgun blast rang out, hurling thirty, what turned out to be, non-life threatening, pellets to his neck and head. Despite this, he testified. Dolly, however, also threatened, did not.

Unfortunately for the prosecution, The Kid was not the best of witnesses. Dubbed "The Talker" by the press, he excitedly spoke far too fast. Despite admonitions and guidance from the judge, The Kid blathered on. In the end, the jury was deadlocked and a mistrial was declared. Unknown to most, except Shondor and the juror he bribed, the outcome was set prior to the trial even beginning. Eventually, the charges were dropped.

Monitoring and reporting the proceedings, *The Cleveland Press* shouted out the outcome of the failed trial—"Another Break for a Bum." That night, Birns, holding court in a local gin mill, probably happily bought a round for the reporter who wrote it.

* * *

When Dolly's case came to trial, she beat the gaming charge but was convicted of the possessing obscene materials one. While at the time of the search it appeared that everyone thought a valid warrant existed, none was ever subsequently produced, leading, in the words of the appellate courts, to "considerable doubt as to whether there ever was any warrant for the search of [the] defendant's home." For Dolly's part, the warrant really wasn't an issue in her trial as she did not challenge the determination that the materials were obscene. Rather, her defense was that she did not possess them; that they belonged to a former boarder, Morris Jones.

After again losing in the state Appeals and Supreme Courts, she turned to the United States Supreme Court, where her attorneys basically argued that Mapp's first amendment rights had been violated. The justices ignored that assertion and instead seized upon a short argument in an amicus—friend of the court—brief filed by the American Civil Liberties Union, which claimed that it was her fourth amendment rights that had been disturbed.

While the fourth amendment exclusionary rule outlawing the introduction of unlawfully seized evidence applied to the federal courts since 1914, it did not apply to the states, unless a state so chose to adopt it. The justices heard the case of Dolly Mapp and the doodle drawing, pamphlets and pictures she allegedly possessed and held that the states were also bound by the rule. If the evidence had been illegally seized from Dolly, it could not be used in evidence against her.

The seismic decision shook the legal world. History had been made. It remains the law today, firmly entrenched and recognized. And it all started with the ever so sassy and assertive Dolly Mapp.

Epilogue

After her legal adventures, Dolly relocated to Queens, New York. In 1970 her home was raided. This time the police had a valid search warrant. $150,000 in heroin and $100,000 in stolen property were seized. Mapp was convicted and sentenced to serve twenty years to life under New York's harsh new sentencing laws. In 1981, her sentence was commuted by a sympathetic New York Governor, Hugh Carey.

As for The Kid, after testifying against Shondor and those accused of the bombing, the IRS moved in and charged him with not paying taxes on his gambling business and seized his bombed out house. This paled however in comparison with his two murder charges. He had been acquitted of the 1954 one, the jury believing that he justifiably killed Hillary Brown who was trying to rob one of The Kid's gambling houses. He wasn't so fortunate on his 1966 indictment, although he was convicted of the lesser charge of manslaughter. He served four years in prison. Upon his release in 1971, he became America's foremost boxing promoter. His name? Don King.

Tidbits

Dolly, whose name was actually Dollree, learned of the Supreme Court's decision before even her own attorneys when a court bailiff, whom she befriended while her case was being heard, called her from Washington with the news.

In 1975, Shondor Birns, who was in his late sixties, met his maker, courtesy of a bomb, ironically his favorite method of elimination. The $843 found on or by him was seized by the IRS. His killer was a former partner, Danny "The Irishman" Greene. Greene, in turn, after many attempts, was also assassinated. The investigation of his killing helped bring down the entire Cleveland mob. A book and movie, both titled *Kill the Irishman*, tell the tale. To the end of her life, Shondor's mother described her son as just a nice Jewish boy.

Virgil Ogletree kept up with his criminal gaming activity and was again indicted in 2003 at the age of eighty-one. Allegedly suffering from dementia, the charges were dismissed. He remained friends with Mapp.

Some of the mobsters who ran Cleveland and Pittsburgh were arrested at the 1957 Apalachin meeting in upstate New York, discussed in Chapter 16 (There is No Mafia).

In addition to Cleveland at the time being an entertainment hub, it also generated much business. At the turn of the century, cars, electricity, railroads, oil and chemicals predominated. In the 1960s, The Port of Cleveland brought in significant trade.

IV

THE (TOILET) SEAT OF GOVERNMENT AND POWER

SOMETIMES THOSE IN GOVERNMENT AND power act in a manner contrary to their position. Such acts are done for a variety of reasons: to cover up misfeasance or malfeasance; to avoid embarrassing situations; to gain publicity or money; or simply due to the belief that legitimate ends justify nefarious means. Such acts have existed since the creation of government.

Perhaps government lawyers purposely lied to the United States Supreme Court because they truly believed in the principle they were espousing. Perhaps radicals had to be legally railroaded because they were simply evil and un-American. Maybe a doctor had to be given an unfair trial because that was the best way to prove him guilty.

Before discussing all of these cases, however, we start with a congressman who took umbrage at the local district attorney sleeping with his wife. He responded by brazenly shooting the illicit lover, who howled for mercy as bullets reigned down upon him. Despite the murder occurring in broad daylight in front of witnesses, he got away with it. When the Civil War broke out a few years later, he joined the Union Army. As a general, he fought at Gettysburg and lost a leg.

The Congressman Who Got Away With Murder

With wealth, power, and political connections, Daniel Edgar Sickles knew how to get what he wanted. The popular Congressman from New York commanded the allegiance of countless friends in high places, including presidents, past and current. When the emotional and volatile Sickles learned that the district attorney of Washington, DC was having an affair with his wife, he took matters into his own hands.

* * *

Sickles was born on October 20, 1819 in New York City. His father, George, was a patent lawyer and politician. Sickles studied at what is now New York University and became a member of the bar in 1846. He quickly entered politics where his star rose rapidly, joining the New York State Assembly. As evidence of his standing, the mayor himself presided over Sickles' marriage in 1852 to a girl half his age, the mid-teened Teresa Bagioli. Teresa was the prized granddaughter of Lorenzo Da Ponte, a wealthy professor. Years earlier, Sickles' parents had sent him to live in the Da Ponte household to prepare for his education. There he met his future wife, a mere infant at the time. She obviously made a lasting impression on him.

Marriage, however, did not tame his wandering eye, which was strong and constant. He bedded numerous women, regardless of their social or marital status. On one occasion, he reputedly took a prostitute with him to meet the Queen of England and introduced the working girl as his wife. Teresa, young and pregnant at the time, had not accompanied him on the trip. She later gave birth to their only child, a girl, whom they named Laura.

The Sickles family relocated to our nation's capital, courtesy of New York's 3rd Congressional District, which elected him to Congress in 1856. There, he and his wife entertained Washington's finest, including President Buchanan, at their rented house the Stockton Mansion. The receptions were magnificent. It was at one of these soirees that Teresa, youthful and charming with a lovely round face, met the handsome and also connected Philip Barton Key, the local district attorney. A widower and popular escort, Key beckoned from a prominent family. His father, Francis Scott Key, wrote "The Star-Spangled Banner" while his uncle, Roger Taney, served as the Chief Justice of the United States Supreme Court.

Sickles, when he was away at work, entrusted Key with squiring Teresa around town. Their

Dan Sickles, Congressman, General, playboy and killer, 1862. (*Library of Congress*)

travels eventually landed in the bedroom. Despite rumors of their romance, Key denied it all, insisting that his affection was merely fatherly in nature. He was after all, like Dan, twice as old as young Teresa.

The tryst continued. Sadly for them, they failed to recognize that their servants had eyes and often remembered what they saw, especially if it involved the sexual peccadillos of their masters. On one occasion, the duo was seen leaving a prestigious costume party and sharing a drunken sexual encounter inside a carriage. When Sickles was away, Key traveled to the Stockton Mansion, where he stayed late. Key and Teresa also met at cemeteries and frolicked among the dead. In November 1858, Key rented a home on Fifteenth Street, where neighbors often saw Teresa frequenting. Key hung a white ribbon or string from the upstairs window to signal that it was safe to come in.

* * *

Upon receiving an anonymous letter, Sickles soon learned what everyone already knew—his wife was having an affair. The missive, dated February 24, 1859, identified Key by name. It closed with, "I do assure you he has as much the use of your wife as you have. With these few hints I leave the rest for you to imagine." Key received a similar letter warning him that the public knew of his affection for Teresa.

Like lightning striking a mighty oak, Sickles, despite his numerous extramarital affairs, blew apart at the revelation. Emotional and grief stricken, he confronted his young wife and forced her to write a confession. She wrote, in part, that she "Usually stayed an hour. There was a bed in the second story. I did what is usual for a wicked woman to do."

As if a wounded animal, Sickles groaned and wept throughout the ordeal, uttering, "I am a dishonored and ruined man." Despite his hurt, he refused to leave his wife.

* * *

The following day, despite Key's knowledge that the affair had been discovered and the peril the emotional Sickles presented, he, like an obedient and loyal lap dog, still longed for his paramour. With Teresa suffering and Sickles mourning, Key was spotted wandering near their mansion. Key, who at forty was a year-and-a-half older than Sickles, even waved a white handkerchief to signal his lover.

It was Dan however, not Teresa, who spotted Key and became enraged. In short order, he followed and confronted the district attorney, winding up in front of the White House. "Key, you scoundrel, you have dishonored my house! You must die!"

Sickles drew a pistol and fired. A near miss inflicting only a minor injury to Key's hand. A scuffle. Sickles pulled back and drew another gun. "Don't murder me!" Key cried. From a few feet away, Sickles shot Key in the upper leg. Key collapsed to the ground, screaming for mercy. "Don't shoot me! Murder! Murder!"

Sickles again pulled the trigger. Click. A misfire. He pulled it yet again. This time a bullet went surging into Key's body just below his heart. Sickles stepped even closer. Click. Another misfire. A bystander jumped in. Too late.

The Congressman offered a simple justification for the slaughter: "He has violated my bed."

A murder in broad daylight in front of witnesses heralds in a new criminal defense, 1859.

* * *

Sickles fled a few blocks, to the house of his friend and mentor, the elderly Attorney General Jeremiah Black, and surrendered. He freely confessed and was sent to jail after making a stop home, where the police allowed him to go upstairs to meet with Teresa. The details of that conversation are lost. One report, however, indicated that he simply uttered, "I've killed him." After having a brandy, he was whisked away.

Sickles landed in a dingy prison with narrow cells, which did not deter countless politicians and friends from visiting him. Fellow Congressmen, cabinet members and even Vice President Breckinridge swarmed to meet and console their beleaguered friend, who cried at the state of his marriage. He also wished that Key had put up a fight, which would have made the slaying more honorable. "We could not live together on the same planet," Sickles said of his victim.

While capable of making bail, Sickles refused, either out of pride or the solitude of his stark surroundings. Earlier he had confiscated Teresa's wedding ring, later returning it with the band broken. His young daughter, Laura, was told that her father was away on business. President Buchanan, informed of the shooting, worried about the political fallout.

* * *

With the speed of the bullets leaving Sickles' gun, the news of the shooting shot throughout the nation, monopolizing the headlines. Public opinion was mixed, with gossip running rampant. News of Teresa's forced confession spread. Some thought it proof of a premeditated killing. A ravaged Teresa, who in the eyes of her father dishonored the family, fled from Washington to New York with Laura.

Sickles assembled an impressive legal team, including future Secretary of State Edwin Stanton and James Topham Brady, an insanity expert. That temporary insanity had not been used before was no impediment to it being used now. Robert Ould inherited the role of district attorney from his slain boss. Key's relatives hired John Carlisle, a prominent Washington lawyer, to assist Ould.

* * *

Foreign journalists, joining their American counterparts, flocked to the opening of the trial at City Hall on April 4, 1859. The room was crowded, hot and muggy. No women were allowed inside other than witnesses. Sickles was marched into the court and placed in a small, penned-in holding area. Lending support, Dan's father and father-in-law sat nearby.

Ould's opening remarks portrayed the defendant as a walking arsenal. He asked the jurors to look beyond his social status and find that a premeditated killing occurred, with the pain of Teresa's infidelity no excuse.

The defense countered that Sickles was a hero doing away with Key, a sexual predator. Brady portrayed his client as being driven to temporary insanity, pushed over the edge by an unfaithful wife. Letters that Key wrote regarding the earlier rumors of the affair were admitted as evidence supplementing the live testimony of witnesses placing Key and Teresa together as lovers. Sickles shed tears as the witnesses testified.

The state countered with Congressional transcripts, showing Sickles' sound mind days before the shooting. Prosecutor Carlisle also wished to introduce evidence of Sickles' visit to a Baltimore hotel with another woman; the judge disallowed it.

* * *

After a nearly month-long trial, working even on Easter Sunday to more quickly end the lengthy proceeding, the jurors set off to decide Sickles' fate. They didn't need much time. In barely over an hour, they returned to a loud, packed and stirring courtroom. Spectators climbed on benches and tables to catch a glimpse at the jurors' faces, hoping to gain a clue as to the verdict. The judge called for order. Silence settled in, gripping the courtroom. A well-dressed Sickles stiffened in anticipation as he stood and faced the jury.

Not guilty.

Sickles' popularity, political connections and crafty lawyers combined to save him. Vindicated in slaying an adulterer, he became the first defendant in America to successfully use the defense of temporary insanity. His supporters and attorneys rejoiced and celebrated across town late into the night. Jurors joined in. Days later, Dan recounted the shooting and casually admitted that he had every intention of killing Key.

Epilogue

Sickles returned to New York to recuperate and reconciled with Teresa despite the disapproval of the public. With the outbreak of the Civil War, he joined the Union army as a general. At Gettysburg in July 1863 he violated orders and repositioned his soldiers in a manner that led to massive casualties. He himself was seriously wounded, losing his right leg. Despite his questionable decisions, he was awarded the Medal of Honor, although it took some thirty-four years of campaigning to receive it.

After the war, he served as the military governor of South Carolina and helped manage North Carolina. Teresa died of tuberculosis shortly thereafter, in January 1867, at a still-young thirty-one.

Sickles went on to serve as ambassador to Spain and unsuccessfully negotiated a deal for the US to purchase Cuba. He had an affair with the deposed Queen Isabella II and later married Caroline de Creagh, the adopted daughter of an Irish-Spanish family, in 1871. They had two children, a son and daughter, before separating in 1879 due to Sickles' continued womanizing. Laura, now grown up, struggled in New York City and became estranged from Sickles. She died of alcoholism and possibly tuberculosis in 1891. Her father did not attend her funeral.

Insisting to the very end of his life that his strategy at Gettysburg helped win the decisive battle, Sickles stayed active, dedicating war memorials and traveling and participating in Civil War reunions and events throughout the nation. To that end, he, now old, chaired the New

York Monuments Commission, where he came to be accused of embezzling a large sum of money, approximately $27,000. Perhaps the money was stolen to pay for a statue of him at Gettysburg. Shortly thereafter, in 1914, Sickles, at the age of ninety-four, died of a cerebral hemorrhage and was buried in Arlington National Cemetery.

Tidbits

Key's wife, Ellen, died of unknown causes in 1855 shortly after the birth of their youngest child. Oddly, Key lived separately from his four young children, possibly because they reminded him too much of Ellen. Given his wealth, servants were available to raise the children. Virginia Clay, wife of Senator Clement Claiborne Clay of Alabama, observed that the widower Key was: "the handsomest man in all Washington society."

Dan's right leg was mangled by a cannonball during the fiercest moments of a Confederate attack at Gettysburg. As he was carried by stretcher to a hospital, he grinned and puffed on a cigar on the way to the operating table. His amputated leg, along with a cannonball similar to the one that shattered it, is housed at the National Museum of Health and Medicine in Silver Spring, Maryland.

After the war, Sickles had occasion to return to New York City where he attended the opera one evening. There he spotted the presence of a young man, sitting below him, whose face looked strikingly familiar. When the man's eyes met his, Sickles was certain of the man's identity. Robert Key had enough of a resemblance to his slain father to distract Sickles from his beloved opera. Neither man, however, gave any sign of recognition.

It remains unclear why Laura became estranged from her famous father. She was married at one point but later abandoned. As a young woman living in New York, she scratched out a living selling her paintings. She spent the allowance money that Sickles sent her on alcohol.

Our Next Tale

Whether it was Louie Lepke or Kid Twist breaking legs for either management or labor, labor unrest has been a significant part of our nation's history. In the early years, it was often management exploiting the put upon worker. When radicals jumped in to aid the oppressed, they were met head on by the government and the police, ever on the look-out against subversives and anarchists. In Chicago, when the unrest turned violent, strong steps were taken. They included convicting the innocent.

26

Chicago Blows Up

The city was simmering. Just the day before, workers were shot and killed by the police. And now, on May 4, 1886, the workers again assembled, calling for an eight-hour work day. Their employers bristled at the outrageous demands and proclaimed that anarchists and socialists were behind the turmoil. Marches were held and speeches were made. And more tragedy awaited.

* * *

The fight between laborers and their employers for better working conditions is as old as our nation itself. Following the Civil War, industrial production grew rapidly and Chicago, a major trade hub, soon found herself at the epicenter of the labor movement. Capitalists grew rich and powerful, often at the expense of the tens of thousands of unskilled workers, many of them immigrants, who arrived in America in search of a better life. Instead they found discrimination, exploitation, cramped tenements, disease and dangerous jobs paying minimal wages. At present in Chicago, their six-day, ten-hour, back-breaking work day garnered them $1.50. With every powerful institution against them—the courts, the politicians, the police and private militias—they were powerless. Unless they united.

* * *

Many players populated the field calling for eight-hour work days and safety improvements. Some labor unions sought to peacefully bring about change; others were more rabid. Led by self-proclaimed anarchists, they believed the battle to be a far larger one—that capitalism lay at the center of all economic inequity—the solution required a forceful one.

On the other side stood the capitalists and businessmen, wary of change and decreased profits and scared of revolutionaries preaching violence. The Chicago police, who one would think shared the ideals of the workers, instead joined the other side; in place to ensure law and order. Plagued by allegations of corruption, they eagerly used force against the protesting workers; so did the Pinkertons and leg-breakers, the infantry in the fight against the worker.

* * *

A national trade union set May 1, 1886 as the day the eight-hour work day would become the standard. On that date, workers throughout America rallied and walked off their jobs. Chicago was at the forefront with thousands of workers participating.

Leading the charge stood German-born August Spies (pronounced "Speez"), the editor of the revolutionary German-language newspaper *Arbeiter-Zeitung (Workers' Times)*. Albert Parsons, a Texan and former Confederate soldier aided his comrade. Both were gifted speakers, dedicated to radicalism.

* * *

The marches on Saturday, May 1st, were peaceful. Late that night, Parsons took the train to Cincinnati to speak to the workers there. The following day, a Sunday, Chicagoans rested, their exuberance saved for Monday, where the atmosphere surrounding the strikers and locked-out workers was almost festival-like with games played and beer consumed; women and young girls from the sewing shops sang in the streets.

That afternoon, on the southwest side of Chicago, Spies spoke to German and Bohemian workers outside the McCormick Reaper Works. With the police hovering nearby, Spies urged resistance and solidarity. During his oratory, the closing bell blared, releasing both those who chose to work and those hired as replacements.

Like the start of a twisted competition, within seconds three great forces came together—the strikers, the workers and the police. Upon the bell's blaring, the strikers had surged away from Spies and rushed to the factory gates, which was depositing its workforce. Like acid on skin, two mean and ugly groups converged. Jostling became punching which became rioting. Screams and shouts and grunts filled the air. Then gunshots. Fired by the police. Workers killed, the number forever in dispute—two or six?

Left: August Spies, an anarchist more interested in his cause than his life.
Right: Albert Parsons, another anarchist who unjustly died for his beliefs.

Witnessing the carnage, an enraged Spies sprinted to his newsroom and gathered his forces. In what later would be dubbed the Monday Night Conspiracy, they planned a response. Spies ominously wrote that if the McCormick protesters had been armed "with good weapons and one single dynamite bomb not one of the murderers would have escaped his well-deserved fate."

Meanwhile, Louis Lingg and William Seliger were busy making bombs.

*   *   *

On Tuesday, May 4th, the strikes resumed, paralyzing Chicago. A protest at Haymarket Square was planned for that night, with Spies once again a featured speaker. Also, once again, the police were out in force.

At the anointed hour, Spies hopped atop a hay wagon to speak. The area reeked of manure and rotting vegetables. Spies denounced the lies suggesting that he instigated the McCormick incident and lambasted the working conditions of the workers. Parsons, who had returned from Cincinnati, followed and spoke about the need for better wages. Three thousand jam-packed workers cheered his remarks, which ended with a call to arms. Despite the challenge, Mayor Carter Harrison, who earlier decided to attend the gathering, concluded that nothing violent was likely to occur and left.

With the Haymarket demonstration on the West Side, bomb makers Lingg and Seliger toiled on the North Side, loading their deadly devices into a trunk, which traveled to a nearby hall where the troops awaited their ammunition.

Samuel Fielden, another anarchist, next addressed the Haymarket crowd, inciting it: "Keep your eye on the law! Throttle it! Kill it! Stop it! Do everything you can to wound it!"

It was now late, 10:20 p.m., and getting colder. The crowd had noticeably thinned, now only five hundred strong. As Fielden concluded his fiery speech, a large column of police advanced through the crowd, ordering everyone to disperse. Fielden assented.

All was calm. And then a hissing sound. In the sky, a sizzling object arching its way through the dimly lit night, headed toward the front line of officers. A policeman with military experience immediately recognized the missile and cried out, "Look out Boys! For God's sake, there is a shell!"

The bomb detonated with a loud crackle. Relentless gunfire followed. Seven cops died.

*   *   *

The officers involved claimed that they were fired upon first. Others maintained that no one other than the police did the shooting, unloading their revolvers into both the crowd and each other. Public sympathy for those killed ran strong. Unknown were the many casualties of the workers, the dead and wounded quickly carried away by those fearful that all involved would be implicated, charged and jailed. What was known was that the bomb killed Officer Mathias Degan. Six fellow officers died as a result of bullet wounds. Numerous others suffered serious injuries.

The city was at war, with civil liberties, like Degan, suffering a mortal blow. With the niceties of search warrants and legal process tossed aside, the police sought to impose order. Chicago residents laid low, the usually bustling Haymarket Square eerily quiet, people cowering and nourished by a press preaching conspiracy, and avoiding danger in the form of howling foreign lowlifes, intent on violence and mayhem. Gun sales soared. Police rampaged meeting halls, saloons and homes in pursuit of the guilty. In short order, as in Bogie's *Casablanca*, the usual suspects were rounded up. Nearly two hundred arrests were made, including August Spies and three of his fellow *Arbeiter-Zeitung* associates—assistant editor Michael Schwab, typesetter Adolph Fischer, and office manager Oscar Neebe. Labor strikes by and large came to a halt.

* * *

Eight men were indicted: Spies and his three employees; bomb maker Louis Lingg; speakers Albert Parsons and Samuel Fielden; and militant radical George Engel, who was home playing cards when the riot occurred. None were accused of throwing the fatal bomb. Instead, they were all charged with conspiring to murder, their deadly plan hatched in response to the McCormick shootings.

A mountain of evidence, including dozens of witnesses who were promised money in exchange for testimony, was marshaled by the prosecutor, Julius Sprague Grinnell; in preparation for what many thought was the worst crime on American soil since President Lincoln's assassination in 1865.

* * *

Lawyers were hired. Preparations made. And finally the trial, starting on June 21, 1886, in the Cook County Courthouse. Judge Joseph Eaton Gary presided over a sensational proceeding that foreshadowed the infamous murder trial of anarchists Sacco and Vanzetti three decades later in Boston. Reporters and spectators overfilled the courtroom. Nearly a thousand potential jurors were screened; after three weeks, a jury was selected. Although most were rather ordinary—a salesman, a railroad worker, a hardware store dealer, a school principal—many openly harbored a bias against the defendants.

On July 15th, Prosecutor Grinnell, with an intimidating face and wide mustache, launched his attack, arguing that Spies had provoked the McCormick incident and then organized a group to battle the police at the Haymarket. That the identity of the bomber was unknown was not a hindrance, he continued, as whoever planned and aided the crime was just as guilty as the one who tossed the fatal bomb.

The prosecution took advantage of the many turncoats who testified against their once-friendly fellow anarchists. Louis Lingg's partner William Seliger testified and went uncharged as did Godfried Waller, who chaired the Monday night enclave and testified to the formulation of a murderous plan to fight the police. The trigger to set the plan in action—the use of the German word "Ruhe" (rest) in Spies' newspaper. The May 4th edition of the paper was produced. It contained the damning word. Overplaying his hand, the prosecutor elicited improbable testimony from one witness who had Spies lighting the fuse of the bomb. Physical evidence aided the prosecution in the form of boxes of dynamite found at the homes of some of the defendants and their anarchist newspapers advocating destruction and death. Bomb material seized from Lingg's house matched that found in the remnants of the killer bomb.

The defense countered that as none of the defendants had been charged with perpetrating a murder, none could be found guilty of conspiracy to cause it. Several witnesses, including the mayor, were called, disputing some of the testimony of the state's witnesses. Many indicated that none of the defendants threw the bomb; indeed some of the accused were not even in the area at the time. Four of the defendants—Spies, Parsons, Fielden and Schwab—testified on their own behalf.

Sadly, whether due to the incompetence of counsel—"their willingness to vindicate anarchism rather than to save the necks of their clients"—or overcome by the overzealousness of their convictions, the defendants did not aid their cause. Spies admitted to owning and using dynamite, "out of curiosity. [...] I wanted to experiment with dynamite just the same as I would take a revolver and go out and practice." Lingg's attorney, in his opening statement, oddly argued that "It may seem strange why he was manufacturing bombs. The answer to that is, he had a right to have his house full of dynamite." He also asserted that his client had no intent to kill any police officer "except in self-defense."

＊　＊　＊

Closing arguments began on August 12th. The defense claimed that the prosecution's witnesses were not credible and that the allegations that Spies had orchestrated the bomb throwing remained unproved. Prosecutor Grinnell, in part, appealed to the fears of the jury, urging them to help protect America from anarchists.

On the afternoon of August 19th, the jurors retired to their hotel. The next morning nearly a thousand spectators ringed the courthouse. The verdict came quickly. Guilty of murder. The defense was shocked. Albert Parsons stood, smiled and bowed to the audience.

After, the jurors were swarmed by reporters, who heaped praise on them despite their admitted biases. Wealthy businessmen arranged for cash rewards for a duty well-done. Newspapers boldly declared that the trial, which had dominated their pages, had been perfectly fair.

＊　＊　＊

At sentencing, the defendants spoke and over the course of days decried the injustices against them. Spies said that he was ready to die a martyr. "Call your hangman!" he challenged the judge. The other defendants followed and lashed out at the treatment they had received.

Judge Gary took Spies at his word and sentenced him and six of his cohorts to death. Only Oscar Neebe, against whom existed scant evidence, escaped the noose, receiving a fifteen-year prison sentence.

＊　＊　＊

The bomb that killed Officer Degan also grievously wounded the eight-hour movement, which came to a halt. The defendants appealed to the Supreme Courts of Illinois and the United States and met with failure. As the anarchists awaited their fate, newspapers and public sentiment started to shift somewhat, presenting the defendants in a more sympathetic light.

The trial came to be depicted as a disgraceful sham with rights ignored, testimony purchased, and witnesses browbeaten; the defendants proven guilty of being anarchists, not murderers.

In some quarters, the convicted were viewed even more favorably, as martyrs. Countless visitors followed, lending support and words of encouragement. One, the lovely Nina Van Zandt, even notoriously married the imprisoned August Spies.

As the date for their executions—set for November 11, 1887—approached, protests erupted worldwide. Only a request for clemency could save them. True to their ideals, Parsons, Engel, Fischer, and Lingg demanded their release, not clemency. Spies offered to die if the lives of the others were spared.

On November 10th, Lingg cheated his accusers, chomping on a dynamite cap somehow smuggled into his cell. Over six hours, with part of his face partially blown away, he gradually descended the ladder of death in agony. That same day, Governor Oglesby acted on the clemency request of the remaining prisoners—Fielden and Schwab. It was granted. Their lives were spared.

* * *

Parsons spent his last night on earth entertaining his prison guards with song, conversation, and autographs. The following day at high noon with hundreds in attendance, he, along with Spies, Fischer, and Engel, all hooded and dressed in white with their hands bound behind them, marched to the gallows. From behind his shroud, Spies cried out, "The time will come when our silence will be more powerful than the voices you strangle today." As Parsons started to speak, in mid-sentence the trap door opened, plunging the four to a needlessly painful death as, due to the faulty manner in which the nooses were tied, they ever so slowly strangled.

Epilogue

In 1893, Governor John Peter Altgeld pardoned Fielden, Schwab, and Neebe, declaring the trial a mockery of justice. Released, the three lived quiet lives until their deaths.

That same year, Lucy Parsons, the wife of Albert, succeeded in having a graveyard monument built as a memorial for her husband and his comrades. The monument is listed on the US National Register of Historic Places and is a gathering place for activists. Seven of the eight defendants are buried in the Waldheim Cemetery (now the Forest Home Cemetery) in Forest Park, Illinois. The eighth, Samuel Fielden, is buried in Colorado, where he purchased a ranch and married, after his release from jail.

May 1st became the rallying day for workers throughout the world. In America, proponents of the eight-hour workday saw many of their goals achieved when Congress, in 1938, passed the Fair Labor Standards Act, which established a national minimum wage, guaranteed overtime pay in certain jobs, and placed restrictions on child labor.

To this day, the identity of the bomber remains forever a mystery. So too, the exact involvement, if any, of the eight defendants.

Tidbits

Among the many bombing tossing suspects, some pointed the finger at Michael Schwab's brother-in-law Rudolph Schnaubelt, who was nowhere to be found, having fled the country.

Until her death in her late eighties, Lucy Parsons, who became a celebrity in the labor movement, remained active in the fight for social reform, including preserving the memory of her beloved husband Albert and the other anarchists. Frail and blind, she died in a house fire on March 7, 1942.

A statue celebrating the police was erected in Haymarket Square in 1889 but experienced a bitter history of vandalism and destruction. In 1969 radicals used dynamite to blow the statue apart. After its repair in 1970 it was again blown up. After much turmoil, the statue was again fixed and relocated to Chicago Police Headquarters.

In 2004, a memorial was built and dedicated in Haymarket Square to all those who lost their lives there on May 4, 1886.

Captain Schaab of the Chicago Police Department met great criticism for his role, many believing he fabricated, and even planted, evidence. Governor Altgeld, in his pardon of the three jailed anarchists, blasted senior police officials for threatening and terrorizing witnesses and procuring false testimony. At sentencing, Oscar Neebe decried Schaab as a leader of police corruption, ransacking houses and stealing property.

Judge Joseph Gary presided over the second murder trial of Adolph "The Sausage King" Luetgert, discussed in Chapter 21. Luetgert is buried in the same cemetery as seven of the Haymarket defendants.

The mayor, Carter Henry Harrison, was the son of the mayor at the time of the great Chicago World's Fair in 1893, when H. H. Holmes was committing many of his murders, discussed in Chapter 20.

The decision of the Illinois Supreme Court was long—over two hundred and fifty pages. The US Supreme Court's decision ran fifty-one pages. Both were thorough, detailed, well-written and, with history the judge, wrong.

Our Next Tale

The abuse workers suffered came in many forms, including lax safety regulations. In perhaps our saddest story, a fire broke out, needlessly killing scores of young, mainly Jewish and Italian, female garment workers, who came to America in search of a better life. Instead, they found death and tragedy. And injustice. Those responsible for the calamity got off.

27

Down Came the Bodies in a Shower

Ida Brodsky was fifteen, Kate Leone and Rosaria Maltese, fourteen. They were the youngest. Provindenza Panno was the oldest at forty-three, just a few years older than Jacob Bernstein and Catherine Maltese, the mother of Rosaria and twenty-year-old Lucia. The vast majority were in their teens or early twenties. Anna Altman, Jennie Franco and Rosie Grasso were all sixteen, two years younger than Ida Kanowitz, Jennie Stein and Rosina Cirrito. Most were children really, overwhelmingly Jewish or Italian, and recent immigrants, working long hours to make it in their new land, America. They all had one last thing in common. They were all dead, all one hundred forty-six of them. Killed on a late Saturday afternoon on March 25, 1911.

* * *

It was the end of a seemingly endless, mind-numbing, six-day-long workweek. The young ladies were tired. Their fatigue was tempered however by the realization that life in their native lands was far worse. Indeed that was the very reason their families emigrated, to come to America, the land of opportunity. Work hard and succeed.

The owners of the Triangle Shirtwaist Factory were a testament to what hard work could accomplish. Isaac Harris and Max Blanck themselves had emigrated from Russia in the 1890s and began working in the garment industry in New York City. Harris, a tailor, worked in immigrant sweatshops while Blanck worked as a garment contractor. Blanck married Harris's cousin, and the two met shortly thereafter. They became partners, founding the Triangle Shirtwaist Company in 1900. Harris knew the details of shirtwaist production while Blanck worked as the salesman. They installed mechanical sewing machines and priced their shirts at three dollars each. In 1902 they moved the company to the ninth floor of the Asch building with Harris designing the layout of the sewing floor to minimize conversation and increase productivity. In 1906, the company expanded to the eighth floor.

Their lifestyles accelerated with the great success of their business. They both moved into brownstones overlooking the Hudson River on the Upper West Side where servants, including chauffeurs, catered to their every need. They expanded their trade into New Jersey and Pennsylvania. By 1908, sales had hit the lofty one million dollar mark, the largest manufacturer of women's blouses in the area. Harris and Blanck became the "Shirtwaist Kings."

Owners Max Blanch (left) and Issac Harris of the
doomed Triangle Shirtwaist Factory. (*Kheel Center,
Cornell University, http://www.ilr.cornell.edu.trianglefire*)

Profits derived from producing the least expensive shirtwaists in the largest quantity. For the
nearly five hundred workers, one as young as ten, and overwhelmingly Italian and Jewish,
this translated into a daily working grind of twelve to fourteen hours in which they earned
two dollars. The owners kept inventory of the materials, hiring a foreman to monitor the
workers and routinely inspect the women's bags when they left to ensure that nothing was
being stolen. Blanck ordered that a secondary exit door be locked as an additional safeguard
against theft and to prevent workers from taking breaks. The degradation and exploitation
had been on-going and festering.

★ ★ ★

In September 1909, the Triangle Shirtwaist factory workers voted to organize under the
United Hebrew Trades (UHT) rather than continue participating in the company-sponsored
association. A stiff management response resulted; those who organized the union vote were
fired. In response, on October 4th, hundreds of Triangle workers walked off their jobs and
began picketing. Through the use of thugs and the police, Harris and Blanck disrupted the
protests through beatings and intimidation.

The ante now raised, Clara Lemlich, a strike leader, called for a city-wide general strike of
those employed in the shirtwaist industry. Twenty thousand responded to her impassioned call
and joined the strike, creating the largest single work stoppage in the history of New York City.

The protestors called for increased wages, improved working conditions, less draconian
work hours, and the power to unionize. Even some of the richest joined their cause. J. P.
Morgan's daughter, Anne, and fellow millionaire and socialite, Alva Vanderbilt Belmont,
not only joined the picketers, but encouraged others to also do so. They also challenged the
tactics and brutality of the police, who had arrested over seven hundred strikers. With the
approaching holiday season, Harris and Blanck grew concerned and offered to increase wages

and shorten the work day. In return they demanded that the strikers drop their union-only mandate. The strikers refused, which did not sit well with Anne Morgan, who intoned, "I am heartily in favor of these strikers, but these fanatical doctrines are all the more dangerous because they tend to tear down all the good in our present social state." Consequently, she resigned from the strike committee. The strike continued.

By February 1910, however, the shirtwaist manufacturers, except Triangle, accepted the demands of the workers. When the Triangle workers finally went back to work, they obtained higher wages and fewer working hours, but had lost the fight on unions.

* * *

Saturday, March 25, 1911, was a typical one. In early, work all day, breaks—including those to eat and to use the bathroom—discouraged and kept to an absolute minimum. As the day wore on, the excitement grew of a free Saturday night and Sunday. The thoughts of the young workers turned to anticipated plans of delight and fun. A date? An evening with family and friends? The exhilaration of that new-fangled invention called a movie or even Coney Island?

At four or so, right before quitting time. On the eighth floor. A cigarette carelessly and mindlessly tossed into a scrap bin full of discarded cuttings. The smallest of sparks, growing and growing, until, at 4:40, a fire.

Foreman Samuel Bernstein and his assistant, Max Rothberg, rushed to the incendiary pile and attempted to dash it with buckets of water. Too feeble an attempt for too great a challenge. The fire grew, quickly. Now raging.

The cry of fire. Panic quickly following. Workers running in all directions seeking refuge from the ongoing inferno. Many ran to a fire escape, not realizing that it was rusty and decrepit. As

The tragic and heartbreaking Triangle Fire of Saturday, March 25, 1911. (*Kheel Center, Cornell University, http://www.ilr.cornell.edu.trianglefire*)

twenty mounted it, it shuddered and quickly collapsed, plunging them to their deaths. Others scrambled to a closed door, which Dora Miller was able to partially open. But with the mass of a panicked herd behind her, pressing her, pressing the door, until quickly it again slammed shut. Trapped. Miller noticed a nearby glass panel and started frantically smashing it, striking it, until finally a hole large enough to wiggle through. Nearly two dozen followed her. One by one entering the openings. And then no more, the rest overcome by onrushing flames which devoured them.

Others ran to the two elevators and stairs. A bookkeeper, her wits sharpened by the emergency, grabbed a telephone and called to those on the tenth floor, alerting them of the coming disaster. Quickly, the owners Max Blanck and Isaac Harris escaped by making their way to the roof and jumping onto the nearby building next door.

The worker who received the call on the tenth floor fled without hanging up the phone, preventing anyone from calling the ninth floor to alert the two hundred workers there. They learned of the fire far too late, upon its hellish arrival. With rational thought a quick casualty, screams and pandemonium erupted, those trapped frantically searching for a way out. Fighting with one another in an effort to escape, pushing friends aside, throwing them down, hitting them, acting in the most primal urge to survive, to move to the front of an imaginary exit.

To the elevators, both of them. Now jammed. Elevator operators frantically moving up and down, three times to carry the far too many. One came to a screeching halt, buckling under the intense heat. The second grinding to a stop due to the weight of the hurtling bodies from above landing on its ceiling; the trapped from above had pried open the closed elevator shaft to escape the intense heat and either shimmied down the thick steel cable or merely jumped down the blackened chamber, landing with great thumps on the top of the elevator, stopping it.

Flames prevented workers from using one stairway; another was locked, sealed to prevent theft. The foreman who held the stairway key had already escaped, failing to unlock the door. While the building itself was fire proof, it served as a fire trap. Those inside weren't getting out. Thousands of people gathered outside to watch the unfolding and horrific tragedy.

Those on the ninth floor found themselves with two deadly options—either burn to death or die jumping from the windows. Over fifty chose to jump. Some young ladies embraced each other, holding on tightly, as they leapt. One man held a woman out at arms-length and dropped her; then another and another; he kissed the fourth before letting her go. "They were all as unresisting as if he were helping them into a street car instead of into eternity." After the kiss, he himself jumped.

A young girl hung by her fingertips to the windowsill of the tenth floor for three minutes before flames "licked at her fingers" causing her to drop. Another girl jumped from a window but her dress caught a wire, snatching her. The crowd stared as she hung, slowly twisting, until her dress slowly charred until nothing was left to hold her, sending her crashing to the ground.

Some found themselves trapped against ever blackening windows. As they burned, they pressed harder against the glass until it shattered. "Down came the bodies in a shower— burning, smoking, flaming bodies, with disheveled hair trailing upward." In a sense, they were human torches.

As the soon dead rained down and piled up, firefighters were forced to move away to avoid the bombardment of bodies and turned their hoses away from the burning building and onto

The police and on-lookers can only look up with shock and helplessness as the bodies rain down. (*Kheel Center, Cornell University, http://www.ilr.cornell.edu.trianglefire*)

the burning bodies. Further futility and anguish set in upon the realization that their fire ladders only extended to the sixth floor.

Blankets and nets were quickly set up in a vain and useless attempt to catch the jumpers, hurtling down at ever increasing speeds from high above into feeble materials unable to capture the great weight. The bodies blew through the tissue paper of what was mesh and cloth, shelling the pavement and mashing upon impact.

"Horrified and helpless, the crowds—I among them—looked up at the burning building, saw girl after girl appear at the reddened windows, pause for a terrified moment, and then leap to the pavement below, to land as mangled, bloody pulp."

* * *

It is almost difficult to comprehend that such mayhem, death and horror, which to many went on for an eternity, lasted but a short time, basically over in a mere thirty minutes. As for those witnessing the abyss, "[t]he emotions of the crowd were indescribable. Women were hysterical, scores fainted; men wept as, in [convulsions] of frenzy, they hurled themselves against the police lines." Another put it more simply, "I looked upon the heap of dead bodies and I remembered these girls were the shirtwaist makers. I remembered their great strike of last year."

With the fire extinguished, the grim task remained for the firefighters making their way into the building. On the ninth floor, near the elevator and stairways, heaps of young girls greeted them. So too, "bodies burned to bare bones, skeletons bending over sewing machines."

Outside, doctors frantically checked the masses of bodies for any signs of life as the police fought to hold at bay the ever increasing hordes of hysterical relatives, intent on overrunning the blockade to gain a view at a loved one. The police, who in the strike of 1910 beat the workers, now found themselves filling some of those very same people into coffins, ambulances and patrol wagons. Sarah Kulpa, who was the lone surviving jumper from the building, clung to life over six agonizing days, before finally succumbing on March 30th.

* * *

One hundred and forty-six lives were lost—129 women and seventeen men. Fifty-three jumped or fell from the windows. Nineteen fell down the elevator shaft. More than twenty died from the collapsed fire escape and at least fifty burned to death.

The morning after Armageddon, corpses were lined up, one after another, row after row, for identification in a makeshift morgue. Hundreds of grievers searching for their loved ones showed up, joined by tens of thousands of others, either curious, grief-stricken, or merely there to gawk.

Of all of the dead, six remained unidentified. On April 5, 1911, the city buried them in a shared grave at the Cemetery of the Evergreens in Brooklyn. Despite the inclement weather, hundreds of thousands attended the funeral march for those dubbed "the unknowns."

* * *

Triangle owners Max Blanck and Issac Harris were charged with manslaughter due to a violation of the labor code which mandated that doors not be locked during working hours. As the trial started on December 4, 1911, the courthouse was filled with angry relatives of the dead, screaming out "Murderers! Murderers! Give us back our children!"

Over one-hundred witnesses testified over three weeks that the doors were locked. The defense asserted that the witnesses were coached by the prosecution because their wording hardly varied during the retellings. In less than two hours, the jury acquitted Blanck and Harris. The prosecution had not proven to their satisfaction that the two had known that the doors were locked.

The verdict was met with disbelief and anger. The defendants had to be hustled out from the judge's private exit due to the angry crowds. One verbalized the thoughts of many, crying "Justice! Where is justice?" The enraged masses chased the defendants to a nearby subway station, where they were able to scurry away.

Civilly, Harris and Blanck faced twenty-three individual suits. In the end they settled, for $75 per person. The surviving families received $75 each for the death of their child, their wife, their loved one. Under the terms of the insurance policy, however, Blanck and Harris received what came out to be $400 per life. In the end, like the good businessmen they were, they profited handsomely from the deaths of their young workers.

The Triangle Building as it looks today as a NYU
Facility, 2013. (*Photo by author*)

Epilogue

In 1913, the Triangle Shirtwaist Factory was relocated. Later that year Blanck was charged with locking one of the doors during working hours, forcing him to pay a twenty dollar fine. The judge apologized for the imposition. Blanck was also issued a warning the following December when a factory inspection revealed scraps thickly piled in flammable wicker baskets. A year later, the owners were again fined when they were caught sewing Consumer's League labels, which certified that the garments were manufactured under decent workplace conditions, into their clothing. The factory finally closed in 1918, never being able to replicate their pre-fire profits due in large part to the burned reputations of Harris and Blanck.

Public outrage over the fire led the New York Legislature to create safety committees, one of which Frances Perkins, who later became Secretary of Labor under Franklin Roosevelt, helped head. Various safety laws resulted, including fireproofing requirements, automatic sprinklers, alarm systems, fire extinguishers, improved eating and toilet facilities, prohibiting smoking and limiting work hours.

In 2011, after a multi-year painstaking investigation, the six unidentified bodies were finally identified.

Tidbits

In addition to the three members of the Maltese family killed, the fire also killed six sets of sisters, two brothers, and a mother and son.

The scene was truly horrifying, the worst that many seasoned police and fire men had ever seen. Bodies were headless, unrecognizable, burned to a crisp or splattered. Two young ladies "charred beyond all hope of identification" had died so deeply embraced that they were initially placed together in one coffin.

Most maddening is that it was so close to all of the employees leaving for the day. Indeed many of the victims were already in coats and sweaters as they prepared to leave. A mere ten or fifteen minutes and most would have lived, escaping the fatal fire.

The new style blouses that the Triangle manufactured grew in popularity given that they were looser fitting, more comfortable and less restrictive than the Victorian styled rigid dresses of the time. Arguably, the new style symbolized the changing times of women in society.

To this day the fire and its victims are remembered. In 2008, the Remember the Triangle Fire Coalition was created to permanently honor those who died.

Clara Lemlich, who called for the city-wide strike, had emigrated from Russia in 1903 and became an outspoken socialist leader of the garment union. She married twice, her first husband dying after almost forty years of marriage. She had three children, one who, like her, was an active member of the Communist Party. Lemlich died in 1982 at the age of ninety-six in a nursing home, where she urged the workers to organize.

Harris returned to his roots, again becoming a tailor. Blanck continued to own other clothing companies, none of which netted him the profits of the Triangle Factory.

The tragedy has been alluded to in books, theaters, movies and even music.

During the early labor disputes of the 1900s, the unions hired gangsters such as Big Jack Zelig, Joseph "Joe the Greaser" Rosenweig, Pincus "Pinchy" Paul and Benjamin "Dopey Benny" Fein as enforcers to battle the thugs hired by management. Once in, as earlier discussed, they didn't leave.

Our Next Tale

Another sad constant throughout American history has been racism. Minorities thought to be acting inappropriately with whites were often handled in a brutal manner, if not by the authorities then by vigilante groups. So when the white wife of a naval officer in Hawaii told of being raped by a group of locals, the moorings flew off the boat. And Clarence Darrow, so often protecting the poor and downtrodden, instead stood on the other side, representing the abusers.

28

Thalia Lied, Joe Died

A decade before Pearl Harbor, the Massie affair shook the Hawaiian Island like no other catastrophe. The reverberations were felt all the way to Washington, DC, where Congress considered withdrawing its fleet, with potentially devastating economic effect. That lies and racism played a key role was of no moment. And at the center of the hailstorm sat Thalia Massie, the lovely twenty-year-old spoiled housewife from a wealthy and connected family.

* * *

For members of the American elite in pre-statehood Hawaii, the islands were a paradise waiting to be conquered. By the end of the 1800s, the United States had annexed the islands as an official territory. The mainland controlled the destiny of the native population with a powerful Navy presence and oppressive business strategy that enriched whites while disenfranchising local minority workers. Today's multicultural tourist hotspot was once a cauldron of white supremacy, racial tension, and economic oppression, and it was in this environment that Thalia Massie, the wife of a naval officer, instigated a series of events that would change the islands forever.

Thalia was born in Washington, DC in 1911, to Granville Roland Fortescue, a cousin of Teddy Roosevelt, and Grace Hubbard Fortescue, a leader in societal circles, who was obsessed with the family's reputation. It was thus an event when her sixteen-year-old daughter Thalia married the dashing twenty-two-year-old Tommie Massie, who was born in Kentucky and recently graduated from the Naval Academy, on Thanksgiving Day 1927 in Washington. Stationed in Pearl Harbor, his new wife joined him in the 1930s.

As a trendy socialite on the islands, Thalia considered herself superior to even her equally aristocratic friends. Such high-mindedness made her somewhat of an outcast, which had little effect on her active, boozy social life. Her rocky marriage, fueled by drunkenness and pettiness, suffered as a result, with fights occasionally publicly displayed. That she often openly flirted further angered her volatile husband.

The lives of the well-connected, privileged couple tragically detoured on the night of September 12, 1931, when they attended an alcohol-fueled party organized by some naval personnel at a local tavern in Waikiki, Honolulu. Thalia soon grew out of control, bickering

A family of privilege, arrogance and pettiness—Mrs. Granville Fortescue with daughter Thalia Massie and son-in-law Lt. Thomas Massie. (*Library of Congress, NYWT&S gift*)

with both her husband and one of his superior officers, who she slapped prior to stomping away. Walking down Kalakaua Avenue in the direction of the beach, her destination was known only to her. Tommie, still partying, assumed that his wife had merely gone home.

The black void into which she traveled that evening is unknown to this day. When she emerged an hour or so later, she was badly beaten, a broken jaw highlighting a visibly bruised face. She told those whose car she had flagged down, that she had been abducted and beaten by a group of five or six Hawaiian men. She refused an offer of medical attention. When gently asked whether she had been violated, she replied that she had not.

Upon arriving home and soon facing her husband, her story changed, now claiming that in fact she had been gang raped; her efforts to ward off her attackers being of no avail. Rightfully concerned, Tommie contacted the police, despite Thalia's request to the contrary.

When the police arrived and questioned the victim, she was unable to give any substantive details of the rape. It had simply been too dark and she had been too traumatized. She could neither provide details about the perpetrators nor their vehicle.

Several hours later, after prompting by the police, Thalia's memory was mysteriously jolted alive. She now vividly recalled the appearances of her attackers and even furnished a nearly complete license plate number. A group of local men, all in their young 20s—Horace Ida,

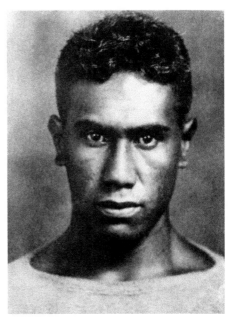

Joseph Kahahawai, the victim of being a minority in hostile times. (*Library of Congress, NYWT&S gift*)

Joe Kahahawai, Benny Ahakuelo, David Takai, and Henry Chang—were shortly charged with the crime.

Initially, Ida wasn't surprised when he was brought in for questioning. A few hours earlier, he had nearly crashed into another car after he and his four friends attended a party. A heated argument ensued with the other driver and his wife, who reported the incident to the authorities. Armed with this information, the police sought to connect the two incidents, ignoring whether in fact they were related. The five thus were not charged with, as they thought, the earlier altercation but a far more serious one—assault and rape—involving a woman they had never seen before.

* * *

With the script neatly written by the police, the case appeared strong notwithstanding the protestations of innocence from the five men, who insisted that they were elsewhere on the island and could prove it. Captain John McIntosh led the investigation and was intent in quickly solving a potentially incendiary crime. The naval authorities lent support, with Rear Admiral Yates Stirling, Jr., intimating that true justice be meted out via a lynching. The national press quickly picked up the story and supported the authorities in their fight against Hawaii's dark and savage criminal underbelly that carried out terrifying attacks against pristine and innocent young women. That such sexual assaults on the island were rare, mirroring the low crime rate of the area itself, were troubling facts to be ignored and replaced by more acceptable myths.

* * *

As the case proceeded to trial, the rock of duplicity was lifted in part; the dirty story beneath exposed to the light of truth and common sense. Doctors who had examined Thalia had not found a scintilla of evidence suggesting rape. There were no vaginal bruises, swelling, blood, or semen found despite the victim's claim to have been violently assaulted by a group of men. Moreover, how could Ida and his friends have committed the crime when they were involved in an altercation across town, a distance away, at nearly the same time? When they were arrested, they too bore no signs of a sexual struggle. Neither blood nor semen was found on any of their clothes. And what to do with three witnesses claiming to have seen Thalia after she left the club followed by a white man shortly before the alleged rape occurred? They would testify at trial that they provided this information to the police.

The police response was simple. Bury everything that was inconvenient; along with the rumors of a false claim of rape to cover up marital infidelity and cheating; a lover who beat Thalia or perhaps even an enraged husband.

* * *

Thalia's mother Grace, who had left the states and moved to Hawaii, was enraged by the innuendos swirling around her daughter and started a public campaign to support her and preserve the family's image. Her wingman in her endeavor was the local naval commander himself, Admiral Stirling, who had a reputation to protect.

While their efforts were partially successful, the prosecution against the five was difficult. With all of these discrepancies brought out by the defense before a racially-mixed jury, the case tumbled down onto itself. After a draining three-week trial with four days of deliberations, the jury could not unanimously agree upon a verdict. A mistrial was declared on December 6, 1931. The jury was split 6-6, with those voting to acquit disgusted by the obvious attempt to manufacture and hide evidence. The five accused rapists remained free on bail.

Americans on the island as well as the mainland were infuriated by the non-verdict. Newspapers stirred the pot of hysteria, claiming all naval wives in Hawaii were at risk. Their husbands could not sit idly by. If the law could not bring the guilty to justice, the Navy certainly would.

The locals lived under a cloud of violence. For Horace Ida, the threat became a reality. In a prelude of worse things to come, Ida was abducted at gunpoint by a group of military men and taken to a nearby dairy farm, where he was beaten and abandoned.

The Massies, egged on by the family's matriarch Grace, took it one step further. The attacks on her family harmed her; the non-verdict was a body blow. Justice had to be served, and if no one else was capable of acting, she surely would. She hatched a vicious scheme, convincing Tommie and his fellow sailors Albert "Deacon" Jones and Edward Lord to do her bidding. Joe Kahahawai, who was thought to be the most vulnerable of the group, would be kidnapped and beaten, a confession his sole salvation.

Setting the plan in motion, Grace created a phony police summons while her cohorts all assumed their roles. Tommie played the role of the chauffer—complete with gray suit, cap, and goggles—of Grace's rented Buick. Lord and Jones staked out the courthouse where they learned that Kahahawai had business.

The kidnappers waited for their target. When Joe appeared, he was shown the fake summons and pushed into the car. Shoddy planning ignored the reality of witnesses being in front of an open courthouse. Eddie Uli'i, Joe's cousin, saw his cousin snatched away and immediately notified the police.

Kahahawai was driven to Grace's bungalow in Manoa where he was beaten. What exactly occurred during the interrogation remains unclear. The outcome wasn't. Kahahawai's abductors had no intention of letting their hostage walk free. The heads became hotter. The violence escalated. Finally a gun was taken out. Confess or be shot. I didn't rape her. The gun fired. One time, to the chest. Joe was dead.

Scrambling, his killers moved and thought quickly. Where to dump the body? Someone suggested in a remote section of the island where discovery was unlikely. The corpse was wrapped in a sheet and placed in Grace's car with the shades pulled down, hiding the interior.

Sometime around ten, after hearing a radio transmission of an abduction, two policemen spotted the car described in the call. A chase commenced. The Buick picked up speed. Another police car joined in. Shots were fired, one hitting the car's taillight. Finally, the Buick was forced off the road. With a body in the back seat, Grace, Tommie, and Lord were arrested for murder. Their fourth cohort—Jones—had stayed behind to clean up the crime scene, including disposing of the murder weapon, a .32-caliber Colt automatic. He raced to the Massie house where he met Thalia and her sister Helene, who volunteered to dispose of the murder weapon.

The police arrived and questioned a visibly drunk Jones and arrested him. Thalia and Helene were taken into protective custody although neither was suspected of any wrongdoing.

Shortly, Tommie, Jones, Lord and Grace were charged with murder. Despite the depravity of the crime, the four received preferential treatment, then and throughout the trial that would follow. Public opinion against "the rapists" remained strong even after the rape mistrial and Kahahawai's killing. The mainland newspapers continued to beat the drum of a violent island unsafe for white women. While some papers complained of the injustice of the murder and the lack of evidence of the rape, they were drowned out. Racial tensions, already high, started to now overheat.

Grace meanwhile remained impervious and defiant. She freely told a reporter from the *New York Times* of the crime and of how she had "slept better" for it. Her only regret was their bungling effort to discard of the corpse. Grace was confident of acquittal, an attitude reflecting the racial attitudes permeating the island. Sympathy for them ran strong.

On top of this, they hired the most famous criminal attorney of his generation, Clarence Darrow, to represent them. Darrow, well past his prime at seventy-five, badly needed the money and, almost as badly, wanted to travel to the oasis of Hawaii. He was bothered though. A leader of the downtrodden, a member of the American Civil Liberties Union and a strong supporter of the NAACP, he would have felt far more comfortable defending the earlier falsely-accused rapists. He swallowed hard, took his hefty legal fee and set about defending the seemingly indefensible. The state had a dead body surrounded by the defendants and a confession made in a newspaper.

The trial started on April 4, 1932. While Darrow would have preferred an all-white jury, sympathetic to the plight of their fellow white citizens, he had to settle for seven white males being joined by three men of Chinese heritage and two of Hawaiian. Women were not allowed to serve.

In addition to journalists flocking in to report on the spectacle, the public clamored to attend. Many camped out early; the wealthy sent servants to wait on line. Tickets were distributed, which, if sold, commanded a hefty price.

At trial, John Kelley, the nattily-attired prosecutor, dressed in a white tropical suit, presented an overpowering case of guilt to the jury, finishing with Kahahawai's tearful and highly sympathetic mother. It was clear that the defendants had killed Joe. Indeed, Darrow would later so acknowledge in his memoirs. "All the attorneys for the prosecution, and those for the defense, as well as the judge, knew that legally my clients were guilty of murder."

But Darrow was a master and countered the avalanche of evidence by arguing that while Thomas was indeed the killer, he blacked out in a fit of rage when the decedent confessed to the rape and unknowingly shot the rapist. In other words, he was driven temporarily insane.

The prosecution contended that whoever killed Kahahawai was irrelevant as all of the defendants acted jointly, in concert and together, and were thus all guilty of his murder. Darrow disagreed, arguing that if the person who pulled the trigger was not guilty by reason of insanity, then all the defendants should go free as they could neither share that insane intent nor even be aware of what an insane person would do. Tommie, a hardworking sailor serving his nation, Darrow argued, was himself worthy of great sympathy. A man facing the criminal who brutalized his wife.

Keeping with that theme, Darrow called Tommie as his first witness and set about characterizing the actors, Thalia versus Kahahawai; the former virtuous and innocent, the latter dark and evil. Darrow carefully guided an, at times, choked up witness into describing his anguish over Thalia's injuries and victimization, and of how he participated in kidnapping Kahahawai to get an admission. Tommie testified that Kahahawai initially steadfastly denied the crime, confessing only after held at gunpoint. "Yes, we done it," Kahahawai told the group. After that, blind rage overcame him and he remembered nothing thereafter, not even pulling the trigger. He came out of his fog when he was arrested.

After a calling a series of minor witnesses, Darrow continued on his main attack. Two psychiatrists, expert witnesses, from the mainland testified that the agony and stress of Thalia's ordeal caused a chemical reaction in her husband that made him lose control. The media reacted sympathetically to the ploy, given, among other things, the military standing of the accused and the need to uphold the honor of American women everywhere.

As a well-prepared attorney—and Darrow was always the best—he could not envision what would transpire next. Disaster.

He called Thalia Massie as his final witness. Her appearance was highly anticipated and would close out the trial. Spectators strained to catch a glimpse of the silent star at the center of the controversy; the sun around whom all others revolved. On this day she was dressed modestly with her hair tied back. As she demurely took the stand and recounted her horrifying ordeal, all sound left the courtroom as her quiet agony rang out. She told of the loving care she received from her supportive husband. Some spectators wept as she told her compelling story. Grace openly cried.

On cross examination, after prosecutor Kelley reiterated the affectionate state of her marriage, he dramatically confronted her with a questionnaire she had earlier filled out when seeing a psychiatrist. That the paper should never have been used due to the confidentiality of the patient-doctor relationship did not deter the prosecutor, who had received it from a sympathetic colleague of the psychiatrist who had treated Thalia. The document, which revealed a highly strained relationship, directly contradicted her in-court assessment of the state of the marriage.

Instantaneously Thalia's demeanor on the stand dramatically changed. It was as if turning a switch, causing a lit room to be plunged into darkness. She became enraged, turning from the sweet witness to a shrew. She shrieked, "Where did you get this?" after Kelley handed the paper to her. Before the startled prosecutor could react, she ripped it to pieces, yelling all the while. Her supporters yelled their approval and applauded her actions. The judge called for order.

The prosecutor closed by thanking Thalia for showing her true colors. As she left the stand, she collapsed into the arms of her husband, crying, "What right has he got the say that I don't love you?"

The theatrics were a fitting end to what would become Hawaii's most famous criminal trial. During closing arguments, Kelley attacked Darrow's use of the insanity defense and reminded jurors of the plain facts surrounding Kahahawai's slaying. Darrow rose to the challenge, speaking for four hours.

In an exposition of oratorical brilliance that marked his career, Darrow argued that Thalia's brutal rape had tortured the Massie family enough, and that finding the defendants guilty of murder would do no good. Even if the jurors didn't believe the insanity defense, Darrow argued, casting off the defendants to prison for the rest of their lives would be pointless.

With speculations abounding, the jury returned its verdict on April 29th. Guilty. Of manslaughter. The killing was not premeditated. Darrow and his clients, so confident of an

Those who unjustly killed in the name of honor—Edward Lord, Albert Jones, Mrs. Granville Fortescue, Thalia Massie, and Thomas Massie, 1932. (*Library of Congress, NYWT&S gift*)

acquittal, were stunned, as were those who were convinced that the facts demanded a murder conviction. The sentence awaiting each defendant—ten years.

Darrow, having suffered for many what would have been a devastating loss, set to rendering it but a momentary setback. Sensing the pressure from all sides to put the entire incident behind, he marshaled his substantial forces. Calls were made to military strongmen, powerful local businessmen and members of Congress, which cried for marital law to tame a wild frontier. Caving to the pressure, Governor Lawrence Judd commuted the sentences of the four killers from ten years to one hour, to be served in the governor's office. To totally end the affair, the rape charges against Horace Ida and the other three remaining and still living defendants were dropped.

Days later, the entire group—Thalia and Tommie, mother Grace and the two other sailors Jones and Lord, along with lawyer Darrow—left the island for good. They were treated to a hero's welcome when they arrived home.

* * *

Later that year, on prosecutor Kelley's recommendation, Governor Judd hired the prominent Pinkerton Detective Agency to conduct an independent investigation into Thalia's original rape claims. After three months of thorough fieldwork, the agency concluded that Thalia was not only never raped, but that the five men had no opportunity to even commit the crimes alleged.

Epilogue

Thalia's accusations and the subsequent honor killing of Joe Kahahawai played a pivotal role in reshaping race relations on the islands and changing the political landscape. In the immediate aftermath, minorities of various backgrounds coalesced to overthrow the ruling oligarchy.

As for Thalia and her husband, they divorced shortly thereafter. Both suffered significant mental health problems. Tommie suffered a breakdown in 1940 and was discharged from the service. He worked a series of random jobs before dying in 1987 just before his eighty-second birthday. Thalia, after numerous suicide attempts, finally succeeded in 1963, dying at fifty-two due to an overdose of barbiturates in Florida. Her mother, the stately Grace continued her luxurious and active lifestyle until dying in 1979 at age ninety-five.

One of the sailors who participated in the killing, Deacon Jones, later claimed that it was he, not Tommie, who pulled the trigger. As for the four accused rapists—Horace Ida, Benny Ahakuelo, David Takai, and Henry Chang—they lived quiet lives, never publicly speaking of the matter other than a brief interview that Ahakuelo gave to a journalist. For them, the tumultuous ordeal was perhaps better left undisturbed, buried deep in the rich Hawaiian soil along with the remains of their murdered friend Joe Kahahawai.

Tidbits

Joe Kahahawai was born in rural Maui in 1909. He earned a football scholarship to a Catholic preparatory school but never graduated and worked odd jobs because of the Great Depression. He also boxed professionally.

Grace Hubbard Fortescue married Army Major Granville "Roly" Fortescue, a first cousin of President Theodore Roosevelt. She was the granddaughter of Gardiner Greene Hubbard, the first president of the National Geographic Society. Grace's father, Charles John Bell, was a first cousin of inventor Alexander Graham Bell, credited with inventing the telephone.

Clarence Darrow also defended John T. Scopes in the Scopes "Monkey" Trial and teenage killers Leopold and Loeb, discussed in Chapter 13.

The report that discredited Thalia's rape claim was produced by the Pinkerton National Detective Agency (also featured in Chapter 20), which is said to have coined the term "private eye." The final report was almost three hundred pages. It concluded: "It is impossible to escape the conviction that the kidnapping and assault was not caused by those accused." The Pinkerton report was initially suppressed by authorities, but the results of the investigation were leaked to the press.

Our Next Tale

Why do we lie? A cheating spouse. A company treasurer with his hand in the till. A mechanic who negligently worked on the brakes of a car, which got into an accident as a result. When questioned and confronted, more lies.

Our government officials are often no different. When caught in an embarrassing or illegal position, fabrications are often the response. While the reasons for such actions are often quite understandable, they are invariably wrong. In many cases, the cover-up grows to be far worse than the earlier transgression. Watergate comes to mind.

In our next chapter, a military airplane, in 1948, flew a secret mission. It crashed. Nine people died. To cover up its malfeasance, the newly created Air Force, in a time of national crisis, lied about its causes. Officials looked at a document and then lied about what they had read; first to a federal district court judge, then a panel of judges sitting on the Court of Appeals, and then to the United States Supreme Court, which bought the fabrication and made a seminal ruling felt to this very day. Fifty years later, given the opportunity to right a wrong, the court passed.

29

The Bastard Birth of the State Secrets Privilege

As Judy sat at her computer, she typed in the words describing the military airplane crash that killed the father she never knew. Given that it had been more than a half-century since the tragedy, she did not expect to find much. Seconds after pushing the button sending her request into the black hole of the web universe, she leaned back, waiting with trepidation, for the inevitable negative response. She was thus shocked when a website advertising access to all military airplane accident reports from 1918 to 1955 popped up.

Barely able to contain her excitement, she contacted the website, explaining what she was asking for. After a bit of rifling through his small, musty, and overcrowded office, Mike Stowe, who loved everything that flew for the military, located the document, and informed Judy that for sixty-three dollars, she could have a copy of the lengthy 220-page report and the fifteen photographs accompanying it.

When the package arrived, Judy anxiously embraced it, barely believing that what she was holding had fifty years earlier been marked Top Secret. Maybe now, answers to questions that had gnawed at her family would emerge from the darkness.

★ ★ ★

With World War II raging, intense pressure existed at every level to build an effective bomber. If corners had to be cut, so be it due to the demands of combat. With B-29s rolling off of the assembly lines, it became readily apparent that their engines were a disaster, which everyone, save perhaps the public, knew. Simply, the engines frequently overheated and caught fire. Worse, the magnesium-constructed crankcases, which made the planes faster and lighter, were highly flammable. While steps were taken to contain the problem, seemingly nothing worked.

Even after B-29s dropped two atomic bombs on Japan, the problems persisted. So too the urgency. With one world war ended, another, led by Soviet Union, appeared to be on the nearby horizon. To help meet the perceived threat, Project Banshee—to create long-range guided missiles—came into being.

For a very young Bob Reynolds, the opportunity to work on the project was a challenging Godsend. Having recently graduated from Purdue University with a degree in mechanical engineering, the twenty-one-year-old found a job with RCA. He also met and married, after a three-month long courtship, eighteen-year-old Patricia of Indianapolis. Soon RCA relocated the two to Florida, where Al Palya, the project manager awaited.

Palya, born in 1907, possessed a number of unique and often unrelated talents, which explains why it took him longer than usual to graduate from college. He played in bands and sang, made travel films of national parks, photographed, did carpentry, and knew Morse code. He courted his future wife, Elizabeth, for three years before marrying her in 1937. In time, as he worked himself up the RCA ladder, two sons and a daughter were born. Judy was born on August 16, 1948. Her father Al would die seven weeks later.

* * *

The B-29s were again being modified and repaired to accommodate Project Banshee. Plane number 45-21866 was tended to on June 19, 1947. The maintenance report, among other things, indicated "Shields not installed." No reason was given for not installing heat shields that the Air Force mandated. Perhaps nothing was done because nothing could be as the B-29 was out of production and spare parts were hard to come by.

Five days later when the plane took off, it unsurprisingly immediately suffered serious problems, so much so that the plane had to return to the base it had just left twenty minutes earlier. The aircraft was inspected and found unfit to fly, with three of the four engines basically inoperable. Repair was estimated to take six weeks. It would take a lot longer. And never be successfully completed.

* * *

At 1:20 pm on October 6, 1948, thirteen men entered B-29 number 45-21866, to test whether the system developed by Al Palya and his team could successfully guide an unmanned missile

A Boeing B-29 Super Fortress, a flying coffin for many.

to a target. As the plane departed Robins Air Force Base in Georgia and headed to Orlando, Florida, one wonders what those on-board were thinking. For some, it was yet another in a long line of mundane assignments; for others, excitement, as significant scientific and military breakthroughs were potentially at hand. That trouble with the aircraft and crew loomed was probably not a thought on their collective minds.

The plane a week earlier had again been deemed unfit to fly. Heat shields were still lacking. The crew, in violation of regulations, barely knew each other. Captain Ralph Erwin had neither flown before with his co-pilot, Captain Herbert Moore, Jr., nor the flight engineer, Sergeant Earl Murrhee. For unclear reasons, the flight, which was scheduled to depart at 8:30 that morning, had been delayed several hours.

When the plane finally lifted off, those in it tended to their specific jobs, giving little thought as to how they came to be there. Al Palya wasn't even supposed to be on the flight but went along for morale purposes. A similar decision had been made by his partner Walter Frick, who at the last minute was called away on other business. Bob Reynolds, who with his wife Patty, had already leased an apartment in New Jersey in anticipation of a transfer there, replaced him. Thirty-four-year-old civilian engineer-physicist William Brauner, of Pennsylvania's Franklin Institute, an RCA sub-contractor, had never before even been on a B-29. Given his background as a resistance fighter in his native Austria, which he fled in 1938 with the Nazis hot in pursuit, fear was an emotion probably lacking. He too went to Purdue University where he met his future wife Phyllis, a chemistry instructor, who had earlier earned a master's degree from Wellesley College. The father of four-year-old Susan with another baby on the way, Bill was proud of his service to his new nation, which he loved and admired.

Ten others joined Palya, Reynolds and Brauner, including two other civilian engineers, Eugene Mechler, also of the Franklin Institute, and Richard Cox, who worked for the Air Force. Shortly, nine of the thirteen would be dead.

* * *

Forty minutes into the flight, as the plane cruised to 18,000 feet over Waycross, Georgia, engine #1 suddenly failed. Captain Erwin, who had flown B-29s during the war and was familiar with its many shortcomings, continued to guide the plane upward, concerned, but confident of its three remaining engines. Deciding to shut down #1, engine #4 was accidentally shut down. While doing so, a smoldering #1 burst into flames. Engine #2 started to lose power. Fire leaped across the left wing. Parachutes were donned. As the plane started to plummet, Erwin shouted, "Stand by to abandon ship!" With that, he opened the bomb-bay doors, which catastrophically braked the plane causing it to lose power such that it could no longer fly. As air barreled through the opening, centrifugal forces slapped the crew into paralysis. Clawing away at the gravity pinning them down, the men scrambled to bail out. Four made it. The plane violently tumbled, shedding its parts as it flew faster and faster to the earth beneath it. Engines fell away, a wing ripped off. Finally a thunderous clap. And oblivion.

* * *

Patty Reynolds, aged twenty, was now a widow; a pregnant Phyllis Brauner was left with her four-year-old daughter; Betty Palya now had to raise three young children, including seven-week-old Judy.

The military honored its dead and commended the men on lives lost for a grateful nation. And everything went back to normal. Except for the widows, whose finances mirrored that of the falling plane. They had little money. And lots of questions that were not being answered. It was almost unpatriotic to sue the government, but given their predicament they did just that. And the attorney who agreed to handle their suit was as atypical as the plaintiffs themselves. Charles Biddle and his mainline, white-shoed law firm represented the wealthy, powerful and privileged, which was of no surprise given the significance of the Biddle family in settling Philadelphia and guiding the nation's currency in its infancy. In taking the case, Biddle thought he was lending a hand to three young widows. Little did he realize that his undertaking would have an everlasting effect on the legal history of the country, still strong today.

*   *   *

In the year following the crash, twelve other B-29s went down, killing dozens, and causing the remaining aircrafts to be grounded. Despite this, and the knowledge of the many problems with the planes, the government, when sued, claimed that it had not been negligent. With suit in federal district court came discovery, and the plaintiffs, who had no idea why the plane crashed, sought a copy of the Air Force's official accident investigation report. In response, the Government argued that the air craft had been engaged in "a highly secret mission" and the release of the crash report, even to a judge privately viewing it, would jeopardize our nation's security.

Judge William H. Kirkpatrick did not buy the government's argument and ordered the production of the report, which was a brave stance given, in the words of President Harry S. Truman, the "wave of hysteria" engulfing America. Communism was on the march. Over a short period, China had been overrun and conquered; East Germany fell; Hungary elected a Communist government; eight Communist countries allied themselves in what would become the Warsaw Pact; and, most terrifying, the Soviet Union had THE BOMB. Against this backdrop, the case proceeded through the courts.

The government responded with a motion for rehearing, forcibly arguing that the release of the report would not only be adverse to the public interest, but would indeed hamper "national security, flying safety, and the development of highly technical and secret military equipment." The judge answered by saying, let me, and me alone, see the report to determine whether those concerns are legitimate. The government refused and, after another hearing, the judge found for the plaintiffs and ordered damages in the amount of $225,000 (somewhat under two million dollars today). The widows had won. The victory would be short-lived.

*   *   *

The Court of Appeals agreed with Judge Kirkpatrick's ruling and observed that "[i]t is but a small step to assert a privilege against any disclosure of records merely because they might prove embarrassing to government officers." By allowing judges to privately review the materials, all were protected as "judges may be depended upon to protect with the greatest of care the public interest in preventing the disclosure of matters which may fairly be characterized as privileged."

The United States Supreme Court, before which the case landed upon the government's appeal, had a markedly different response, recognizing that the government, in "a time of vigorous preparation for national defense," had a compelling interest in not turning over a report that "certainly [...] would contain references to the secret electronic equipment which was the primary concern of the mission." Military secrets could not be divulged, even alone to a judge, and if, as a result, three widows could not ascertain the cause of the crash that killed their husbands, that was the price to be paid to protect America's citizens from its many enemies around the world.

And thus, the official birth of the state secrets privilege.

Epilogue

On September 14, 1950, the accident report, and other supporting materials, came up for a routine classification review. The Air Force reduced its classification from top-level Secret to third-level Restricted. No one involved in the case learned of the change.

Since the time of its release in 1953, the Reynolds decision has been successfully cited hundreds of times to support the government's claim of national security, most recently in Guantanamo Bay. That judges were often forced by Reynolds to fly blind, attempting to evaluate claims of the privilege without being allowed to privately review the evidence at issue, was, once again, the high price of security.

In time the privilege expanded, ultimately embracing, in 1978, the mosaic theory wherein the DC Circuit Court of Appeals upheld the government's claim of privilege as to documents sought by Vietnam War protestors who had been subjected to surveillance and wiretapping. As intelligence gathering, the Court reasoned, "is more akin to the construction of a mosaic than it is to the management of a cloak and dagger affair" even seemingly innocuous bits and pieces of information may be classified.

While the Reynolds case ultimately settled for $170,000—less than the original judgment—the families of the victims never knew the cause of the crash. Until over fifty years later when Judy Palya Loether ripped open the envelope containing the cherished report.

This is what she discovered—heat shields never installed, faulty engine design, a plane unfit to fly, several recurring maintenance problems improperly addressed, combustible coverings, pilot errors, and insufficient training. As for national security, it contained nothing.

* * *

The families returned to the nation's highest court, asking it to acknowledge that facts were wrongfully withheld and seeking to correct those errors. The request was denied. The family then unsuccessfully filed a new action in federal court; an adverse decision there was again upheld by the Supreme Court in 2006. That same year, the American Bar Association adopted a resolution calling on Congress to regulate the state secrets doctrine. Testimony before the ABA delegates revealed that "The Reynolds decision was based on a lie that took five decades to unravel."

Tidbits

In 1952, Betty Palya married Bill Sacker, a butcher who served with the Marines during WWII and had a baby girl, Jeannie, in 1954. Patty Reynolds, at twenty-two, also remarried, had three children and led a busy and productive life. Phyllis, with her two children returned to Massachusetts, earned a PhD in chemistry at Boston University and taught for over three decades at Simmons College. Her highly distinguished career culminated with the creation of both the Phyllis A. Brauner Memorial Lecture and the Phyllis A. Brauner (chemistry) Memorial Book Prize. Having never remarried, she died, at eighty-four, in 1990, the same year that eighty-eight-year-old Betty also passed on.

Of the five civilians, two survived the crash—Richard Cox, who as an employee of the government could not sue, and Eugene Mechler, who despite having not been briefed on exiting the plane during an emergency, somehow found his way out.

The Air Force officially came into existence on September 18, 1947. Prior to that it had been the Army Air Forces.

The origin of the state secrets privilege is often traced back to the Aaron Burr treason trial of 1807 wherein Burr sought to gain access to a letter sent by a general to President Jefferson.

Adding to the tension at the time of the original suit was the start of Senator Joseph McCarthy's witch hunt for communists in the government.

Our Final Tale

There is perhaps no greater sin in our criminal justice system than convicting an innocent man. For murder no less. In a tale that many believe was the inspiration for the television show and movie *The Fugitive*, about an innocent Dr. Richard Kimble being wrongfully convicted of murder, we examine his true life counterpart and a rabid press intent on seeing that "justice" was done. As with Dolly Mapp, the case ultimately landed in the United States Supreme Court, which issued yet another landmark decision, still in force to this day. Sadly, the man at the center of all of the attention was destroyed in the process.

30

Who Whacked the Doctor's Wife?

The headline of the Cleveland Press wailed: "WHY ISN'T SAM SHEPPARD IN JAIL?" After all, everyone knew he was guilty. Even the judge, before the trial started, confided to a newspaper reporter that Sheppard was "guilty as hell. There's no question about it." The police even had a motive—Sheppard's longtime affair with his fetching assistant, the twenty-four-year-old Susan Hayes, who worked with him at the hospital.

Sheppard had always been a pillar of his community—the hometown football, basketball, and track star and elected class president who married his high school cheerleading sweetheart, became a doctor, and joined the family business. That he steadfastly maintained his innocence, gave numerous statements to the police, with whom he cooperated, and testified at length at the inquest was of no moment. Before his eyes, the entire town slowly turned against him.

✳ ✳ ✳

Saturday, July 3, 1954. A brutal day for the handsome and athletic Dr. Sam, as he was affectionately known by his many patients. Earlier that day, a child had been struck by a truck and rushed to the 110-bed hospital founded and operated by the Sheppard family. Despite Sam's efforts, the boy died, leaving Sheppard to console the boy's furious and distraught parents. Later on, Sheppard had to return to the hospital to check on yet another patient.

By the end of the long day, the thirty-year-old physician couldn't wait to be with his pregnant wife and their adorable seven-year-old son, Chip, in their lavish lakefront home. To celebrate the holiday, that evening would be spent in the company of a few close friends, soothed in food and cocktails liberally provided. So comfortable with the company or, perhaps indicative of yet another difficult and trying day, Sheppard dozed off on the living couch after his guests left.

Marilyn's screams cut through Sam's sleep, jolting him awake. He sprinted upstairs toward the sound, charging into their dimly lit bedroom. He managed to glimpse a large form wearing a white top before being struck from behind and knocked out. He never saw it coming.

Groggily, he came to, sprawled out on the floor where he had landed. The metallic tinge of blood in the air hit him. His eyes scanned the hazy room, falling upon the pale, lifeless body of his wife. Fearing for the safety of his son, he ran to his bedroom and saw that he was safe. At that moment, he heard a sound from downstairs. Bolting back down the stairs, he saw the silhouette of a "bushy-haired" man by the living room windows facing Lake Erie. He gave chase, pursuing the intruder down the many wooden steps and confronted him on the darkened beach. The two grappled in the sand, and once again, Sheppard received a blow to the head, rendering him unconscious.

Upon awakening, he found himself face down. Curiously, his shirt was missing and his lower body was in the water. Light seeped through the haze of dawn. As Sheppard struggled to his feet, pain shot throughout his body. Hobbling back to his house, he called his neighbor Spencer Houk, who was both the mayor and butcher of their small suburban Cleveland town. Sam was shouting through the phone, his words hitting the drowsy Houk like a cold gust of air. "My God, Spen, get over here quick! I think they've killed Marilyn." Hearing Sheppard's panicked words, Houk rushed over with his wife Esther.

They arrived to find Sheppard slumped over in a chair. Esther rushed upstairs to check on Marilyn. A grisly scene greeted her. The bedroom was painted red. Marilyn lay on one of the two twin beds, the one closest to the door, a halo of blood surrounding her head. Her pajama bottoms were dangling from one leg around her knee exposing her genital area while her gown was pushed up around her neck revealing her breasts. Marilyn's face was unidentifiable, a mass of matted hair and blood. Blood splattered the walls behind the bed and the closet door, further evidence of the brutal attack, a clear overkill. Nearby, Sam's medical bag lay overturned on the floor, its contents spilled out haphazardly.

Downstairs, evidence of an attempted burglary scattered the rooms. Sheppard's trophies had been smashed. His desk drawers were open and the contents suspiciously arranged in piles on the floor. It seemed as if they were meant to give the impression of a burglary, yet the scene lacked the disheveled quality of a true ransack, and upon closer inspection, nothing had been taken.

As for Sam, his injuries, as reported by his family's hospital, were also serious. He was in shock after the incident, suffering a swollen eye, a cracked vertebra, a concession, and possible contusion to his spinal cord. Two of his teeth were slightly chipped. For the rest of the summer, he would wear a neck brace.

Despite his many injuries, and lacking any marks to indicate a struggle with his wife, Sheppard was the immediate and sole suspect—the only one on the scene, a staged burglary, and a womanizer. A clear case of domestic violence. Sam was pressured at the outset to confess. So sure of his guilt, the police seemingly performed a rather rudimentary examination of the house: fingerprints were insufficiently taken; a trail of blood and other forensic evidence were not properly tested; and the crime scene was left unsecured, allowing reporters to walk around willy-nilly. One even stole family pictures to run in the newspaper the next day. The autopsy, as many argued, was performed in a manner that suggested the crime had already been solved.

Marilyn had suffered thirty-five wounds to her face and body. The autopsy revealed fifteen crescent-shaped lacerations on her skull, some exposing bone. Her nose was shattered and parts of her front teeth had been ripped away. The autopsy further revealed that, while her skull had been cracked, none of the blows were powerful enough to push bone into her brain. She had wounds to her left hand and wrist. A fingernail was torn off and a finger on her right hand was broken. She obviously put up a valiant fight. Her cause of death was asphyxiation, from choking on her own blood.

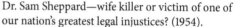

Dr. Sam Sheppard—wife killer or victim of one of our nation's greatest legal injustices? (1954).

Coroner Gerber would testify at trial that Marilyn died around 3:00 a.m., severely damaging Sheppard's account of the murder. As Mayor Houk was not contacted until 5:45, nearly three hours later, the police surmised that Sheppard had plenty of time to destroy the evidence, including his missing blood-covered t-shirt. The assistant coroner, who had actually performed the autopsy, opined in his report, however, that the time of death was more likely to have occurred between 4:30 and 4:45 a.m. Unfortunately, the report and the time estimation were buried, perhaps to hide an unhelpful fact damaging to the state's case. So well hidden the report that it took nearly half a century to surface.

*   *   *

As the police marshaled the evidence, the press, which initially had been sympathetic to Sheppard, started to beat the drum for his being charged. With each passing day the pressure intensified. As the judge and prosecutor were both running for office, both felt the heat. At all junctures, the press had a voice and front row seat to all of the proceedings, as well as access to the witnesses. When an editorial demanded to know why an inquest had not been held, one was called within twenty-four hours. The inquest was broadcast live from the high school gymnasium over the course of three days. While Sheppard's attorney, William Corrigan, was allowed to be present, he wasn't permitted to participate. When he attempted to innocently intercede, he was forcibly ejected from the proceeding to the loud cheers of the partisan crowd. Sheppard testified and foolishly denied that he and Susan Hayes had engaged in an affair.

Finally, on the Friday evening of July 30th, at 10:30 p.m., Sheppard was arrested and hustled off to court for his arraignment. By the time he showed up, everyone—reporters, newscasters and photographers, as well as hundreds of spectators—had heard of the main event and stood

Susan Hayes, the other woman, whom Sheppard foolishly lied about. (*Special Collections, Michael Schwartz Library, Cleveland State University*)

outside the court, awaiting the arrival of the town's notorious celebrity. Night became day with the explosion of flashbulbs and blinding klieg lights when the star appeared. The suspect, having been denied a temporary delay for his counsel to arrive, was quickly arraigned. In short order, his case was presented to the grand jury, which formally charged him with first degree murder. The state announced that it would be seeking the death penalty.

There was no lull leading up to the trial in October, just a few weeks prior to the election involving the judge and prosecutor. Meanwhile, the press, still in control of the proceedings, commanded a birds-eye view. Reporters were given the front three rows in the courtroom. The families of the defendant and victim were relegated to the last row. Every room in the courthouse had been taken over by the media.

The jurors were neither sequestered nor shielded, their names and addresses revealed to the public at large. Over the course of the nine-week trial, jurors and parties alike were attacked by an onslaught of shouting reporters at the courthouse doors. The daily proceedings, including testimony that had been excluded from the court record, were printed verbatim in the newspapers, to which the jurors had ready access.

State's spokesmen were allowed to publicly refute what the defense brought up at trial and comment generally on the proceedings. When Sheppard took the stand, testifying to the mistreatment he received at the hands of the homicide detectives, Captain Kerr of the Homicide Bureau, who never even testified at the trial, publicly denounced Sheppard to reporters. The following day, a newspaper headline blared: "Kerr Called Dr. Sam a Bare-faced Liar." Rumors and innuendo were often reported as fact. Even New York City turned its focus on the trial, broadcasting fictitious and damaging stories about Sam. The bombastic Walter Winchell reported on his wildly popular radio show that a female inmate, arrested for robbery, claimed that she, too, had an affair with the Lothario Sheppard and bore him a bastard child. Although many pro-Sheppard articles appeared, they paled in comparison with the conflicting view and merely added to the carnival-like atmosphere of the proceedings.

Time and again, Sheppard's attorney Corrigan unsuccessfully pled with the court to stem the on-going avalanche of negative publicity. Motions at the outset for a change of venue, or to postpone the trial until the furor quieted down, or to closely question prospective jurors for bias were routinely rejected. In one motion, in which Corrigan revealed a poll he had taken concerning the negative pretrial publicity, he was met with a rebuke from both the judge and the press, which categorized his call for jury questioning "jury tampering." His efforts to secure an unbiased jury were lambasted as "non-judicial, non-legal and nonsense." A debate on a local radio station concluded the defendant was guilty, solely because he had hired a high-powered criminal defense attorney to defend him.

After two months of trial, the case went to the jury, which finally was sequestered. The jurors, however, were allowed to make phone calls. On December 21, after five days of deliberation, Sheppard was found guilty of second-degree murder and sentenced to life imprisonment.

The verdict devastated the Sheppard family. On January 7, 1955, just weeks after the verdict, Sheppard's mother, Ethel, committed suicide. Sheppard's father, Richard, died only ten days later from cancer. In shackles, Sheppard was allowed to attend both funerals.

* * *

After years of jail and endless appeals, Sheppard's attorney, Bill Corrigan, died in 1961 at the age of seventy-five. Fortuitously, a new attorney, one destined for greatness in the courtroom, fell into Sheppard's lap. Just twenty-seven and barely out of law school, F. Lee Bailey took the case, initially charging no fee. It wound up in the Supreme Court of the United States. In a momentous decision, the Court overturned Sheppard's conviction on the sole ground of the pervasive and unfair pretrial publicity, saying "[criminal] trials are not like elections, to be won through the use of the meeting-hall, the radio, and the newspaper."

Sheppard was tried again. Bailey represented him. The trial lasted two weeks. Sheppard was found not guilty.

Who Did It?

If Sheppard didn't kill his wife, who did? Over the years, various theories have abounded. Two involve known killers.

Perhaps the strongest case is the one against Richard Eberling, the Sheppard's window washer in 1954. Born out of wedlock in 1929, Richard was an odd boy, who grew into a man "with no masculine interests." He grew up living with various foster parents, one of whom sexually abused him when he was nine-years-old. In 1959, when Eberling was arrested for larceny—he routinely robbed the houses in which he cleaned their windows—the police discovered a stolen ring belonging to Marilyn in his possession. Eberling admitted taking it two years earlier while cleaning the house of Sam's brother. Eberling also volunteered a startling

A young Richard Eberling who many believed murdered Marilyn Sheppard, 1959.

revelation—placing drops of his blood throughout the Sheppard house—explaining that he had merely cut his hand two days before the murder while working on a window. Despite this puzzling admission, nothing further was done. (Nor was anything done when a corroded flashlight, which was dented as if it had "[struck] something repeatedly," was found in Lake Erie and turned over to the police.)

In the decades to follow, Eberling moved up the social latter. Having smartly acquired land, he sold it in parcels to land developers. Through these transactions, he became a millionaire and soon traveled in richer circles. Working as an interior decorator, he found great success, ultimately working on historically preserving Cleveland's City Hall. Eberling was at heart, however, a criminal, engaging in various, often lucrative scams. Many involved getting into the good graces of wealthy, lonely, and elderly women and forging their names onto bogus wills naming him as their heir.

One such swindle involved Ethel Durkin. When she was slow in dying, Eberling murdered her. Five years later, in 1989, he was convicted of the crime. He was also a suspect in the brutal murder of Ethel's sister, Myrtle Fray, in 1962, a homicide scarily similar to Marilyns'. As Eberling confessed to an associate that he had murdered Durkin, he also indicated that he, while wearing a wig, had also killed Marilyn. In an interview shortly before his death in 1998, Eberling out of the blue stated that, "I fully expect to be convicted of killing Marilyn Sheppard."

Another theory has it that Marilyn was killed by an ex-Air Force pilot, Major James Arlon Call, who apparently had been visiting his sister in the Cleveland area at the time of the murder. A picture discovered after the homicide depicts Marilyn speaking with someone who looked similar to Call at a car race. Several witnesses claimed to have seen a "bushy haired" man resembling Call in the neighborhood on the day before the murder near the Sheppards' residence. In August 1954, while Call was hiding in the Adirondack range in New York after

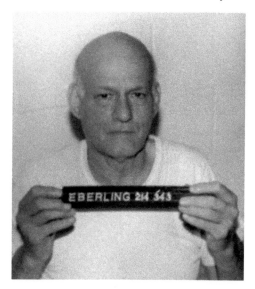

Eberling, years later, still in jail for other crimes and still protesting his innocence.

having gone AWOL from the military, he fired on officers who had come to investigate a break-in at the cabin in which Call sought refuge. One officer was killed and two wounded. Call escaped, finally captured one hundred days later in Reno, Nevada. Despite suspicions that Call might have murdered Marilyn, the lead was never pursued. Call died in 1974.

Perhaps the least likely scenario was the one successfully put forth by Sheppard's attorney, F. Lee Bailey, which implicated the very next door neighbors whom Sheppard first turned to after he staggered back to his house from the lake. The wily attorney borrowed the theory from a book written shortly after the first trial, which suggested that Marilyn's murder involved two people. Bailey theorized that Marilyn Sheppard and Spencer Houk were having an affair. After Sam fell asleep on July 3rd, Houk returned for a sexual tryst. Marilyn was known to leave a particular upstairs light on when Sam was not at home. On this night the light was on even though Sam was there. The theory continues that an enraged Esther Houk, aware of the affair, confronted them and proceeded to bludgeon Marilyn with a heavy duty flashlight. A crime scene investigator confirmed that Marilyn had been struck numerous times with a blunt object by someone of less than average strength. Bailey further alleged that Spencer struck Sam as he entered the room. This threadbare story, however, fails to account for the fact that Houk was injury-free despite Marilyn having fought her attacker, perhaps even biting him. Indeed, one reason Sam was ultimately exonerated was due to his not suffering such wounds. Furthermore, this notion does not account for the lake struggle, in which Sam described the assailant as solid and strong. Spencer, who walked with a limp, unlikely possessed the agility to even run to the beach.

Lastly, other speculations opine that Marilyn was the victim of a sexual attack. Given the viciousness of the crime, her vain struggle, and her disheveled clothing, it's surprising that rape was never as seriously considered at the outset as it should have been. One could easily envision an intruder breaking into the house and trying to rape her. When she resisted, she was killed.

Epilogue

A host of television shows and movies flowed from the Sheppard affair. Perhaps the most famous were the 1960s television show, *The Fugitive*, and the 1993 hit movie by the same name. The movie featured Harrison Ford playing the convicted Dr. Richard Kimble, who after his escape en route to prison, searched for the one-armed man who had truly murdered his wife. While awaiting his retrial, and out on bail, in 1964, the real Dr. Sheppard married his second wife, Arianne Tebbenjohanns, a wealthy and bored, German blond bombshell who had corresponded with him while he was in jail. The press had a field day with the outspoken Fraulein, especially when it was revealed that she was the sister-in-law of the late Joseph Goebbels, the notorious propaganda minister under Adolph Hitler. That Ariane was not a Nazi and had little to do with Goebbels was occasionally lost in the telling of the story. The marriage, like the Third Reich, lasted a short time. They were divorced in 1968, Ariane revealing that she greatly feared her husband.

Sheppard's attempt to return to medicine was short-lived. His skills having deteriorated, he quickly abandoned the profession. His behavior became erratic as he turned to alcohol and drugs. In 1969, he remarried, this time to twenty-year-old hairdresser Colleen Strickland. Her father, George, was in the wrestling business and convinced Sam to join him. He did, and performed under the ring name of Sam "the Killer" Sheppard.

A heavy drinker and broken man estranged from his family, Sam Sheppard died a year later, on April 6, 1970, of liver failure. He was forty-six.

The 3 Wives of Sheppard—the murdered Marilyn's wedding picture of 1945; Ariane Tebbenjohanns, whose half-sister was married to Nazi propaganda chief Joseph Goebbels; and his last wife, Colleen Strickland, the young daughter of his wrestling partner. (*Corbis*)

Tidbits

In 1999, Sheppard's son Chip unsuccessfully sued the state of Ohio claiming that his father had been wrongfully convicted. After a ten-week trial, an eight person jury quickly found for the state, which contended that Sheppard was the most logical suspect in that he was upset that his wife was pregnant, wanted to continue having affairs, feared the ramifications of divorce and killed to get out of the marriage (shades of Bathsheba Spooner and Adolph Luetgert).

Bill James, in his book, *Popular Crime: Reflections on the Celebration of Violence*, surmises that Eberling was the killer, but acted at the behest of Sheppard.

Sheppard was tried in the same courtroom as Dolly Mapp.

In a twist that the very perverse Dr. H. H. Holmes might well have appreciated, Sheppard's middle name was Holmes.

In 1963, Marilyn Sheppard's father also committed suicide.

The family-owned hospital in which Sam worked was originally built about a half-century before by a self-made millionaire, Washington Lawrence, who had been orphaned at an early age. The mansion in which his family lived carried with it a fair share of intrigue—a lavish wedding, a tragic elevator accident and a murder scandal, arising out of, again like H. H. Holmes, an insurance scam. Turned into condos in the 1980s, ghosts of Lawrence, as well as a former hospital resident, have allegedly been seen in the facility.

In many of our tales, pretrial publicity perversely affected the proceedings. As the court declared, "In this atmosphere of a 'Roman Holiday' for the news media, Sam Sheppard stood trial for his life." Such helter-skelter, free-for-all interference from the press was common. Adolph Luetgert, while clearly guilty, was just as clearly declared so by the media prior to his trial. Theoretically even worse, the reporters in cases we have examined, William Desmond Taylor for instance, often rummaged through the crime scene doing who knows what. Fortunately, such practices today have been curtailed.

Acknowledgements

I am indebted to the many people who assisted me in completing this book. A huge amount of research was required and I cannot begin to repay the many research assistants who helped along the way: Kevin Manganaro, Amal Bala, Ariella Gragg, Kate Hart, Ben Piper, Gina Plata-Nino, Dustin Dow, Nathan Band, Tim Ferriter, Sarah McDougall, Matt O'Connor, Lindsay Smith, Jamie Wells, Marianne Salza, Patty Ramirez, Kelli Untiedt, Alan Guichard, Jennifer McGann, Mark McMahon, Nathan Breen, Alvin Kwong, Jackson LaVelle, Shannon Dale, Sydney Turnbull, Jessica Gordon, Kerry Ellard and Cory Lewis.

Others helped by sharing their incredible knowledge on certain of the characters I wrote about. They include Bruce Long, who knows more about William Desmond Taylor than anyone; Jonathan Eig, an expert on Al Capone and Eddie O'Hare; and Stephen Puleo for his insight on writing non-fiction.

Thanks also to Alan Sutton and Heather Martino of Fonthill Media; Esmond Harmsworth of Zachary Shuster Harmsworth; my sister Sue Kantrowitz and Jeff Garmel of WGHB; Wendy Murphy; Fran Fecteau; Suzanne Hoey of the Worcester County Law Library Trust; Jane Winton (Curator) and Tom Blake of the Boston Public Library); Christine Ogsbury of the *Village Voice*; Miranda Sarjeant of Corbis; Vern Morrison of Cleveland State University; and, most of all, my wonderful family, Marianne, Matt, Sara and Laura.

And, lastly, thanks to all of my colleagues and my other lunch friends—Steve, Joe, Kevin, Bob, Paula, Peter, Jen, Cat, Carol, Krista, Gerry, John and Jon, Nick and Nicki, Martin, James, Tim, Mike, George, Pat, Scott, Bill, and Mitch—who make coming to work in Boston so enjoyable.

To those I have inadvertently missed, I apologize.

Sources

Needless to say, this work is not one of scholarly, intricate, and intimate research. Indeed, nearly all of the sources utilized were secondary in nature. Typically, each chapter is based upon one or so primary sources with multiple additional sources used to address different aspects of the story. As many websites typically go offline or change addresses, and in the interest of space and the realization that most readers have little concern with a multiple and lengthy list, I have not included the dozens used. A full compilation, however, is available on my website, www.rmarckantrowitz.com. One admittedly quite helpful site—Wikipedia—was utilized to confirm dates of birth, locations, personalities, backgrounds, etc.

Chapter 1 (White-Nesbitt-Thaw)
Baker, Paul: *Stanny: The Gilded Life of Stanford White* (Free Press 1989).
Editors of Life (eds.): *The Most Notorious Crimes in American History* (Life Books 2007).
Langford, Gerald: *The Murder of Stanford White* (Bobbs-Merrill Company 1962).

Chapter 2 (Arbuckle)
Edmonds, Andy: *Frame Up: The Untold Story of Roscoe "Fatty" Arbuckle* (William & Morrow Co. 1991).

Chapter 3 (Taylor)
Giroux, Robert: *A Deed of Death: The Story of the Unsolved Murder of Hollywood Director William Desmond Taylor* (Knopf 1990).
King, Ed: "I Know Who Killed Desmond Taylor," in *True Detective Mysteries* (Oct. 1930).
Kirkpatrick, Sidney D.: *A Cast of Killers: The Sensational True Story of Hollywood's Most Scandalous Murder-Covered Up for Sixty Years and Solved at Last by the Great Film Director King Vidor* (E. P. Dutton 1986).
Long, Bruce: "Official Documents," *Taylorology.com.*

Chapter 4 (Harlow)
Marx, Samuel & Vaderveen, Joyce: *Deadly Illusions: Jean Harlow and the Murder of Paul Bern* (Random House 1990).
"Jean Harlow, Film Star, Dies in Hollywood at 26 After an Illness of Only a Few Days," *New York Times,* June 8, 1937, at 1, 30.
"Paul Bern a Suicide; Wed Jean Harlow," *New York Times, Sept. 6, 1932, at 1.*

Chapter 5 (Errol Flynn)
McNulty, Thomas: *Errol Flynn: The Life and Career* (McFarland 2011).

Chapter 6 (Lana Turner)
"Complete Testimony of Inquest," *Los Angeles Times*, Apr. 12, 1958.
Crane, Cheryl & Jahr, Cliff: *Detour: A Hollywood Story* (Arbor House 1988).
Pero, Taylor & Rovin, Jeff: *Always Lana* (Bantam Books 1982).
Wayne, Jane Ellen: *Lana: The Life and Loves of Lana Turner (St. Martin's Press 1995).*

Chapter 7 (Bob Crane)
Graysmith, Robert: *Auto Focus* (Berkley Boulevard Books 2002).

Chapter 8 (Parkman-Webster)
Potier, Beth: "Murder at Harvard: Medical College Case Riveted 19th Century Boston," *Harvard University Gazette* (2002).
Stone, James W.: *Report on the Trial of Professor John W. Webster* (Phillips, Sampson & Company 1850).
Sullivan, Robert: *The Disappearance of Dr. Parkman (Little, Brown & Company 1971).*

Chapter 9 (Minor)
Winchester, Simon: *The Professor and the Madman: A Tale of Murder, Insanity, and the Making of the Oxford English Dictionary* (Harper Collins 1999).

Chapter 10 (Fisk)
Brands, H. W.: *The Murder of Jim Fisk: For the Love of Josie Mansfield* (Anchor Books 2011).

Chapter 11 (Gunness)
Langlois, Janet L.: *Belle Gunness: The Lady Bluebeard* (Indiana University Press 1985).
Schechter, Harold & Everitt, David: *The A to Z Encyclopedia of Serial Killers* (Pocket Books 1997).

Chapter 12 (Ponzi)
Zuckoff, Mitchell: *Ponzi's Scheme* (Random House 2005).

Chapter 13 (Leopold and Loeb)
Baatz, Simon: *For the Thrill of It: Leopold, Loeb, and the Murder That Shocked Chicago* (Harper Collins 2008).
Farrell, John A.: *Clarence Darrow: Attorney for the Damned* (Doubleday 2011).

Chapter 14 (O'Hare and Capone)
Eig, Jonathan: *Get Capone: The Secret Plot That Captured America's Most Wanted Gangster* (Simon & Schuster 2010).
Ewing, Steve & Lundstrom, John B.: *Fateful Rendezvous: The Life of Butch O'Hare* (Naval Institute Press 1997).
Kobler, John: *Capone: The Life and World of Al Capone* (Da Capo Press 1971).

Chapter 15 (Kid Twist)
Elmaleh, Edmund: *The Canary Sang But Couldn't Fly: The Fatal Fall of Abe Reles, the Mobster Who Shattered Murder, Inc.'s Code of Silence* (Union Square Press 2009).
Turkus, Burton B. & Feder, Sid: *Murder, Inc.: The Story of the Syndicate* (DaCapo Press 1992).

Chapter 16 (Apalachin)
"20 Apalachin Convictions Ruled Invalid on Appeal," *Toledo Blade*, Nov. 29, 1960.
Adams, Jack: "Hoodlums Run Into Black Days Since Federal Drive Started," *The Tuscaloosa News*, Mar. 8, 1959.
Raab, Selwyn: *Five Families: The Rise, Decline, and Resurgence of America's Most Powerful Mafia Empires* (Thomas Dunne 2005).

Chapter 17 (Bathsheba Spooner)
Lundquist, Weyman I.: "*The Bathsheba Spooner Murder Trial*," *Litigation*, 1998, Vol. 24, Issue 3, at 57–71.
Navas, Deborah: *Murdered By His Wife* (University of Massachusetts Press 1999).

Chapter 18 (Helen Jewett)
Cohen, Patricia Cline: *The Murder of Helen Jewett: The Life and Death of a Prostitute in Nineteenth-Century* (Vintage Books 1998).
Stashower, Daniel: *The Beautiful Cigar Girl: Mary Rogers, Edgar Allan Poe and the Invention of Murder* (Dutton 2006).
Wilkes, George & Howard, H. R.: *Lives of Helen Jewett, And Richard P. Robinson (1849)* (Kessinger Publishing 2009).

Chapter 19 (Mary Rogers)
Stashower, Daniel: *The Beautiful Cigar Girl: Mary Rogers, Edgar Allan Poe and the Invention of Murder* (Dutton 2006).

Chapter 20 (H. H. Holmes)
Larson, Erik: *The Devil in the White City: Murder, Magic, and Madness at the Fair that Changed America* (Crown Publishers 2003).

Chapter 21 (Adolph Luetgert)
Loerzel, Robert: *Alchemy of Bones: Chicago's Luetgert Murder Case of 1897* (Univ. of Illinois Press 2003).

Chapter 22 (Grace Brown)
Brandon, Craig: *Murder in the Adirondacks: An American Tragedy Revisited* (North Country Books 2006).

Chapter 23 (Gein)
Gollmar, Robert H.: *America's Most Bizarre Murder: Edward Gein* (Pinnacle Books 1984).
Schechter, Harold: *Deviant: The Shocking True Story of Ed Gein, the Original "Psycho"* (Pocket Books 1989).

Chapter 24 (Dolly Mapp)

Dash, Samuel: *The Intruders* (Rutgers Univ. Press 2004).

Long, Carolyn N.: *Mapp v. Ohio: Guarding Against Unreasonable Searches and Seizures* (Univ. Press of Kansas 2006).

Zotti, Pricilla H.: *Injustice for All: Mapp vs. Ohio and the Fourth Amendment* (Peter Lang Publishing Inc. 2005).

Chapter 25 (Sickles)

Hessler, James: *Sickles at Gettysburg: The Controversial Civil War General Who Committed Murder, Abandoned Little Round Top, and Declared Himself the Hero of Gettysburg* (Savas Beatie 2010).

Keneally, Thomas: *American Scoundrel: The Life of Notorious Civil War General Dan Sickles* (Anchor 2003).

Chapter 26 (The Haymarket Affair)

Green, James: *Death in the Haymarket: A Story of Chicago, the First Labor Movement and the Bombing that Divided Gilded Age America* (Pantheon 2006).

Chapter 27 (Triangle Fire)

Kavieff, Paul R.: *The Life and Times of Lepke Buchalter: America's Most Ruthless Labor Racketeer* (Barricade Books Inc. 2006).

Von Drehle, David: "The Fire Next Time. A century after the deadliest factory fire in New York City history, the lessons for reform still hold true," *Time Magazine, Apr. 4, 2011.*

Chapter 28 (Thalia Lied, Joe Died)

Stannard, David E.: *Honor Killing: How the Infamous 'Massie Affair' Transformed Hawai`i* (Viking 2005).

Chapter 29 (State Secrets)

Fisher, Louis: *In the Name of National Security: Unchecked Presidential Power and the Reynolds Case* (University Press of Kansas 2006).

Siegal, Barry: *Claim of Privilege (Harper Perennial 2008).*

Chapter 30 (Sheppard)

DeSario, Jack P. & Mason, William D.: *Dr. Sam Sheppard on Trial, Case Closed: The Prosecutors and the Marilyn Sheppard Murder* (Kent State University Press 2003).

Neff, James: *The Wrong Man: The Final Verdict on the Dr. Sam Sheppard Murder Case* (Random House 2001).

Index